Ten Theories of
Human Nature

Ten Theories of
Human Nature
Third Edition

LESLIE STEVENSON
DAVID L. HABERMAN

New York   Oxford
OXFORD UNIVERSITY PRESS
1998

OXFORD UNIVERSITY PRESS

Oxford   New York

Athens   Auckland   Bangkok   Bogota   Bombay   Buenos Aires
Calcutta   Cape Town   Dar es Salaam   Delhi   Florence   Hong Kong
Istanbul   Karachi   Kuala Lumpur   Madras   Madrid   Melbourne
Mexico City   Nairobi   Paris   Singapore   Taipei   Tokyo   Toronto   Warsaw

and associated companies in
Berlin   Ibadan

Published by Oxford University Press, Inc.
198 Madison Avenue, New York, New York 10016

Oxford is a registered trademark of Oxford University Press

Library of Congress Cataloging-in-Publication Data
Stevenson, Leslie Forster.
    Ten theories of human nature / Leslie Stevenson, David L.
Haberman. — 3rd ed.
        p.   cm.
    Rev. and expanded ed. of: Seven theories of human nature, 2nd ed.
1987.
    Includes bibliographical references and index.
    ISBN 0-19-512040-X (hardcover). — ISBN 0-19-512041-8
(pbk.)
    1. Philosophical anthropology.   I. Haberman, David L., 1952–
II. Stevenson, Leslie Forster.   Seven theories of human nature.
III. Title.
BD450.S766   1998
128—dc21   97-40922
                                                                          CIP

CLOTH 10 9 8 7 6 5
PAPER 19 18 17 16 15 14 13 12 11

Printed in the United States of America

*To my daughters, Sonia and Lydia, who have, of
course, taught me much about
human nature*
L. S.

*To my parents, Reuben and Ruth,
in many ways the sources of my own
human nature*
D. H.

Contents

Preface   ix

PART I
INTRODUCTION

Chapter 1   Rival Theories—and Critical Assessment
of Them   3

PART II
THREE ANCIENT RELIGIOUS TRADITIONS

Chapter 2   Confucianism: The Way of the Sages   25
by David L. Haberman

Chapter 3   Upanishadic Hinduism: Quest for   45
Ultimate Knowledge
by David L. Haberman

Chapter 4   The Bible: Humanity in Relation   68
to God

PART III
FIVE PHILOSOPHICAL THINKERS

Chapter 5   Plato: The Rule of Reason   89
Chapter 6   Kant: Reason and Freedom, History   110
and Grace
Chapter 7   Marx: The Economic Basis of Human
Nature   130
Chapter 8   Freud: The Unconscious Basis of Mind   149
Chapter 9   Sartre: Radical Freedom   169

PART IV
TWO SAMPLES OF SCIENTIFIC THEORIZING ABOUT HUMAN NATURE

Chapter 10   Behavioral Psychology: Skinner on
              Conditioning   189
Chapter 11   Evolutionary Psychology: Lorenz on
              Aggression   207

PART V
CONCLUSION

Chapter 12   Toward a Unified Understanding: Nine
              Types of Psychology   225

              Index   235

Preface

In the early 1970s, as a raw young lecturer at St. Andrews University, I found myself faced with large numbers of first-year students who were required, under the traditional Scottish system, to take a philosophy course. (St. Andrews has since wisely decided that a compulsion to do philosophy comes better from within than from without.) I wondered what was appropriate for such an audience of conscripts, most of whom would study no further philosophy. My response was to broaden a conventional philosophy of mind course into a discussion of various theories of human nature (and I am grateful to my then head of department, Len Goddard, for allowing me to do so). The first edition of this book emerged from that pedagogical experience.

It is now a quarter of a century since first publication, and the book is still found useful for introductory courses in many institutions in various countries. The second edition had a new final chapter but made only cosmetic changes elsewhere, rather complacently leaving the seven main chapters almost untouched (I was also under a mistaken impression that economy required minimal changes to the typesetting). Time has moved on—philosophical scholarship has advanced, feminism and postmodernism have become very influential in the humanities, scientific research in psychology and biology has proceeded apace, and there is now yet another wave of evolutionary theorizing about human nature.

After twenty-five more years of study—and life—I might be expected to find something more to say about human nature. But the subject is infinite, the task is daunting, and my knowledge and abilities are finite. I realize that it is a rare privilege to be read by so many thousands of students, and Robert Miller of Oxford University

Press has persuaded me to accept a corresponding responsibility to improve the book as best as I now can.

The first question was whether to stick with the magic number seven. The idea of expounding some non-Western theories was attractive. But I am not qualified to do this myself: it needs someone with the relevant expertise, in sympathy with the spirit of the project and prepared to write at introductory level, utilizing the four-part structure of theory of universe, theory of humanity, diagnosis, and prescription that readers and instructors seem to have found helpful. I am delighted to say that David Haberman of Indiana University at Bloomington has met these criteria perfectly and has contributed two new chapters on Confucianism and Hinduism, which will, I trust, considerably add to the range and cross-cultural appeal of the book. The other chapters remain my own work—the authorial "I" thus refers to Leslie Stevenson.

Of course, once one starts suggesting more theories for consideration, there is no knowing where to stop—Aristotle, Stoicism, Islam, Aquinas, Hobbes, Spinoza, Hume, Nietzsche, Heidegger, Chomsky, and on and on! Feminism demands more of a response than the very minimal adjustment I made in the second edition. But it seemed difficult to pick out a single representative feminist figure or theory for consideration. What we have tried to is to indicate what each of the theories says or implies about women, and we have used gender-neutral language throughout.

I have decided to add a chapter on Kant, the philosopher on whom I have spent the most time in the rest of my work, though it is only recently that I have begun to appreciate the more practical side of his thought. Much of Kant's writing is formidably abstract and technical, but I have tried to give an intelligible summary of his theory of human faculties, the basis of his approach to ethics, politics, and religion, his recognition of radical evil in human nature, and his hopes for progress in human affairs. My own inclination is to defend a suitably modernized version of his late-Enlightenment appeal to reason, in contrast to the postmodernist or culturally relativist approaches that have recently become fashionable.

In the case of the original seven theories, I have rewritten each chapter very thoroughly this time around, extending them by up to half the original length and (I hope) deepening the treatment while still keeping the level introductory. But I am painfully aware that I cannot claim to be an expert on any of these topics and that my discussion tends to stop where the going gets difficult, which is of course the fate of an introductory book.

Comments from various referees have saved me from errors and have suggested more adequate treament in some places. I am especially grateful to Julia Annas for making me realize how much I had missed in Plato's *Republic*, above all the moral argument based on his tripartite theory of "the soul," still very relevant for us today. My previous account was surely overly influenced by Popper's criticism of Plato's political program. I am grateful to Allen Wood for comments on my chapter on Kant, to Richard W. Miller on Marx, to an anonymous referee on Freud, and to Stephen P. Stich on Skinner and Lorenz. In returning to these themes, I also hear in my mind faint echoes of the booming voice of Isaiah Berlin lecturing in Oxford many years ago (one of the inspirations for my taking up philosophy in the first place).

Various readers have made the point that Skinnner and Lorenz are outdated figures: there is indeed nothing so dated as the recent past! I would agree that *sub specie eternitatis* neither of them will probably deserve to be up there in a pantheon with the others treated here. But to survey more recent would-be scientific theorizing about human nature seemed too tall an order for my knowledge and for the intended length of this book. So after some hesitation, I have decided to retain updated treatments of Skinner and Lorenz. I hope that critical discussion of them (and, in particular, of their extrapolation from animals to humans) will equip students to look at more recent theorizing with a similarly sceptical eye. In the new concluding chapter I offer a brief overview of some recent developments and distinguish no fewer than nine different kinds of psychology.

The former two introductory chapters have been rolled into one. I have tried to make the epistemology and the philosophy of science there a bit less primitive, but it is the function of other books to provide systematic introductions to those areas. This seemed to be the place in which to touch, if only briefly, on the challenge of relativism, which has rolled over so much of humanistic academia since the first edition of this book.

With the addition of chapters on Confucianism, Hinduism, and

Kant and the decision not to give proportionate attention to very recent theorizing, the book has in effect grown backward rather than forward. Though that may reflect my own philosophical specialization, perhaps it is no bad thing to offer a contrast to the prevailing obsession with being up to date with the very latest research and speculation. In our rush toward the future, there is surely a danger of a parochialism of the present that forgets the wisdom of the past.

I would like to thank Anne Cameron and Barbara Orton for typing the second edition onto disk for me to word-process and Nora Bartlett for assistance with the final editing. I would like affectionately to remember here my father, Patric Stevenson (died 1983), for his fastidious attention to matters of style in the first edition, which must have contributed to its success, and which I hope has rubbed off, via me, onto subsequent editions. I would also like to thank Robert Miller for his continued encouragement and support in the writing of this revised and expanded edition.

St. Andrews   L. S.
August 1997

Ten Theories of
Human Nature

Introduction

CHAPTER

1

Rival Theories—and Critical Assessment of Them

1. Rival Conceptions of Human Nature

So much depends on our conception of human nature: for individuals, the meaning and purpose of our lives, what we ought to do or strive for, what we may hope to achieve or to become; for human societies, what vision of human community we may hope to work toward and what sort of social changes we should make. Our answers to all these huge questions depend on whether we think there is some "true" or "innate" nature of human beings. If so, what is it? Is it different for men and women? Or is there no such "essential" human nature, only a capacity to be molded by the social environment—by economic, political, and cultural forces?

On these fundamental questions about human nature there are disagreements aplenty. "What is man that Thou art mindful of him . . . Thou hast made him a little lower than the angels, and hast crowned him with glory and honor," wrote the author of Psalm 8 in the Old Testament. The Bible sees human beings as created by a transcendent God with a definite purpose for our life. "The real nature of man is the totality of social relations," wrote Karl Marx in the mid-nineteenth century. Marx denied the existence of God and held that each person is a product of the particular economic stage of human society in which he or she lives. "Man is condemned to be free," said Jean-Paul Sartre, writing in German-occupied France in the 1940s. Sartre was an atheist, too, but he differed from Marx in holding that our nature is not determined by our society, nor by anything else. He held that every individual person is completely free to decide what he or she wants to be and do. In contrast, recent sociobiological theorists have treated human beings as a product of evolution, with our own biologically determined, species-specific patterns of behavior.

It will not escape the notice of contemporary readers that these three quotations from the Bible, Marx, and Sartre all use the masculine word "'man" (in English translation), where presumably the intention was to refer to *all* human beings, including women and children. Such usage has been widespread and is often defended as convenient shorthand, but it has recently come under criticism for contributing to questionable assumptions about the dominance of male human nature and the consequent neglect or oppression of female nature. There are important issues here, which involve much more than linguistic usage. We touch on feminist themes at some points in this book, but we do not address them head-on: there is no chapter on specifically feminist theories of human nature. We strive to avoid sexist language in our own writing, but it can hardly be avoided in quotations.

Different conceptions of human nature lead to different views about what we ought to do and how we can do it. If an all-powerful and supremely good God made us, then it is His purpose that defines what we can be and what we ought to be, and we must look to Him for help. If, on the other hand, we are products of society, and if we find that our lives are unsatisfactory, then there can be no real solution until human society is transformed. If we are radically free and can never escape the necessity for individual choice, then we have to accept this and make our choices with full awareness of what we are doing. If our biological nature predisposes or determines us to think, feel, and act in certain ways, then we must take realistic account of that.

Rival beliefs about human nature are typically embodied in different individual ways of life, and in political and economic systems.

Marxist theory (in some version) so dominated public life in the communist-ruled countries of the twentieth century that any questioning of it could have serious consequences for the questioner. We can easily forget that, a few centuries ago, Christianity occupied a similarly dominant position in Western society: heretics and unbelievers were discriminated against, persecuted, even burnt at the stake. Even now, in some countries or communities, there is a socially established Christian consensus that individuals can oppose only at some cost to themselves. In the Republic of Ireland, for example, Roman Catholic doctrine has (until recently) been accepted as limiting policy on social matters such as abortion, contraception, and divorce. The Catholic Church exerts similar strong influence in postcommunist Poland. In the United States, an informal protestant Christian ethos affects much public discussion, despite the official separation of Church and State.

An "existentialist" philosophy like Sartre's may seem less likely to have social implications, but one way of justifying modern "liberal" democracy is by the philosophical view that there *are no* objective values for human living, only subjective individual choices. This assumption (which is incompatible with both Christianity and Marxism) is highly influential in modern Western society, far beyond its particular manifestation in French existentialist philosophy of the mid-century. Liberal democracy is enshrined in the American Declaration of Independence, with its separation of politics from religion and its acknowledgment of the right of each individual freely to pursue his or her own conception of happiness. (It should be noted, however, that someone who believes there *are* objective moral standards may still support a liberal social system if he or she thinks it unwise to try to *enforce* them.)

2. Christianity and Marxism Compared

Let us look a bit more closely at Christianity and Marxism as rival theories of human nature. Although they are radically different in content, they present some remarkable similarities in structure, in the way that the parts of each doctrine fit together and give rise to ways of life. First, they each make claims about the nature of the universe as a whole. Christianity is, of course, committed to belief in God, a personal being who is omnipotent, omniscient, and perfectly good, the Creator, Ruler, and Judge of everything that exists. Marx condemned religion as "the opium of the people," an illusory system of belief that distracts them from their real social problems. He held that the universe exists without anybody behind or beyond it and is fundamentally material in nature.

Both Christianity and Marxism have beliefs about history. For the Christian, the meaning of history is given by its relation to the eternal. God uses the events of history to work out His purposes, revealing Himself to His chosen people (in the Old Testament) but above all in the life and death of Jesus. Marx claimed to find a pattern of progress in human history that is entirely internal to it. He thought that there is an inevitable development from one economic stage to another so that just as the economic system of feudalism had been superseded by capitalism, so capitalism would have to give way to communism. Both views see a pattern and meaning in history, though they differ about the nature of the moving force and the direction.

Second, following from the conflicting claims about the universe, there are different descriptions of the essential nature of individual human beings. According to Christianity, we are made in the image of God, and our fate depends on our relationship to God. All people are free to accept or reject God's purpose and will be judged according to how they exercise that freedom. This judgment goes beyond anything in this life, for we each survive physical death. Marxism denies life after death and any such eternal judgment. It also plays down individual freedom and says that our moral ideas and attitudes are determined by the kind of society we live in.

Third, there are different diagnoses of what goes wrong with human life and humankind. Christianity says that the world is not in accordance with God's purposes, that our relationship to God is disrupted because we misuse our freedom, reject God's will, and are infected with sin. Marx replaces the notion of sin by the concept of "alienation," which also suggests some ideal standard that actual human life does not meet. But Marx's idea seems to be of alienation from oneself, from one's own true nature: his claim is that human beings have potential that the socioeconomic conditions of capitalism do not allow them to develop.

The prescription for a problem depends on the diagnosis. So, last,

Christianity and Marxism offer completely different answers to the ills of human life. The Christian believes that only the power of God Himself can save us from our state of sin. The startling claim is that in the life and death of Jesus, God has acted to redeem the world. Everyone needs to accept this divine forgiveness and can then begin to live a new, regenerate life. Human society will not be truly redeemed until individuals are thus transformed. Marxism says the opposite—that there can be no real improvement in individual lives until there has been a radical change in society. The socioeconomic system of capitalism must be replaced by communism. This revolutionary change is said to be inevitable, because of laws of historical development; what individuals should do is to join the progressive movement and help shorten the birth pangs of the new age.

Implicit in these rival prescriptions are differing visions of a future in which humankind is redeeemed or regenerated. The Christian vision is of people restored to the state that God intends for them, freely loving and obeying their Maker. The new life begins as soon as the individual accepts God's salvation and joins the Christian community, but the process must be completed beyond death, for individuals and communities are forever imperfect in this life. The Marxist vision is of a future in this world, of a perfect society in which people can become their real selves, no longer alienated by economic conditions but freely active in cooperation with one another. Such is the goal of history, although it should not be expected immediately after the revolution; a transitional stage will be needed before the higher phase of communist society can come into being.

We have here two systems of belief that are total in their scope. Traditionally, Christians and Marxists claim to have the essential truth about the whole of human life; they assert something about the nature of all human beings, at any time and in any place. And these worldviews claim not just intellectual assent but practical action; if one really believes in either theory, one should accept its implications for one's way of life and act accordingly.

As a last point of comparison, note that for each belief system, there has been a human organization that claims the allegiance of believers and asserts a certain authority on both doctrine and practice. For Christianity there is the Church, and for Marxism the Communist Party. Or, to be more accurate, there have long been rival Christian churches and a variety of Marxist or communist parties. Each makes competing claims to follow the true doctrine of its founder, defining rival versions of the basic theory as orthodox and following different practical policies.

3. Other "Ideologies" about Human Nature

Many people have noted this similarity in structure between Christianity and Marxism, and some have suggested that the latter is as much a religion as the former. There is food for thought here for believers of both kinds, and for the uncommitted person, too. Why should such very different accounts of the nature and destiny of man have such similar structures?

But there are many more views of human nature than these two. The theories of the ancient Greeks, especially of their great philosophers Plato and Aristotle, still influence us today. Since the rise of modern science in the seventeenth century, a variety of thinkers has tried to apply the methods of science (as they understood them) to human nature—for example, Hobbes, Hume, and the French thinkers of the eighteenth-century Enlightenment. More recently, Darwin's theory of evolution and Freud's psychoanalytic speculations have fundamentally affected our understanding of ourselves. Modern biology and psychology offer a variety of allegedly scientific theorizing about animal and human nature. Some distinguished scientists, including Skinner and Lorenz, have offered their own diagnosis of the human condition, supposedly on the basis of their scientific expertise.

Outside the Western tradition, there have been Chinese, Indian, and African conceptions of human nature, some of which are still very much alive. Islam, often seen as "oriental," is closely related to Judaism and Christianity in its origins. Islam in particular is undergoing a resurgence of popular strength, as the peoples of the Middle East express their rejection of some aspects of Western culture, and it has also gained influence among African Americans. As the influence of Marxist theory wanes, some in Russia have looked for guidance to their Orthodox Christian past and others to a variety of modern forms of spirituality; in China, Confucianism has been given some official revival.

Some of these views are embodied in human societies and institutions, as Christianity and Marxism have been. If so, they are not

just intellectual theories but ways of life, subject to change, to growth
and decay. A system of beliefs about human nature that is held by
some group of people as giving rise to their way of life is standardly
called an "ideology." Christianity and Marxism are certainly ideologies in this sense; even value-subjectivism can, as noted earlier, form
an ideological basis for political liberalism.

An ideology, then, is more than a theory, but it does involve some
theoretical conception of human nature. What we propose to do in
this book is to examine certain influential theories that claim to have
practical implications for human affairs. Not all of them are ideologies, since not all have a corresponding group of people who hold
the theory as giving rise to their way of life. But the theories we have
selected to discuss all exhibit the main elements of that common
structure we have seen in Christianity and Marxism:

1. a background theory about the world;
2. a basic theory of the nature of human beings;
3. a diagnosis of what is wrong with us; and
4. a prescription for putting it right.

Only theories that combine such constituents offer us hope of solutions to the problems of humankind. For instance, the single assertion that everyone is selfish is a brief diagnosis but offers no
understanding of why we are selfish and no suggestion as to whether
or how we can overcome selfishness. The statement that we should
all love one another is a brief prescription, but it gives no explanation of why we find it so difficult and no help in achieving it. The
theory of evolution, although it has a lot to say about human beings
and our place in the universe, does not in itself give any diagnosis
or prescription.

The theories we examine include those of Christianity and Marx.
We also look at Hinduism and Confucianism, the ancient traditions
of India and China, which are still very influential. We look at the
philosophy of Plato (mostly as expressed in his *Republic*, one of the
great books of all time and still a very readable work) and of Kant
(one of the very greatest philosophers of all). Among twentieth-
century thinkers we examine Freud (whose psychoanalytical theories
have affected so much of the thought of the twentieth century); the

French existentialist philosopher Sartre; B. F. Skinner (an American psychologist who claimed to have the key to how human behavior is conditioned); and Konrad Lorenz (an Austrian biologist who tried to explain human nature in terms of Darwinian evolution).

In each case we try to sketch the essential background briefly, but we cannot possibly survey the many varieties of each kind of theory, especially in the case of a "theory" drawn from an entire religious culture rather than from a single thinker. With the modern psychological or biological theories, we cannot hope to be up to date with all the very latest developments, for the frontiers of science and speculation are constantly moving. But perhaps it is more important in an introductory book to concentrate on fundamental questions of methodology, concepts, and values, in the hope of equipping readers to apply these lessons to new theorizing in the future. So we try to summarize clearly the key ideas of each theory, interpreting them through the four-part structure outlined earlier. We suggest a careful selection of further reading relevant to each theory.

4. The Criticism of Theories

As well as expounding the basic ideas of each theory, we want to suggest some of the main difficulties that they face. So in each chapter there is some critical discussion that will, we hope, encourage readers to think further for themselves. (In some chapters the criticism follows the exposition; in others it is intertwined with it.) Before we begin our main business, let us review the prospects for rational assessment of such controversial matters. Once again, we can usefully look first at the cases of Christianity and Marxism, to see what tends to happen when we criticize theories of human nature.

The most basic Christian claim about the universe, that God exists, is, of course, faced with many skeptical objections. To take one of them, the suffering and evil in the world surely count against the existence of God, as traditionally conceived. For if He is omniscient, He must know of the evil, and if He is omnipotent, He must be able to remove it, so if He is perfectly benevolent, why does He not do so? In particular, why does God not answer the prayers of believers for the relief of manifold sufferings all over the world?

The basic Marxist assertion about the world—that there is an inevitable progress in human history through stages of economic development—is just as open to skepticism. Is it at all plausible that such progress is inevitable; does it not depend on many noneconomic factors, which are not predetermined, such as contingencies of politics and wars? In particular, communist revolutions have not occurred in the heart of capitalism—the United States and the industrialized countries of Western Europe—and the communist regimes of Eastern Europe collapsed in the late twentieth century. So isn't there direct evidence against Marx's theory?

Christian and Marxist claims about the nature of individual persons also raise large philosophical problems. Are we really free and responsible for our actions? Or is everything about us determined by our heredity, upbringing, and environment? Can the individual person continue to exist after death? In the face of the universal and obvious fact of human mortality, the alleged evidence for survival is highly controversial. But can the materialist view that human beings are made of nothing but matter be true, in the light of our distinctive mental powers to perceive and feel, think and reason, debate and decide?

Doubts also arise about the respective prescriptions for human problems. The Christian claim that a particular man is divine, and is the means of God's reconciliation with the world, defies human rationality. The Marxist belief that communist revolution is the answer to the problems of humanity attaches almost as great significance to a particular historical event. In neither case is the cosmic claim supported by the subsequent history of those communities, institutions, or nations in which the regeneration is supposed to be taking effect. The Christian churches down through the ages, and the various communist-ruled countries in the twentieth century, show a mixture of good and evil like that evident in all other human history. Neither Christian nor communist practice has eliminated disagreement, selfishness, persecution, tyranny, torture, murder, and war.

5. Defenses Against Objections—"Closed Systems"

These common objections to Christianity and Marxism are very well worn by now. What is interesting is that belief has not disappeared in the face of them. Christianity has suffered an erosion of influence over the past few centuries, but it is still very much alive. In one form or another, it retains the power to convince and convert. Admittedly, Marxism now has far fewer supporters than it had formerly (except, perhaps, in China), but it held the allegiance of many people for much of the twentieth century, despite its obvious problems of principle and of practice. Even now, some would argue that the regimes of Eastern Europe did not properly put Marx's theory into practice and that his basic ideas may still be valid.

How could anyone continue to believe in Christianity or Marxism, in the face of the standard objections? First, believers look for some way of explaining them away. The Christian says that God does not always remove evil or answer our prayers—what seems bad to us may ultimately be for the best. Some Marxists suggested that communist revolutions did not occur in the West because the workers were "bought off" by the concession of higher standards of living and did not realize that their true interest was in the overthrow of capitalism. To the doubts about the respective prescriptions, the believers can reply that the full regeneration of human nature is still to come and that the terrible things in the history of Christianity or communism are only a stage on the way to perfection. By thus explaining away difficulties in theory and appealing to the future for vindication, believers may maintain their commitment with some show of plausibility. The theorists of churches and "People's Republics" became well practiced at such justification of the ways of God, or of the ruling Party.

Second, the believer can take the offensive by attacking the motivation of the critic. Christians tend to say that those who persist in raising intellectual objections to Christianity are being blinded by sin, that it is their own pride that prevents them from seeing the light. The Marxist may claim that those who do not recognize the truth of Marx's analysis of history and society are deluded by their "false consciousness," and that the capitalist mode of production tends to prevent those who benefit under it from acknowledging the truth about their society. So, in each case, a critic's motives can be analyzed in terms of the very theory being criticized, and the believer may thus try to dismiss the criticism. In the case of Freudian theory, which offers its own distinctive ways of explaining human actions and attitudes, this method of counterattack against criticism has been very widely employed.

These are two typical ways in which a belief can be maintained in the face of intellectual difficulties. If a theory is defended by these devices:

1. not allowing any evidence to count against the theory, i.e., always finding some way of explaining away putative counterevidence; or

2. answering criticism by analysing the motivations of the critic in terms of the theory itself

then we say that it is being held as a "closed system." It appears that Christianity, Marxism, and Freudian theory *can* be held as closed systems—but this is not to say that all Christians, Marxists, or Freudians hold their belief in that way.

Why should people want to maintain a belief in the face of conceptual dificulties and counterevidence? Inertia, and unwillingness to admit that one is wrong, must play a large part here. If one has been brought up in a certain belief and its associated way of life, or if one has been converted to it and followed its precepts, it takes courage to question or abandon one's life-commitment. When a belief is an ideology, used to justify the way of life of a social group, it is difficult for the members of that community to consider it objectively. There are strong social pressures to continue to acknowledge it, and it is very natural for believers to maintain it as a closed system. People will tend to feel that their belief, even if open to some theoretical difficulties, contains some vital insight, some vision of essential truths that have practical importance. To question it may be to threaten what gives meaning, purpose, and hope to one's life and to endanger one's social position.

6. The Hope for Rational Discussion and Evaluation

Is it possible, then, to discuss various theories of human nature rationally and objectively, as we are setting out to do in this book? For when such theories are embodied in ways of life, belief in them seems to go beyond mere reasoning. The ultimate appeal may be to faith or authority, to community membership, loyalty, or commitment: there may be no answer to the questions "Why should I believe this?" and "Why should I accept this authority?" that will satisfy someone who is not already a member of the relevant group or tradition, or attracted by it. In the contemporary world, rival traditions and ideologies are as influential as ever. Religious, cultic, political, national, ethnic, psychotherapeutic, and gender-based dogmas are asserted with various degrees of aggression or politeness, crudity or sophistication. The media of the so-called "global village" seem to bring different cultures together in the sense only of confrontation, not of dialogue. The attractions of certainty, commitment, "identity," and membership in a strongly defined community are as strong as ever.

In reaction to this, skepticism is tempting. These days it tends to take the intellectual form of "cultural relativism" or "postmodernism," according to which no particular cultural tradition (or conception of human nature) has any more rational justification than any other. One of the most influential prophets of this trend was the nineteenth-century German philosopher Friedrich Nietzsche, who has been described as a "master of suspicion" because he was always ready (like Marx before him and Freud after him) to diagnose an unacknowledged ideological commitment or psychological need behind supposedly "objective" claims to truth or morality. If we jump to the conclusion that there can be no objective, rational discussion of rival theories of human nature, the project of this book may seem doomed from the start.

I want to suggest, however, that such despair would be premature. For one thing, not all the theories we discuss are the ideologies of any identifiable social group, and in those cases there is less likelihood of their being defended in this closed-minded way. But more important, even if a belief does become an ideology and is held as a closed system, rational evaluation of it is still possible for those who are prepared to try it. For we can always distinguish what someone says from that person's motivation for saying it. The motivation may be relevant, if we wish to understand the personality of the speaker, or perhaps something about his or her society. But if we are concerned primarily with the truth or falsity of what is said, and with whether there are any good reasons for believing it, then motivation is irrelevant. The reasons that the speaker may offer for something are not necessarily the best available reasons for it. There is nothing to stop us discussing what is said on its own merits.

Despite Nietzsche's scorn for the theory of knowlege and moral philosophy (wittily expressed as it often is), he displays a double standard at work in his own thought, for he has to presuppose that he has some way of knowing or justifying what he himself asserts. "The falseness of a judgment is to us not necessarily an objection to a judgment," he wrote, "the question is to what extent it is life-advancing, life-preserving, species-preserving, perhaps even species-breeding." On the one hand he describes a judgment as *false*, and on the other he suggests that it can have some other sort of life-enhancing virtue. But how does he *know* that it is false? One may, of course, accept a proposition and act on it while acknowledging that it *may* turn out false—such is the usual human condition. But if Nietzsche thinks an assertion is false or a moral judgment unacceptable, he should have some idea of what *justifies* him in that view. Nobody can opt out of reasoning and justification: we all have to make our own judgments in the light of evidence available to us, including what other people say on the matter.

The second feature of closed systems—the technique of meeting all criticism by attacking the motives of the critic—is thus rationally unsatisfactory. For if what is being discussed is whether the theory is true or whether there are good reasons for believing it, then the objections that anyone produces against it must be replied to on their own merits, regardless of their possible motivations. Someone's motivation may be peculiar or objectionable in some way, and yet what the person says may be true and justifiable by good reasons. (Criticism is not refuted by dislike of the critic. The most annoying critics are those who are—at least partly—*right!*) And if motivation *is* considered, to analyze it in terms of the theory under discussion is to assume the truth of that theory and thus to beg the question. An objection to a theory cannot be rationally defeated just by reasserting part of the theory.

7. Validity of Statements

The first feature of closed systems, the dismissal of all evidence against the theory, must be looked at with some suspicion. We often feel that such "explaining" is only "explaining away," that it is not very convincing except to those already disposed to believe in the theory. (Consider how Christians try to solve the problem of why God does not prevent suffering, and Marxists the problem of why revolutions did not occur in the West.) We must try to decide when such explaining is rationally justifiable and when it is mere "explaining away." To do this, we must distinguish various different *sorts* of statement that may be made as part of a theory.

7.1 Value Judgments

First, a statement may be a value judgment, saying what *ought* to be the case, rather than a factual assertion about what *is* the case. For example, suppose someone says that homosexuality is unnatural. It might be objected that in almost every known society there is a certain amount of homosexuality. Suppose the person replies that this does not disprove the point, since homosexuality involves only a minority in each society. Perhaps the objector will suggest that it is possible that a majority of society might indulge in homosexual as well as heterosexual activity (as seems to have been the case for men in ancient Greece). The reply may be "I would *still* say it is unnatural." Such a reply suggests that the speaker is not asserting anything about what people actually do but is expressing an opinion about what they ought to do (this would be confirmed if we find that the speaker reacts with disgust against homosexual activity). If what is being said is thus evaluative rather than factual, evidence about what actually happens does not disprove it. But in order to be in this way impervious to factual evidence, the claim must be recognized as a value judgment, as not even *attempting* to say what is the case. And if so, then it cannot be *supported* by evidence either, for what actually happens is not necessarily what should happen.

Statements about human nature are especially subject to this kind of ambiguity. Indeed, the words "nature" and "natural" should be regarded as danger signals, indicating possible ambiguity or confusion. If someone says "Human beings are naturally X," we should immediately ask "Do you mean that all or most human beings *are* actually X, or that we *should* all be X—or what?" (Let "X" be heterosexual, or altruistic, or kind to children, for example.)

Sometimes what may be meant is something of the form "In conditions Y, human beings *would be* X." Consider, for example, the claim that all properly brought-up children are polite and considerate, or that in a more equal society males would not be so aggressive. But then we have to ask what exactly the relevant conditions Y are supposed to be (what, in the examples, constitutes "proper upbringing" or "a more equal society"?) and what evidence there is to support the hypothetical claims (how can anyone know what would happen in such counterfactual situations?).

Maybe what is meant is something of the form "Whenever human beings are not X, they suffer consequences Z." Here we may have *both* a factual generalization, and an implicit value judgment about the undesirability of Z, and we should ask for evidence for the former and for reasons for the latter. The objectivity of value judgments is, of course, one of the fundamental questions of philosophy, and I am not prejudging it here. I am just pointing to the need for this kind of clarifying question when discussing human nature.

7.2 Analytic Statements

There is a second, quite different, way in which a statement may be impregnable to contrary evidence, and that is if it is a matter of definition. For instance, if someone says that all humans are animals, it is not clear how any conceivable evidence could count against this. Suppose someone claims (contrary to the theory of evolution) that we do not have a common ancestry with animals. Would we not still count as animals, albeit of a special kind—for it can hardly be denied that we live, feed, breed, and die? Suppose robots were made to walk and talk but not to eat or reproduce like us—they would not be animals. We might treat them as persons if they interacted with us in appropriate ways involving desires, feelings, and responsibility for actions, but surely they would not count as human. (Intelligent aliens might also be counted as persons, but they would not be *human*.) It looks as if nothing can be *called* a human being unless it also counts as an animal. If so, the statement that all humans are animals does not make any assertion about the facts but only reveals part of what we mean by the word "human." It is true by definition: in philosophers' terminology, it is "analytic," i.e., its truth depends merely on analysis of the meaning of its terms. If a statement is thus analytic, it cannot be refuted by any conceivable evidence, but neither can it be proven by evidence, for it does not *attempt* to say anything about the world.

A statement that appears to be saying something about the facts of human nature may thus be really only a concealed definition. If a word is already used with a standard meaning in the language, it is misleading to use it with a different meaning, unless explicit warning is given. Sometimes scientific or philosophical theories introduce new terms or use old words in a new way, and it is then necessary to give definitions and to make it clear that they are not factual claims. Not all matters of meaning are trivial. Definitions may have consequences that are not immediately obvious. For instance, it if is analytic that all animals die and that all humans are animals, then it is analytic that all humans die. Analytic statements, then, can have their uses, but only if they are clearly distinguished from "synthetic statements" that make factual claims. (There has been a debate among philosophers about whether the analytic-synthetic distinction is as clear as it first seems, but there is no need to enter into that difficult theoretical question here.) So if someone maintains that all humans are X and dismisses any suggestion that some might not be X, then we should ask "Is it part of your definition of a human being that he or she must be X, or would you allow the possibility of someone not being X?" Only if the person admits it to be merely a matter of definition can he or she be allowed to dismiss all factual evidence without investigation.

7.3 Empirical Statements, Including Scientific Theories

Value judgments and analytic statements, then, cannot be proven or disproven by discovering facts about the world. If a claim *can* be confirmed or disconfirmed by such investigation—ultimately involving perceptual experience, what we can observe by our senses—it is called by philosophers an "empirical" statement. By use of the clarifying questions just suggested, it should be possible to elucidate whether a statement is evaluative or analytic, rather than empirical.

Science certainly depends crucially on empirical reports of observable fact. But scientific theorizing extends to the far reaches of space and time and to the microstructure of matter. Philosophers of science have tried to elucidate what it is that enables *scientific* theories to give us reliable knowledge about such humanly unobservable aspects of the world. Certainly, science must depend on what we can perceive, for example, when an experiment is conducted, but how can scientific theories about imperceptible entities command rational assent? The answer is that they can be tested *indirectly*—they have consequences (in conjunction with other empirical assumptions) whose truth or falsity *can* be observed.

The twentieth-century philosopher of science Karl Popper put the emphasis on falsification rather than verification here. He held that the essence of scientific method is that theories are *hypotheses*, which can never be known for certain to be true but which are deliberately put to the test of observation and experiment, and revised or rejected if their predictions turn out to be false. It may be that absolutely conclusive falsification of a hypothesis, beyond all possible doubt or reconsideration, is no more achievable than conclusive verification. But the main point remains that if a claim is to count as scientific, some possible observable evidence *must* rationally count for or against it, and anyone defending that claim must be prepared to evaluate rationally all evidence that may be relevant to it. In this sense, statements of scientific theory have to be empirical, subject to the test of our perceptions.

7.4 Metaphysical Statements

The difficult cases are those in which a statement does not seem to fall into any of these three categories. Consider once again the Christian assertion of the existence of God and the Marxist assertion of progress in human history. It seems that they are trying to claim some fundamental truth about the nature of the universe. Their proponents will hardly admit them to be value judgments or mere matters of definition. Yet it is not clear that these assertions are genuinely empirical either, for, as we have seen, although there is a great deal of evidence that seems to count against each, their proponents tend not to accept this as disproof but to find ways of explaining it away. Now if a believer in a theory seems ready to explain away *all possible* evidence against it (freely making additions to the theory whenever necessary), we begin to feel that he or she is winning too easily, by breaking the rules of the game.

This is why some twentieth-century philosophers were attracted to "the verification principle," which stated that no nonanalytic statement can be meaningful unless it is verifiable—or at least testable—by perception. This would imply that any "metaphysical" statement that is neither analytic nor empirical is literally meaningless, a kind of concealed nonsense. Such putative statements would not really be statements at all; they could not be true or even false and would suffer from the more radical defect of not expressing any intelligible proposition. Claims about the existence of God or the inevitable progress in history and many others (including ones more directly about human nature, such as those about the existence of an immortal soul or of predetermining causes behind every human action) were indeed dismissed as meaningless by the "logical positivists" (the proponents of the verification principle in the 1920s and 30s). Value judgments were also dismissed as "cognitively meaningless," as expressions of emotion or attitude, not claims to truth.

Many philosophers have since come to the conclusion that this is too short a way with such big questions. Although it is very important to distinguish statements that are analytic or empirical from those that are neither, we cannot simply dismiss the latter as meaningless. They are too mixed a bag, and they deserve individual attention. The stark choice between meaningful and meaningless seems too crude a tool with which to explore claims about the existence of God, progress in history, the immortality of the soul, or determinism behind human choice. Such claims are not, after all, nonsense in the way that "The mome raths outgrabe" is—nor in the different way that "Green ideas sleep furiously" is; nor are they explicitly self-contradictory like "Some leaves are both green and colorless."

However, the challenge remains that any statement that is not a value judgment and is not analytic, and that does not seem to be testable by observation either, is deeply problematic in status. The examples already mentioned suggest that some controversial statements about human nature may not be scientific claims, empirically testable hypotheses, at all. This need not condemn them outright, but it is a very important feature to establish, for they cannot then enjoy the advantages of scientific status—that their defenders can point to the observable evidence and the connecting arguments and challenge those who believe they can rationally reject the claims. Such statements may have some other sort of function, there may possibly be other sorts of reasons for accepting them, but we had better inquire carefully what they are in each case.

Conventional textbooks and courses in philosophy pursue these issues much further (and they remain on the frontier of philosophical research), but the aim of this book is different: to examine theories of human nature in concrete detail. So this is perhaps as much as we can usefully do by way of preparatory methodology here; let us proceed to our critical examination of particular theories.

Three Ancient Religious Traditions

CHAPTER

2

Confucianism: The Way of the Sages

No other single figure has had more influence on Chinese thought and civilization than Confucius (551–479 B.C.). Little is known for certain about this important figure who came to be regarded as "the teacher" in many periods of Chinese history. He was born into the aristocratic yet poor K'ung family in the state of Lu, now part of the province of Shantung. We are told that as a youth he was orphaned early and was very fond of learning. Later in his life he left his home state of Lu and traveled throughout several regions of China offering his service as an adviser to feudal lords; however, he was never successful at obtaining a position that would allow him to put his ideas into practice and so returned to Lu to devote the remainder of his life to teaching. It is useful to keep this failure in mind while considering certain aspects of his teachings. Confucius became honored in Chinese chronicles as the Great Master K'ung, or K'ung Fu-tzu, better known in the West in the Latinized form "Confucius."

By all accounts the text known as *Lun Yu*—usually rendered into English as *The Analects*—is the most reliable source of Confucius's ideas. The *Analects* consists of scattered sayings of the Master that were compiled by his disciples after his death. It is a matter of scholarly debate whether any or all of the *Analects* can be regarded as the actual words of Confucius, and many will argue that some of the chapters are later additions. Although Confucianism is a complex tradition with a long history of development, the *Analects* gives voice to early and central Confucian ideas that continued to define the tradition for many centuries. Therefore, for the purposes of this introduction, I focus exclusively on the *Analects*, treating the text as a whole, and use the name "Confucius" to refer to the source of the sayings recorded in the *Analects*. Two later developments within Confucianism that pertain to theories of human nature are explored toward the end of this chapter.

Theory of the Universe

The main emphasis in the *Analects* is on humanism, not metaphysics. That is to say, Confucius was concerned primarily with basic human welfare and spoke little about the ultimate nature of the world in which we live. When once asked about worship of gods and spirits, Confucius replied: "You are not able even to serve man. How can you serve the spirits?" (XI.12). And when asked about death he said: "You do not understand even life. How can you understand death?" (XI.12). Avoiding metaphysical speculation, Confucius instead advocated good government that would promote the well-being of the common people and would bring about harmonious relations among citizens. Confucius did, however, recognize that there are forces in the universe that determine our lives. He characterized these by employing two related meanings of the term *ming*: the Decree of Heaven (*t'ien ming*) and Destiny (*ming*).

Confucius insisted that we live in a moral world. Morality is part of the very fabric of the universe; for Confucius, there is something ultimate and transcendent about ethical conduct. He once remarked: "Heaven is author of the virtue that is in me" (VII.23). The concept of the Decree of Heaven was widely accepted in China during Confucius's day. The Decree of Heaven was generally understood to mean a moral imperative for governance, based on the belief that Heaven cares profoundly about the welfare of the common people.

Heaven would support an emperor only so long as he ruled for this higher purpose and not for his own benefit. Confucius added to this doctrine by extending the realm of the heavenly mandate to include every person; now everyone—not just the emperor—was subject to the universal law that obliged one to act morally in order to be in harmony with the Decree of Heaven. Ultimate perfection, then, for Confucius, has to do with cultivating a transcendent morality authored by Heaven. It is possible, however, to resist or disobey the Decree of Heaven.

Nevertheless, there are certain dimensions of life that are beyond human control, areas in which human effort has no effect whatsoever. This indeterminate dimension of human life falls under the heading of Destiny, that aspect of Heaven's design that is beyond human comprehension. One's place in life, social success, wealth, and longevity are all due to Destiny. No amount of struggle will make any difference in their outcome; these things are simply determined by one's fate. Whereas the Decree of Heaven can be understood— although with great difficulty—Destiny is beyond comprehension. The distinction between the Decree of Heaven (to which humans can conform or not) and Destiny (which is beyond human agency) is fundamental for Confucius, for if one understands that the material comforts of life are due to Destiny, one will recognize the futility of pursuing them and will devote all one's effort to the pursuit of Heaven's morality. Morality, then—which has nothing to do with social success—is the only worthy pursuit in life. Confucius argued that it is necessary to understand the nature of both the Decree of Heaven (II.4) and Destiny (XX.3), but for different reasons. The Decree of Heaven is the true object of ultimate concern, whereas Destiny is simply to be accepted courageously.

Before we move on to look at Confucius's views of human nature, it is useful to examine another of his concepts: the Way (*tao*). Although the term *Tao* did come to be used in China as an abstract metaphysical principle (especially by the Taoists), for Confucius it primarily meant the "Way of the sages," those ancient rulers of earlier ideal times. The Confucian concept of the Way is linked intimately to the concept of Heaven in that it involves the path of proper conduct. Although it is difficult to discern, the Way of Heaven can be known through the previous actions of the sages. Regarding the sage Yao, Confucius is recorded as saying: "Great indeed was Yao as a ruler! How lofty! It is Heaven that is great and it was Yao who modeled himself upon it. He was so boundless that the common people were not able to put a name to his virtues" (VIII.19). Accordingly, the ancient sages—who modeled themselves on Heaven—become models of the Way to human perfection in the present, the Way to be followed by all people (VI.17). In the end, three related things warrant reverence according to Confucius. He is recorded as saying: "The gentleman stands in awe of three things. He is in awe of the Decree of Heaven. He is in awe of great men. He is in awe of the words of the sages" (XVI.8).

Theory of Human Nature

Confucius seems to have been very optimistic about potential human accomplishments. In fact, the goal of much of Chinese philosophy is to help people become sages. Confucius's remark that "Heaven is author of the virtue that is in me" demonstrates his conviction that human beings have access to the ultimate reality of Heaven's morality. For Confucius, every person is potentially a sage, defined as one who acts with extreme benevolence (VI.30). That is, all human beings have the capacity to cultivate virtue and bring themselves into harmony with the Decree of Heaven. Confucius indicates that the result of following the Way of Heaven is the subjective experience of joy. Optimism regarding human potential, however, is not the same as optimism about the *actual* state of human affairs. The truth is, Confucius went on to attest, that a sage is a very rare being. He declared: "I have no hopes of meeting a sage" (VII.26). Although all human beings are potential sages, in reality this is an uncommon occurrence. Most human beings exist in a dreadful state.

What is it that enables potential sages to be so misled? Confucius said very little directly about human nature, causing his disciple Tzu-kung to remark: "One can get to hear about the Master's accomplishments, but one cannot get to hear his views on human nature and the Way of Heaven" (V.13). His dearth of statements on human nature allowed widely divergent theories to develop in later

Confucianism. Despite his lack of explicit statements about human nature, however, it is clear from Confucius's sayings that in certain areas of life human beings exercise a freedom of will. Although we have no control over our Destiny—we cannot, for example, determine our social status or longevity—we are free to reject or pursue morality and proper conduct. That is, we have the ability to resist or conform to the Decree of Heaven, the very source of virtue. While acknowledging that human beings have no significant choice as to the circumstances of the life they live, Confucius stressed that we do have a choice as to *how* we live in any given situation.

While he did not define human nature in any detail, Confucius insisted that all human beings are fundamentally the same. We simply become differentiated due to our different ways of being. "Men are close to one another by nature. They diverge as a result of repeated practice" (XVII.2). What this means, among other things, is that human beings are extremely malleable. We can become almost anything. We are unfinished and impressible, and in need of constant molding to achieve our ultimate end of moral perfection. In accord with modern sociologists and psychologists, Confucius seems to be suggesting that our environment and ways of being significantly determine our character. Thus his great concern with paradigmatic figures—the sages—and the role they play in shaping the ideal human life. Human life without carefully crafted culture produces disastrous results. The subsequent state of problematic social conditions are taken up in the next section.

Two additional matters are worth mentioning in regard to Confucius's views of human nature. First, the ideal moral figure for Confucius is the "gentleman" (*chun-tzu*). This term is decidedly masculine. While the term might be applied in a manner that includes both genders, it is clear that Confucius used the term in an exclusive way. He has little to say about women, and when he does speak of them he frequently does so in unflattering terms. On one occasion, for example, he lumps them together with "small men" and warns that in one's household both are "difficult to deal with" (XVII.25).

Second, although Confucius informs us that human nature is fundamentally uniform, he does not clarify whether this is a good nature that needs to be guarded carefully or a bad nature that stands in need of serious reform. His lack of specificity on this issue spawned much heated debate in later Confucianism. We see what two major thinkers in the Confucian tradition have had to say about this important issue in the last section of this chapter.

Diagnosis

Although the sayings of Confucius are predominantly prescriptive, they give a clear indication of what is wrong with human life. Generally speaking, the human condition is one of social discord caused by selfishness and ignorance of the past. Stated perhaps more succinctly, human beings are out of accord with the Decree of Heaven. Consequently, human interaction is marred by strife, rulers govern with attention only to personal gain, common people suffer under unjust burdens, and social behavior in general is determined by egoism and greed. Such is the dismal state of human beings.

What are the reasons for these distressing circumstances? At least five causes can be discerned in the *Analects*: (1) people are attached to profit; (2) society lacks the respect of filial piety; (3) the connection between word and action cannot be trusted; (4) ignorance regarding the Way of the sages prevails; and (5) benevolence is absent from human affairs. Let us examine these causes one by one.

Confucius said: "If one is guided by profit in one's actions, one will incur much ill will" (IV.12). One of the central tenets in Confucian thought is the opposition between rightness and profit. "The gentleman understands what is moral. The small man understands what is profitable" (IV.16). Ordinary human behavior is driven by a strong concern for the outcome of a particular action with regard to the self. That is, people typically ask, What will I get out of this action? The common aim in action, then, is a selfish one. Actions are generally performed to increase one's wealth or power. This is what Confucius means by action guided by profit. Even if a person does what is right, if the motivation is a nonmoral purpose— say, to gain rank—that person is still guided by profit. Confucius warns in the *Analects*: "It is shameful to make salary your sole object" (XIV.1). Since he believed that morality should be the sole guide for all action, Confucius contended that action guided by profit leads to immoral circumstances and social disharmony wherein all people are selfishly looking out for themselves alone. Material benefits derived from invested labor are not in themselves bad, but the means by which they are obtained is of critical importance to Confucius. "Wealth and rank attained through immoral means have as much to do with me as passing clouds" (VII.16).

Selfish conduct motivated by personal profit implies a lack of true respect for others in a given society. For Confucius, this lack of respect reveals improper relationships within families, which in turn demonstrates a lack of self-discipline. This occurs because individuals have lost their grounding in morality, leading to problems in the family, which is the very basis of a good society. In this sense, Confucianism is very much a tradition of family values. A son who does not know how to treat his father will be a very poor citizen. Corrupt individuals, then, who have not cultivated the personal virtue necessary for proper familial relationships spread ill will throughout society. On the other hand, "It is rare for a man whose character is such that he is good as a son and obedient as a young man to have the inclination to transgress against his superiors" (I.2).

Another problem noted by Confucius is the fact that there is often a difference between what is said and what is done. Confucius said: "I used to take on trust a man's deeds after having listened to his words. Now having listened to a man's words I go on to observe his deeds" (V.10). Confucius recognizes that people are often untrustworthy. Without a direct connection between word and deed there is no basis for trust, since trust rests on the premise that what is said will be done. Without this basic trust, individuals lose the ability to represent themselves sincerely and to rely on others with any degree of confidence. Accordingly, society loses its footing.

Ignorance of the past is also a major cause of the troublesome human condition. What Confucius means specifically by this is an unfamiliarity with the Way of the sages. It was pointed out earlier that the sages model their lives on Heaven, thereby establishing a paradigm for the path to moral perfection. Without knowledge of the Way of the sages, people are cut off from the moral insight of the past. In such a state they become morally adrift and prone to wrong action. Confucius had so much faith in the Way of the sages that he remarked: "He has not lived in vain who dies the day he is told about the Way" (IV.8).

The most important virtue that a human being can possess for Confucius is benevolence (*jen*). To embody benevolence is to achieve moral perfection. This central Confucian idea is represented by a Chinese character that has been explained pictographically as consisting of two parts: the component for "human" and the component for "two." That is, it represents two people standing together in harmony. Essentially, benevolence has to do with human relationships. Several scholars have argued that *jen* is better translated into English as "human-heartedness" or "humaneness." Regardless, *jen* is a wide-ranging moral term that represents the very pinnacle of human excellence for Confucius. And, according to him, it is definitely within the reach of human beings. "The Master said, 'Is benevolence really far away? No sooner do I desire it than it is here' " (VII.30). The core of a perfected human being, then, is a benevolent heart. Unfortunately, Confucius observes, this virtue is all too rare in the world: "I have never met a man who finds benevolence attractive" (IV.6). Consequently, potential social harmony is replaced with strife.

Prescription

The Confucian prescription for the ills of human existence is based on self-discipline. When questioned about the perfect man, Confucius said: "He cultivates himself and thereby brings peace and security to the people" (XIV.42). The ideal ruler for Confucius rules by personal moral example. But just what does self-cultivation mean in this context? The answer to this question can be found by exploring the proposed solutions to the five ills outlined in the preceding section.

To overcome the human tendency to act out of a concern for profit, Confucius proposed "doing for nothing." Specifically, this involves doing what is right simply because it is morally right, and not for any other reason. For Confucius, the moral struggle is an end in itself; through it, one achieves a union of will with the Decree of Heaven. Acting in order to do what is right, rather than what is profitable, can serve also as a shield against life's disappointments. The state of benevolence is characterized by an inner serenity and equanimity and an indifference to matters of fortune and misfortune over which one has no direct control. Righteousness is its own reward, a joyous reward that transcends any particular social situation. Even if all one's efforts go unrecognized, by following the principle of "doing for nothing" one is never discontented. "Is it not gentlemanly not to take offence when others fail to appreciate your abilities?" (I.1). Furthermore, this principle motivates one to keep working for righteousness in a world that has little appreciation for it. Confucius himself is described as one "who keeps working towards a goal the realization of which he knows to be hopeless" (XIV.38). Faith in the Way of Heaven does not depend on results within the social world of rank and recognition. Remember that Confucius himself failed to secure a political position that would have provided him recognition and allow him to put his ideas into practice. He says in the *Analects* that a man should strive to enter politics simply because he knows this to be right, even when he is well aware that his principles cannot prevail (XVIII.7). This relates to the notion of Destiny discussed in the first section of this chapter. Social success is a matter of Destiny; Confucius therefore concludes that it is futile to pursue it. Moral integrity, however, is within one's control, and in truth it is the only thing in life worth pursuing. One can struggle to understand the ways of Heaven, but it is clear that one should act humanely whatever Heaven sends. Again, it is the cultivation of self that is important, not social recognition. "The gentleman is troubled by his own lack of ability, not the failure of others to appreciate him" (XV.19).

The cultivation of self as a good family member is another of Confucius's prescriptions for a harmonious society. He believed that being a good family member had tremendous influence beyond the boundary of one's immediate family. "Simply by being a good son and friendly to his brothers a man can exert an influence upon government" (II.21). The transformation of society begins with the cultivation of the self within the environment of the family; it then spreads out like ripples caused from throwing a pebble in a still pond. The rules and relationships that govern the family are to be extended to include all of society. Benevolence toward people outside one's family should be an extension of the love one feels for members of one's own family. The most important relationship of all for Confucius is the one between a son and his father. When questioned about filial piety, Confucius advised: "Never fail to comply" (II.5). The manner in which a good son honors a father is by following his ways. "If [after his father's death], for three years, a man makes no changes to his father's ways, he can be said to be a good son" (I.11). This depends, of course, on the virtuous qualities of the father. Confucius is adamant that the father of the family, or by extension the emperor of the state, must rule by moral example. "If you set an example by being correct, who would dare to remain incorrect?" (XII.17).

Confucius was once asked what would be the first thing he would do if he were put in charge of the administration of a state. He replied: "If something has to be put first, it is, perhaps, the rectification of names" (XIII.3). The rectification of names means that there is an agreement between name and actuality. This correction is necessary, because without the agreement between name and actuality, or between word and deed, much is lost. For Confucius, a name carries certain implications that constitute the very essence of the named object. For example, when asked by a duke about good government, Confucius responded by saying: "Let the ruler be a ruler, the subject a subject, the father a father, the son a son" (XII.11). The concept of "son," for example, as we have just seen, is more than a biological designation. The name implies certain attitudes and responsibilities essential to harmonious existence. Moreover, without the connection between word and actuality there is no genuine trust. This is the definition of a lie. After hearing Confucius's remark on good government, the duke exclaimed: "Splendid! Truly, if the ruler be not a ruler, the subject not a subject, the father not a father, the son not a son, then even if there be grain, would I get to eat it?" That is, the word "grain" and the availability of grain are two different things. If there is no connection between them, then one may go hungry because of a locked, or perhaps even empty, granary. Words are easy to produce; if a person or government uses them to conceal the truth, then social chaos ensues. Trust is a critical ingredient of all dependable social interaction. Therefore, the self-cultivating gentleman is "trustworthy in what he says" (I.7) and "puts his words into actions" (II.13).

The antidote for the ignorance of the past referred to in the preceding section is study. Confucianism is a scholarly tradition. In China it is known as the Ju School—the term *ju* comes to mean "scholar"—and is recorded in Chinese sources as the school that delights in study of the Six Classics (*Lui Yi*). From this it is evident that

Confucius placed great emphasis on learning. He advised: "Have the firm faith to devote yourself to learning, and abide to the death in the good way" (VII.13). But what is the content of this learning that allows one to abide in the good way? It is clear from the representation of Confucianism just mentioned that the content of Confucian learning is the Classics, a collection of books that constitutes the cultural legacy of the past. Most important for Confucius, the Classics give expression to the Way of the sages and thus grant access to the exemplary conduct that leads to moral perfection. Because of this, study of the Classics is understood to be a vital element in achieving excellence and a sacred enterprise that expands one's nature. It is also an important aspect of good government. "When a student finds that he can more than cope with his studies, then he takes office" (XIX.13).

Excellence is defined by the Confucian tradition primarily as the embodiment of benevolence. The manner in which one comes to embody benevolence constitutes the last of the five solutions being explored. This process really involves three elements: clinging to benevolence at all times while following the "golden rule" and observing the "rites."

Confucius said: "The gentleman never deserts benevolence, not even for as long as it takes to eat a meal" (IV.5). That is to say, one is to be ever mindful of benevolence in everything one does. The Confucian goal is to let benevolence determine all aspects of life, since it is the perfect virtue that denotes the Decree of Heaven. Confucius himself is described in the *Analects* as one who maintained correctness and benevolence at all times (VII.4). But how is one to know what constitutes benevolence?

The practice of benevolence consists in balanced consideration for others and oneself. One measure of the consideration for others is determined by the treatment one desires for oneself. Confucius says: "A benevolent man helps others to take their stand in so far as he himself wishes to take his stand" (VI.30). In other words, this is the golden rule: "Do unto others what you would have done to yourself." Confucius also states this rule in negative form. When asked to define benevolence, he said: "Do not impose on others what you yourself do not desire" (XII.2). In a general sense, then, one's own self becomes a measure of decent conduct. However, Confucius has more to say about the measure of excellent conduct than this. Even if a person's heart is in the right place, it is possible to offend others because of a lack of knowledge about what is appropriate conduct in a particular situation. Knowledge is a key component to ethical action. Specifically for Confucius, this means knowing ritually correct behavior, or the rites (*li*). These consist of regulations governing action in every aspect of life, as well as ceremonial propriety, such as in making offerings to the ancestors. The rites are designed to teach individuals how to act well and are therefore a critical component in moral education. Knowledge of the rites functions as a guide for action beyond the general decency derived from using one's own self as a measure of conduct. Self-interest must finally be harnessed to the rites in order to achieve moral perfection. "To return to the observance of the rites through overcoming the self constitutes benevolence" (XII.1). Observing these rules, a person transcends self-interest. The rites are a body of rules culled from past moral insights and guide action toward perfection. What are the rites based on, and how does one come to know about them? They are based on the Classics, and one comes to know of them through study. Thus, the interconnectedness of Confucius's ideas comes into focus. Moral perfection, or benevolence, is achieved by following the rites, which are known by studying the Classics, which give expression to the Way of Heaven as embodied by the sages.

Perhaps the most significant passage of all those recorded in the *Analects* is one that gives a summary indication of the path to perfection as it is understood in early Confucianism. "The Master said, 'At fifteen I set my heart on learning; at thirty I took my stand; at forty I came to be free from doubts; at fifty I understood the Decree of Heaven; at sixty my ear was atuned; at seventy I followed my heart's desire without overstepping the line' " (II.4). Here Confucius is saying that at fifteen he took up serious study of the Classics. This gave him access to a knowledge of the Way of the sages and, therefore, an awareness of the rites, the institutional form of their perfect demeanor. At age thirty he was able to take a stand in the rites, or to put the proper conduct of the rites into practice. By practicing the rites, he moved at age forty from mere observation of the rites to true understanding of the rites. This led to a concomitant understanding of the Decree of Heaven by age fifty. At sixty Confucius experienced a union of wills with the Decree of Heaven, so that by age seventy he could follow his own desire—now in harmony with the Decree of Heaven—with the result that he spontaneously acted with perfect benevolence.

Indicated here is the salvific path of paradigmatic action. As perfect beings, the sages naturally act with benevolence. Their benevolence is the external expression of a perfected inner state. As such, their benevolent actions become models of and for perfection for Confucians who desire to achieve the accomplished state of a sage. Again, the Way of the sages is available in the Classics; thus the great attention paid to study in the Confucian tradition. What the sages perform naturally becomes the model for the conscious self-discipline that leads to moral perfection. Proper disciplined action is represented in the Confucian tradition as the rites (*li*). From an outsider's perspective, the natural benevolent action of a sage and of a self-disciplined person who follows the rites appear the same, but the internal motive is different. The sage's behavior is the natural expression of an inner perfected state, whereas the disciplined person's behavior consists of studied actions—the rites—that are modeled on the benevolence of the sages. The goal of disciplined action, however, is to achieve a state wherein perfect moral action becomes natural and spontaneous. This is the state of the "gentleman," and this is what is said to have happened to Confucius toward the end of his life. The sages express moral perfection naturally, whereas the gentleman has achieved perfection by modeling his life on the behavior of the sages. The actions of a gentleman and a disciplined Confucian student may also appear the same from the outside, just as a master musician and a disciplined student appear to be making the same moves. But once again, the motives are different in both cases. The master musician has so internalized the fingering chart of the instrument she is playing that she is no longer conscious of it, whereas the student is still consciously following the fingering chart. Likewise, the gentleman has so internalized the Way of the sages that he now acts spontaneously, whereas the Confucian student who "stands in the rites" consciously follows the proper conduct that the rites represent. In either case, by following the rites, both the gentleman and the diligent student have embodied benevolence, the very pinnacle of moral perfection.

As a paradigmatic tradition, Confucianism produces a chain of perfected moral action that makes the benevolent Way of the sages present for the common people and creates moral examples for those who are not involved in the elite tradition of textual study. It should be clear by now that moral perfection for the Confucian tradition is represented by the sages and that, as the ideal of human perfection, the gentleman has achieved moral perfection by studying the Classics and internalizing the Way of the sages. The Confucian practitioner is ideally moving along this same path. Direct observation of present-day human practitioners takes the place of textual study for those unable to read. To the degree that a practitioner can embody benevolence by following the Confucian rites, the Way of the sages is then present for all of society to observe and to follow. In this way, a line of moral perfection reaches back from the time of the sages and continues into the very present. If all people would follow this Way, Confucius believed, individuals would achieve perfection, society would be radically transformed, and benevolence would rule.

Later Developments

Because Confucius did not spell out his views on human nature in any detail, a major debate arose within the tradition soon after his death regarding this question: Is human nature originally good or evil? Opposing answers were supplied by two leading figures in the Confucian tradition. Representing the "idealistic wing," Mencius (371–289 B.C.) contended that human nature is originally good; representing the "realistic wing," Hsun-tzu (298–238 B.C.) argued that human nature is originally evil. Although we cannot possibly do justice to the entire Confucian tradition here, a brief examination of this debate gives further indication of the complexity of this tradition and adds to our overall consideration of human nature.

The writings and ideas of Mencius rank second in the tradition only to those of Confucius, and, above all, his name is associated with his theory of the original goodness of human nature. In a collection of his sayings recorded in a book that bears his name, Mencius articulates his position on the controversy over human nature that came to be regarded as orthodox for the Confucian tradition and normative for much of Chinese culture. In the *Mencius*, Mencius refutes a philosopher named Kao-tzu, who argues that human nature is intrinsically neither good nor bad and that morality therefore is something that has to be added artificially from the outside. "Human nature," Kao-tzu maintains, "is like whirling water. Give it an outlet in the east and it will flow east; give it an outlet in the west and it will flow west. Human nature does not show any preference for either good or bad just as water does not show any preference for either east or west." Mencius, however, is insistent that human nature is innately good. He counters Kao-tzu by explaining: "It certainly is the case that water does not show any preference for either east or west, but does it show the same indifference to high and low? Human nature is good just as water seeks low ground. There is no man who is not good; there is no water that does not flow downwards" (VI.A.2).

The core of Mencius's theory about innate human nature relates to his understanding of the human heart. For Mencius, the thinking, compassionate heart is a gift from Heaven (VI.A.15). This is what defines our essential humanness and sets us apart from animals. Specifically, the heart is a receptacle of four incipient tendencies or "seeds," as Mencius calls them. He maintains that "Man has these four germs just as he has four limbs" (II.A.6). If unobstructed and nurtured carefully, these seeds sprout into the four virtues so greatly prized by the Confucian tradition, as lofty trees grow naturally from small seeds. The four seeds of compassion, shame, courtesy, and sense of right and wrong develop respectively into the four virtues of benevolence, dutifulness, observance of the rites, and wisdom (II.A.6). And Mencius insists that these four seeds "are not welded on to me from the outside; they are in me originally" (VI.6). For Mencius, our original heart identifies us all as potential sages.

Mencius, however, agrees with many of the philosophers of his time that human beings are creatures of desire. Selfish desire in particular threatens to overwhelm the four seeds that define the source of our higher moral nature. The heavenly gift of the thinking heart is therefore recognized to be fragile and can be lost if not used and cultivated. This, of course, is the norm. Mencius says: "Heaven has not sent down men whose endowment differs so greatly. The difference is due to what ensnares their hearts" (VI.A.7). The ensnarement of the human heart, for Mencius, is the source of all evil; thus the great concern for carefully nurturing its innate qualities. "Given the right nourishment there is nothing that will not grow, and deprived of it there is nothing that will not wither away" (VI.8).

All hope for humanity, according to Mencius, lies in the human heart. Our desiring nature is something we share with all animals, but it is our thinking heart—that special gift from Heaven—that sets us up to be benevolent sages. Mencius offers a proof for the innate goodness of all people. "My reason for saying that no man is devoid of a heart sensitive to the suffering of others is this. Suppose a man were, all of a sudden, to see a young child on the verge of falling into a well. He would certainly be moved to compassion, not because he wanted to get in the good graces of the parents, nor because he wished to win the praise of his fellow villagers or friends, nor yet because he disliked the cry of the child" (II.A.6). What Mencius seems to be saying here is that every person in this situation would have an immediate, spontaneous, and unreflective urge to save the child. This reveals a pure impulse for righteousness over selfish profit. Mencius says nothing about the ensuing action. It may be the case that the man involved would, upon any reflection following the "all of a sudden," engage in calculating thoughts of self-interest. Regardless of what follows, however, the momentary urge indicated in this statement is all Mencius needs to demonstrate what he refers to as the seed of compassion. For him, this proves that human nature is intrinsically good.

Mencius's strongest opponent was Hsun-tzu, an important Confucian writer who was born toward the end of Mencius's life. Hsun-tzu held that our interior world is dominated by dynamic impulses of desire. The basic human problem for Hsun-tzu is that human libidinous urges have no clear limit. Nature has given us unlimited desires in a world with limited resources; hence, social strife arises among necessarily competitive human beings. In a text he composed himself, Hsun-tzu writes: "Man is born with desires. If desires are not satisfied for him, he cannot but seek some means to satisfy them himself. If there are no limits and degrees to his seeking, then he will inevitably fall to wrangling with other men" (section 19, p. 89). This view caused him to formulate a position on human nature diametrically opposed to that of Mencius: "Man's nature is evil; goodness is the result of conscious activity" (section 23, p. 157). Hsun-tzu was well aware of Mencius's ideas but insisted that they were wrong. "Mencius states that man's nature is good, and that evil arises because he loses his original nature. Such a view, I believe, is erroneous" (158). Hsun-tzu replaces Mencius's theory of the four seeds with his own theory of four incipient tendencies for profit, envy, hatred, and desire, which if left in their natural state give rise to the four evils of strife, violence, crime, and wantonness. These, he insists, are innate in all humans, so that the path that follows our own nature leads only to evil. "Any man who follows his nature and indulges his emotions will inevitably become involved in wrangling and strife, will violate the forms and rules of society, and will end as a criminal" (157).

Hsun-tzu goes on to compare the criminal-like human being to a warped piece of wood. "A warped piece of wood must wait until it has been laid against the straightening board, steamed, and forced into shape before it can become straight, because by nature it is warped" (164). Surprisingly, Hsun-tzu is rather optimistic about potential human accomplishments, for he too believed that with the proper education and training all people could become sages. "The man in the street can become a Yu [a sage]" (166). What is it, we might ask, that transforms the warped pieces of wood that are human beings into the straight boards of sages, or at least proper citizens? That is, what constitutes the straightening board for human beings? After his statement about warped wood, Hsun-tzu writes: "Similarly, since man's nature is evil, he must wait for the ordering power of the sage kings and the transforming power of ritual principles; only then can he achieve order and conform to goodness" (164). Hsun-tzu here confirms the absolute value of a fundamental Confucian idea; the straightening board consists of the rites, or what is here translated as "ritual principles." For him, the rites are the products of the sheer intellectual activity of the sages and were designed to curb and channel the boundless desires of human beings. When Hsun-tzu says that "goodness is the result of conscious activity," he means a conscious effort to transform oneself by diligently applying oneself to the rites, those guiding principles created and embodied by past sages. Hsun-tzu is clearly an advocate for culture over nature, for the rites are not an essential part of human nature. Everything that is good is a product of conscious human effort. The fact that we have two arms is natural, but virtue comes only with assiduous human effort. For him, the attentive application of the unnatural rites is the key to achieving human perfection. "In respect to human nature the sage is the same as all other men and does not surpass them; it is only in his conscious activity that he differs from and surpasses other men" (161). The sage, then, for Hsun-tzu, is a human being whose nature has been radically transformed by the Confucian rites.

The contrast between Mencius and Hsun-tzu is dramatic. Mencius believed that morality is naturally present in our hearts, whereas Hsun-tzu believed that it is something artificially instilled from the outside. Nevertheless, we observe an agreement in the ideas of Hsun-tzu and Mencius that identifies them both as Confucians. Both agree that the path to sagehood comprises the Confucian rites, those proper modes of action based on the paradigmatic behavior of past sages. For Hsun-tzu, the rites function as a straightening board to transform warped human beings into straight and benevolent citizens, whereas for Mencius, they function more like a racket press designed to keep a stored wooden tennis racket from warping; although innately present, the heart of compassion can become twisted if not reinforced with the constant observance of the rites. Although the two philosophers disagree sharply in theory, they are in complete agreement regarding practice. Human perfection is achieved through a process of following the paradigmatic actions and insights of past sages.

Critical Discussion

We may conclude this introduction to Confucianism with a few comments designed to bring into sharper focus some possible criticisms already hinted at in our discussion. Besides being a system that is rooted in the common decency of the golden rule, Confucianism is a tradition that teaches obedience to superiors. The relevant superiors are the father of the family, the ruler of the state, and the Confucian scholar who makes accessible the Way of the sages. If the head of the family and state are just men, then all is well. But if such men are unjust, then the entire system is undermined. Confucius himself was aware of this problem and therefore insistent on the moral character of leaders. Nonetheless, his system gives a great deal of power to a few individuals and leaves the majority in a subordinate position.

Confucianism is also a fairly conservative tradition that looks to the past for guidance. This may be seen as an attitude that restricts the creativity of individuals in the present. Furthermore, it is a system dependent on an elite of literati, the Confucian scholars. We might ask, Do scholars have access to the past in a manner that is free of their own ideological agendas? Confucianism, it has been shown, is based largely on a transcendent view of morality. It may be argued that such a view is simply a way for a certain group to give special privilege to its own view of morality. We might then ask, Whose view of the past and whose view of morality is Confucianism based on? Most historians today contend that no view of the past is completely neutral or apolitical. All historical representations involve issues of power.

Many people seem to be excluded from the Confucian enterprise. The common people are represented as an undifferentiated and generally inept mass. Women in particular do not seem to be included in Confucius's educational system. His view of human perfection is decidedly masculine, and all in all he has little to say about the potential of women for self-cultivation. When Confucius does speak about women, he does so in derogatory terms, suggesting that they are generally unruly and resistant to legitimate authority. Although the Confucian path to perfection may be expanded by its advocates to include both genders, the *Analects* poses a problem for readers who believe in the equality of the sexes.

Finally, the pragmatic nature of Confucianism has been criticized by other Chinese philosophers, such as the more metaphysically minded Taoists. The Taoist philosopher Chuang-tzu, for example, criticized the Confucians for their reduction of reality to only that which concerns human social affairs. Chuang-tzu reversed Hsun-tzu's assessment of what is valuable by advocating nature over culture. As a nature mystic aware of the immensity of life in all its forms, Chuang-tzu believed that the Confucians occupied a tragically small world. He also characterized Confucians as people overly concerned with utilitarian matters and countered this preoccupation with a celebration of the usefulness of uselessness. Over the course of time, however, Confucianism has proven to be a much more attractive system to Chinese thinkers for establishing virtuous human society than the more abstract metaphysical thought of Taoism.

For Further Reading

Basic text: *The Analects* (many translations and editions). I have quoted from the excellent translation by D. C. Lau, *Confucius: The Analects* (London: Penguin, 1979). This is a very readable and reliable text that includes a valuable introduction. Another readily available translation is that by Arthur Waley, *The Analects of Confucius* (New York: Macmillan, 1938; New York: Vintage, 1989).

Mencius: I have quoted from the translation by D. C. Lau, *Mencius* (London: Penguin, 1970). This edition also includes an excellent introduction.

Hsun-tzu: I have quoted from the translation by Burton Watson, *Hsun Tzu: Basic Writings* (New York: Columbia University Press, 1963).

For more on Confucianism, see *Thinking through Confucius* by Roger T. Ames and David L. Hall (Albany: State University of New York Press, 1987).

To gain a better understanding of the place of Confucianism in Chinese philosophy, see *A Short History of Chinese Philosophy* by Fung Yu-lan (New York: Macmillan, 1948; New York: Free Press, 1966); *Disputers of the Tao* by A. C. Graham (Lasalle, Ill.: Open Court, 1989); and *The World of Thought in Ancient China* by Benjamin I. Schwartz (Cambridge, Mass.: Harvard University Press, 1985).

3

Upanishadic Hinduism: Quest for Ultimate Knowledge

An introductory examination of Hinduism can be very challenging, since there is no founder, no clear historical beginning point nor central text, as we find in most other religious traditions. Hinduism is an extremely diverse tradition that consists of a wide range of practices and beliefs, making the task of generalization nearly impossible. The term "Hinduism" itself is largely a Western construct designed simply to refer to the dominant religion of the majority of the people who inhabit the South Asian subcontinent. Therefore, in many ways, it is absurd to attempt to represent Hinduism with a single text, for no particular text is accepted as authoritative by all people who might identify themselves as Hindus, and many think of their religion as being grounded in a way of action, rather than a written text. Nevertheless, if one were to seek a "foundational text" to represent significant tenets of Hindu philosophy, a good selection would be one of the principal Upanishads. The group of texts known as Upanishads have played a decisive role throughout Hindu religious history; they have defined central philosophical issues in India for centuries and continue to be a major source of inspiration and guidance within the Hindu world today. One of the objectives of this chapter is to give a sense of the wide range of interpretive possibilities that emerge from early Hindu texts, demonstrating specifically how practices as diverse as world renunciation and forms of worship that embrace the world itself as divine are justified by the same texts.

The earliest Upanishads were composed in northern India in the seventh or eighth century B.C. The term "Upanishad" means literally to "sit near" but has come to mean "esoteric teaching," for these texts represent secret teachings passed on to groups of close disciples by forest-dwelling meditation masters. The Upanishads, which contain highly speculative thought about the ultimate nature of reality, are among the greatest intellectual creations of the world. Although the Upanishads do not present a single philosophical system but rather give voice to exploratory and often contradictory reflections, their overall theme is one of ontological unity, the belief that everything is radically interconnected. The oldest and largest of the Upanishads is the *Brihad Aranyaka Upanishad* ("The Great and Secret Teachings of the Forest"). This text is not the product of a single author but is a compilation of a number of conversations between teachers and students. The *Brihad Aranyaka Upanishad* has a great deal to say about the ultimate nature of the world and the true identity of human beings and thus provides a good starting point for exploring important issues within Hindu philosophy.

Theory of the Universe

We observe in the *Brihad Aranyaka Upanishad* an ardent metaphysical search for the absolute ground of all being. One of the central philosophical tenets of the Upanishads is that there is a single, unifying principle underlying the entire universe. At the level of ultimate realization, the world of multiplicity is revealed to be one of interconnected unity. The attempt to identify that unifying principle can be seen in a famous passage involving the philosopher Gargi Vacaknavi and the great sage Yajnavalkya (3.6). Gargi opens an inquiry into the ultimate nature of the world, challenging Yajnavalkya to identify the very foundation of all existence. She asks the sage: "Since this whole world is woven back and forth on water, on what, then, is water woven back and forth?" Yajnavalkya responds initially: "On air, Gargi." But Gargi is not satisfied with this answer. "On what,

then, is air woven back and forth?" Yajnavalkya supplies another answer, and then another, and still another as Gargi pressed him to identify increasingly fundamental layers of reality. Finally, the sage
reveals to her that the entire universe is woven back and forth on
what he calls "*brahman.*" At this point he claims that he can go no
further; *brahman* is declared to be the end of Gargi's search. Although
other entities were suggested as the possible foundation of all being
(e.g., space [4.1.1] and water [5.5.1]), these were rejected, as the one
ultimate reality and absolute ground of all being came to be identified as *brahman*. *Brahman* was declared to be the highest aim of all
metaphysical inquiry: "All the vedic learning that has been acquired
is subsumed under '*brahman*' " (1.5.17).

The term *brahman* is derived from a Sanskrit root that means to
"grow," "expand," or "increase." Although in early usage it was associated with sacred utterances, over the course of time it came to
be identified with the very force that sustains the world. During the
time of the Upanishads, it settled into its principal meaning of "ultimate reality," the primary cause of existence, or the absolute ground
of being. Another famous passage from the *Brihad Aranyaka
Upanishad* well portrays the metaphysical quest for the unitary
ground of being that ends in *brahman* (3.9.). Since this passage yields
keen insight into Hindu theology, I quote it in full.

The passage opens with the searcher Vidagdha Shakalya questioning the sage Yajnavalkya about the number of gods in existence.
"How many gods are there?" he asks. Yajnavalkya responds first:
"Three and three hundred, and three and three thousand." Not satisfied with this answer Vidagdha continues.

> "Yes, of course," he said, "but really, Yajnavalkya, how many gods
> are there?"
> "Thirty-three."
> "Yes, of course," he said, "but really, Yajnavalkya, how many gods
> are there?"
> "Six."
> "Yes, of course," he said, "but really, Yajnavalkya, how many gods
> are there?"
> "Three."
> "Yes, of course," he said, "but really, Yajnavalkya, how many gods
> are there?"
> "Two."

"Yes, of course," he said, "but really, Yajnavalkya, how many gods
are there?"

"One and a half."

"Yes, of course," he said, "but really, Yajnavalkya, how many gods
are there?"

"One."

When asked by Vidagdha to identify this "one god," Yajnavalkya
concludes: "He is called '*brahman*'."

Although divinity expresses itself in multiple forms, ultimately it
is One. Here again, we witness philosophical inquiry into the ultimate nature of reality that ends with the discovery of the single unifying principle called *brahman*. But if reality is one, how—and
why—did it become many? Creation stories maintained by any tradition tell us much about that tradition. We find in the *Brihad
Aranyaka Upanishad* an account of creation that provides answers to
these questions and serves as a model for much Hindu thought.

"In the beginning there was nothing" (1.2.1). Yet a great deal can
come from nothing, for much of the Hindu tradition holds that the
entire universe came out of this original nothingness. Like the modern "Big Bang" theory, this text describes an expansion from an original dimensionless point of infinite unity; yet, unlike the Big Bang
theory, this account of creation tells us *why* the expansion occurred.

In the beginning there was nothing but the single unitary principle, *brahman*. However, because it was alone, it was lonely and
"found no pleasure at all" (1.4.2). In this state of loneliness, it desired another and so divided itself into two parts, a male and a female. Departing from the original state of abstract neutrality, the male
and female pair began to interact sexually, and from this was born
the entire universe of diverse forms. Thus, the original point of undifferentiated unity divided itself and, exploding outward, produced
the phenomenal world of multiple forms. The *Brihad Aranyaka
Upanishad* calls this "*brahman*'s super-creation" (1.4.6). This account of creation expresses the true nature of reality and the ultimate
aim of beings within that reality. We will have occasion to refer to
this story later, but the important point is to realize that it accounts
for the multiplicity of the world, while recognizing in a fundamental way the radically interconnectedness of the world. The original

unity is never lost; it simply takes on the appearance of multiple forms.

This theory of the origin of the universe recognizes the simultaneity of unity and diversity. The One reality differentiates itself through what the text calls "name and visible appearance" (1.4.7). The world we experience with our senses, then, is a single reality, though it is clothed with a variety of names and appearances. This is aptly expressed in the following verse:

> The world there is full;
> The world here is full;
> Fullness from fullness proceeds.
> After taking fully from the full,
> It still remains completely full. (5.1.1)

Here we have a portrait of divinity that is simultaneously immanent and transcendent. *Brahman* is not only *in* the world, it *is* the world; there is also a dimension of *brahman* that is completely beyond the world of multiple forms. This is asserted in the *Brihad Aranyaka Upanishad* as a teaching about the two aspects (*rupa*) of *brahman* as the form and the formless: "the one has a fixed shape (*murta*), and the other is without a fixed shape (*amurta*)" (2.3.1). *Brahman* as all forms is everything that is solid and transitory, whereas *brahman* as the formless is ethereal and unchanging. A good way to approach this philosophy is to reflect on the double meaning of the phrase "Nothing ever remains the same." The world of concrete things is in constant flux and always changing; things never remain the same. On the other hand, the no-thingness from which all comes is eternal and unchanging; it ever remains the same. It is important to remember, however, that these are not two separate realities but the same reality seen from different perspectives. The world of forms is pervaded by the unified *brahman* as salt pervades the water in which it is dissolved: "It is like this. When a chunk of salt is thrown in water, it dissolves into that very water, and it cannot be picked up in any way. Yet, from whichever place one may take a sip, the salt is there! In the same way this Immense Being has no limit or boundary and is a single mass of perception" (2.4.12).

Before we move on to examine what the *Brihad Aranyaka*

Upanishad has to say about human nature, one additional important point should be mentioned. Several passages insist that *brahman* is inexpressible and therefore impossible to define. We are told, for example, that "it is neither coarse nor fine; it is neither short nor long; it has neither blood nor fat; it is without shadow or darkness; it is without air or space; it is without contact; it has no taste or smell; it is without sight or hearing; it is without speech or mind; it is without energy, breath, or mouth, it is beyond measure; it has nothing within or outside of it; it does not eat anything; and no one eats it" (3.8.8). That is, *brahman* is completely beyond the world we experience with our senses. This is often expressed in the text by saying that *brahman* is "not this, not that (*neti neti*)."

On the other hand, there are passages that identify *brahman* with everything we experience with our senses: "Clearly, this self is *brahman*—this self that is made of perception, made of mind, made of sight, made of breath, made of hearing, made of earth, made of water, made of wind, made of space, made of light and the lightless, made of desire and the desireless, made of anger and the angerless, made of righteous and the unrighteous; this self is made of everything" (4.4.5). In direct contrast to the "not this, not that" view, this passage continues: "He's made of this. He's made of that." These two different ways of describing *brahman* led to divergent understandings of the world and the self, which in turn resulted in significant differences in religious practice. Two of the most important interpretations of the Upanishads are explored in the final section of this chapter.

Theory of Human Nature

The recognition that all of life is interconnected has clear implications for a theory of human nature. According to the *Brihad Aranyaka Upanishad*, our kin are not only fellow human beings but all other beings as well. This text teaches that the essential self of a human being is radically connected to all beings: "The self within all is this self of yours" (3.5.1). The ultimate self—referred to in the Upanishads by the term "*atman*"—is not, therefore, an autonomous unit operating independent of other beings but rather a part of this larger inter-related network of reality. "This very self [*atman*] is the lord and king of all beings. As all the spokes are fastened to the hub and the rim of a wheel, so to one's self are fastened all beings, all the gods, all the worlds, all the breaths, and all these bodies" (2.5.15). The text makes it very clear that the true self not only animates all beings but is inseparable from the whole of reality (2.5.1–14). The self is all, and all is the self.

The Upanishads certainly recognize a self that is transitory and separate from other selves. That is, the self as ego (*ahamkara*) is identified with the body and its social environment. This is the self we immediately think of when someone asks us who we are. This is also the self we ordinarily invest with great meaning and strive to preserve. This, however, is neither the ultimate self nor the true identity of a human being. The essential self is defined as the *atman*. Our ordinary self is simply a finite, conditioned mask covering our true and infinite nature.

Some passages in the *Brihad Aranyaka Upanishad* suggest that the *atman* is undefinable: "About the self (*atman*), one can only say 'not—, not—'. He is ungraspable, for he cannot be grasped. He is undecaying, for he is not subject to decay. He has nothing yet he neither trembles in fear nor suffers injury" (3.9.28). Other passages, however, identify the *atman* with everything: "He's the maker of everything—the author of all! The world is his—he's the world itself!" (4.4.13). In either case, the text goes on to define the *atman* as the immortal, unchanging self; it "is beyond hunger and thirst, sorrow and delusion, old age and death" (3.5.1).

A central teaching of the Upanishads is that the true self is that eternal dimension of reality that is somehow not different from the highest reality of *brahman*: "And this is the immense and unborn self, unageing, undying, immortal, free from fear—the *brahman*" (4.4.24). Since the *atman* is identified with *brahman*, it too is defined as the very source of all life, the root of all existence: "As a spider sends forth its thread, and as tiny sparks spring forth from a fire, so indeed do all the vital functions, all the worlds, all the gods, and all beings spring from this self [*atman*]. Its hidden name is: 'The real behind the real,' for the real consists of the vital functions, and the self is the real behind the vital functions" (2.1.19). In sum, the *Brihad Aranyaka Upanishad* teaches that one's essential self transcends individuality, limitation, suffering, and death.

Another common designation we find for the *atman* is that it is the "inner controller" of all life (3.7.2–23). This designation is connected to perhaps the most notable characterization of the *atman* we find in the *Brihad Aranyaka Upanishad*. The *atman* is not an ordinary object of consciousness but rather the subject of consciousness, or the silent witness of consciousness. The *atman* is the knower of all knowledge, or the "perceiver of perception." "When, however, the Whole has become one's very self [*atman*], then who is there for one to smell and by what means? Who is there for one to see and by what means? Who is there for one to hear and by what means? Who is there for one to greet and by what means? Who is there for one to think of and by what means? Who is there for one to perceive and by what means? By what means can one perceive him by means of whom one perceives this whole world? Look—by what means can one perceive the perceiver?" (2.4.14). As the perceiver of perception, the *atman* is not an object of consciousness and therefore cannot be known in any ordinary way, for it is declared to be consciousness itself. The primary aim of the Upanishads is to bring about a shift in identity from the transient ego self associated with the body to the eternal and infinite self that is not different from the All. In other words, the goal is to realize that the *atman* is *brahman*, although the task of delineating the details of this equation was left to later writers.

According to the Upanishads, our present life is just one in a long, long series of death and rebirth. When our present life ends, we are reborn in a new body. "It is like this. As a caterpillar, when it comes to the tip of a blade of grass, reaches out to a new foothold and draws itself onto it, so the self [*atman*], after it has knocked down this body and rendered it unconscious, reaches out to a new foothold and draws itself onto it" (4.3.3). That is, as a caterpillar moves from one blade of grass to another, so we move from one body to another. Although some later philosophers insisted that it is a different type of self that constitutes the individual self that undergoes reincarnation, reincarnation seems to have been assumed in the Upanishads.

Informed by this assumption, two paths are outlined in the *Brihad Aranyaka Upanishad* as possible postdeath experiences (6.2.15–16). The first option is the path of return to this life. After death, people's bodies are placed on the cremation fire. Those who performed religious sacrifices designed to enhance worldly life pass into the smoke. From the smoke, they pass into the night and eventually end up in the world of the ancestors. From there they pass into the moon, where they are turned into the rain, by which they return to the earth. Reaching the earth, they become food. The food is eaten by a man and then offered in the fire of a woman, where people take birth once again. This is the ongoing cycle of death and rebirth that defines life for most people.

There is another path, however, for the forest-dwelling meditation masters who have achieved the highest knowledge. After death, these are placed on the cremation fire and pass into the flames. From the flames, they pass into the day and eventually reach the world of the gods. From there they pass into the sun. The sun in much Hindu mythology represents the doorway out of this world, and, indeed, we are told that those who achieve the highest knowledge go on from the sun to reach the world of *brahman*, from which they never return to worldly life. This is one of the earliest representations of *moksha*, or "liberation" from the ongoing cycle of death and rebirth. Although these two paths are presented simply as the two postdeath possibilities in the *Brihad Aranyaka Upanishad*, certain later Upanishads make it clear that the path of no return is far superior to the path of return. To return to this world is an indication of one's failure to achieve ultimate knowledge of one's self. A very special kind of knowledge, then, is declared to be the culmination of a successful human life.

Diagnosis

The main problem with human existence is that we are ignorant of the true nature of reality. "Pitiful is the man, Gargi, who departs from this world without knowing this imperishable" (3.8.10). We see from this statement that all success rests on knowing the imperishable *brahman*, but it is extremely difficult to know, since it is that "which sees but can't be seen; which hears but can't be heard; which thinks but can't be thought of; which perceives but can't be perceived. Besides this imperishable, there is no one that sees, no one that hears, no one that thinks, and no one that perceives" (3.8.11). Without knowledge of the unified and infinite *brahman*, one perceives only the ordinary objects of consciousness and therefore suffers the fate of identifying completely with the dying world of fragmentary and transitory forms. "With the mind alone must one behold it—there is here nothing diverse at all! From death to death he goes who sees here any kind of diversity" (4.4.19).

Ignorance of the true nature of reality is tantamount to ignorance of the true nature of our own selves. Or, stated in different terms, the human predicament consists of a severe identity problem: we don't know who we really are. We identify ourselves with the fragmented, seemingly disconnected phenomenal world of diversity, instead of with the One *brahman*. We are creatures of infinity stuck in highly conditioned and finite personalities. While in reality we are kin to the immense universe, we spend our lives overwhelmed and blinded by the limited projects of our own ego. The result of this is alienation: from others, from the very source of life, from the One, and even from our own true self. The human condition is thus an ongoing experience of fragmentation, isolation, and loneliness. Consequently, our social worlds are riddled with crime and hostile conflict, informed by belief in our own individuality, and we are plagued with existential anxiety, rooted in an investment in the disconnected, transitory self.

The life of the lone individual is anything but free, according to the Upanishads. Life grounded in the belief in a separate self is heavily conditioned and determined. The determining factors are identified as *karma* in the *Brihad Aranyaka Upanishad*, the first text to mention this concept so important to later Hindu thought. The sage Yajnavalkya talks about *karma* in this way: "What a man turns out to be depends on how he acts and on how he conducts himself. If his actions are good, he will turn into something good. If his actions are bad, he will turn into something bad. A man turns into something good by good action and into something bad by bad action" (4.4.5). Ordinary human life, informed by the belief in an autonomous self, is revealed to be highly contingent, conditioned by forces determined by previous actions. Yajnavalkya continues: "A man resolves in accordance with his desire, acts in accordance with his resolve, and turns out to be in accordance with his action." What this means is that we are psychologically programmed in such a way that under normal circumstances free action is impossible. We act out of desire, which itself is the result of some prior action recorded in the unconscious mind. That desire manifests itself as a resolve for action. The subsequent action leaves an impression in the mind, which then goes on to determine the nature of another desire, the root of future action. Here, then, is a picture of the human predicament as a cycle of psychological bondage. A great deal of Hindu yoga and meditation aims to free us from this limited and conditioned state.

Prescription

The Upanishads are generally optimistic about the possibility of attaining ultimate freedom. The *Brihad Aranyaka Upanishad*, however, does not outline a single prescriptive path. A major task of later systematic writers was to articulate a coherent interpretation of this and other Upanishads and to delineate a specific path leading to the ultimate state that those texts describe. As we shall see, the divergent interpretations that emerged differed greatly about the nature of the world and the self.

Generally speaking, the Upanishadic path to freedom involves acquiring a special kind of knowledge. Ordinary knowledge will not cut the chains of our bondage. "Into blind darkness they enter, people who worship ignorance; And into still blinder darkness, people who delight in learning" (4.4.10). The Upanishadic texts do not disparage all learning but rather sound a note of caution about the limits of conventional knowledge. What this passage seems to be saying is that it is dangerous to rely too heavily on ordinary knowledge. Ordinary information is fine for operating in the conventional world of multiple forms; however, it is worthless for knowing the ultimate nature of reality and the self.

The *Brihad Aranyaka Upanishad* makes it clear that one must finally let go of any attachment to ordinary ways of knowing. The text tells us that one "should stop being a pundit and try to live like a child. When he has stopped living like a child or a pundit, he becomes a sage" (3.5.1). That is, after gaining significant exposure to the scriptures and becoming an expert in the scholarly sense, one should abandon any reliance on learning and try to return to the simple and spontaneous state of a child. This still, however, does not give clear indication of how one is to achieve ultimate knowledge and freedom. Only in very general terms does the *Brihad Aranyaka*

Upanishad recommend a path of withdrawing from ordinary ways of being and meditating continually on the *atman*. This vagueness is characteristic not only of this text but of other Upanishads as well. It remained for later commentators to spell out in detail exactly what the final state involves and how it can be attained.

Divergent Interpretations

One of the greatest disagreements within Hinduism occurs between those who view ultimate reality as an impersonal absolute and those who emphasize a personal relationship with ultimate reality. Not surprisingly, these two radically different stances have led to widely divergent interpretations of the *Brihad Aranyaka Upanishad*. A complete introduction to later Hinduism would involve a description of an expansive array of religious practices, including domestic rites, temple rituals, pilgrimages, yogic discipline, and so forth, as well as the beliefs that inform these diverse practices. Although such a task is impossible within the limitations of this chapter, the ideas of two leading figures from the Hindu tradition—Shankara and Ramanuja— are examined to indicate the wide range of practices and beliefs that are included under the rubric of Hinduism. Both are identified as Vedanta philosophers, where "Vedanta" means literally the "end of the Vedas," that is, the culmination of the revealed books of wisdom known as the Vedas. This term is primarily taken to refer to the teachings of the Upanishads but also includes the *Bhagavad Gita* and the *Brahma Sutra*. Although there are also schools of Hindu philosophy that are not Vedanta, Shankara and Ramanuja represent two of the most influential schools of Hindu thought and practice. Since both Shankara and Ramanuja wrote commentaries on the *Brahma Sutra*, a text that further investigates the concept of *brahman* introduced in the Upanishads, we can use these two works to explore this fundamental divergence in interpretation.

Shankara's Advaita Vedanta

Shankara (788–820) is one of the best-known Hindu philosophers in India and in the West. Although his philosophical system of Advaita ("Non-Dualism") informs the activities of only a small minority of

Hindus and has tended to overly dominate Western understandings of Hinduism, it represents an important philosophical position within the Hindu world and constitutes one the most popular rationalizations for the act of religious renunciation.

What does it mean to know *brahman*? Perhaps the most pressing question that remained from Upanishadic speculation was: What is the relationship between the ultimate reality of *brahman* and the world of multiplicity we experience with our senses? A concomitant question arose: What is the status of a personal God and the individual soul? Shankara was one of the first Indian philosophers to formulate a consistent and singular viewpoint based on the Upanishads that addressed these important questions. His is a philosophy of unity that ultimately devalues all diversity. For Shankara, *brahman* is the only truth, the world is ultimately false, and the distinction between God and the individual soul is only an illusion.

Brahman, for Shankara, is the sole reality. It is the absolute undifferentiated reality, one without a second (*advaita*) and devoid of any specific qualities (*nirguna*). Since he understands the highest realization of *brahman* to be a state in which all distinctions between subject and object are obliterated, he concludes that the world of diversity must finally be false. Shankara recognizes that the Upanishads speak of two aspects of *brahman*, one with qualities (*saguna*) and one without (*nirguna*), but he maintains that the former is simply the result of perception conditioned by limiting factors. "Brahman is known in two aspects—one as possessed of the limiting adjunct constituted by the diversities of the universe which is a modification of name and form, and the other devoid of all conditioning factors and opposed to the earlier" (1.1.12). In fact, Shankara claims that all apparent distinctions within *brahman* are the result of the superimposition of the frames of reference of the viewer. This brings us to one of the most important concepts in his philosophy: the theory of illusion, or "*maya.*" *Maya* is the process by which the world of multiplicity comes into being; it is the force by which the formless takes form. *Maya* both conceals and distorts the true reality of *brahman* and is manifest epistemologically as ignorance (*avidya*). Its workings cannot be explained in words, since language itself is a product of *maya.* Since all diversity is finally false for Shankara, *maya* is the major obstacle to the highest realization of ultimate knowledge.

What this means is that the world we experience with our senses is not *brahman* and therefore not ultimately real: "The senses naturally comprehend objects, and not Brahman" (1.1.2). By this Shankara certainly does not mean that the world is a figment of our imagination. He was a staunch opponent of subjective idealism. For him the world has an apparent reality; that is, it is existentially real. He writes: "It cannot be asserted that external things do not exist. Why? Because they are perceived. As a matter of fact such things as a pillar, a wall, a pot, a cloth, are perceived along with each act of cognition. And it cannot be that the very thing perceived is nonexistent" (2.2.28). Shankara does recognize the category of the nonexistent and gives as a stock example "the son of a barren woman." Our world, on the other hand, has an apparent reality, and in this sense it "exists." However, since the experience of the world is devalued by the ultimate experience of *brahman* in which all distinctions are obliterated, it cannot be the absolute reality. Just as the contents of a dream are devalued upon waking, so too the experience of the world is devalued upon the waking of ultimate enlightenment. The stock example used to explain this is the snake and the rope. A person erroneously perceives a rope to be a snake in dim light. The fear that the person subsequently feels is real enough, existentially. However, when the light of knowledge illuminates the "snake," it is discovered to be a rope all along. The snake was merely superimposed onto the rope, giving the snake an apparent reality. So too— as the illustration is applied—the world and *brahman*. The world of multiplicity is ordinarily superimposed onto the nondual *brahman*, with the result that we live in an illusory world. The experience of the world, however, is revealed to be false in the ultimate knowledge of *brahman*. This theory allows philosophers to disassociate the problematic world from the true reality, just as reflections of the moon in various pots of water are finally disassociated from the moon.

The same argument is applied to two other important differentiated entities: the personal God and the individual soul. Shankara defines the personal God as *brahman* with attributes. But since all attributes are the product of the limiting factors of ignorance, God, too, is finally declared to be an illusion. Worship of the personal God, however, is highly beneficial, for although God is not the highest reality, it is the highest reality conceivable for creatures still enmeshed

in the cosmic illusion of *maya*. That is, the personal God is a necessary component of spiritual experience, since it provides a transition
between the world and *brahman* for those who are still attached to
the world. In the end, however, one must give up this sense of sep-
arateness and reintegrate all gods back into one's self.

A related concept for Shankara is the individual soul (*jiva*). By
now it should be clear that all diversity for Shankara is considered
to be the result of illusory perception, so it will come as no surprise
to learn that he ultimately rejects the individual soul as illusory.
Although the *jiva*, or individual soul, involves a higher level of realization than the ego-identity associated with the body, in the final
analysis it, too, is unreal. The true self for Shankara is the *atman*, defined as pure consciousness. Like the world and God, the individual
soul is merely an apparent reality, whose appearance is the result of
viewing the self through the limiting factors of ignorance. He writes
that the self "is endowed with eternal consciousness, . . . it is only
the supreme Brahman Itself, which while remaining immutable, appears to exist as an individual soul owing to association with limiting adjuncts" (2.3.18). Though in everyday experiences we feel
ourselves to be agents of our own actions, this, too, is an illusion.
This means that the true self is eternally free from the conditioning
effects of *karma*; to be free one needs only to realize that bondage
is a mental construct. Shankara also maintains that the self is beyond
all experience, since this involves a difference between the experi-
encer and that which is experienced. Therefore, at the highest level
of realization, the individual soul, the subject of all experience, dis-
appears as an illusion; the true self is declared to be identical with
brahman, the absolute unified ground of being.

The goal of all spiritual endeavor for Shankara is the realization
of this ultimate fact. The highest level of the knowledge of *brahman*
involves the obliteration of all distinctions between the knowing subject and all known objects in the state of absolute identity. A favored
metaphor for the ultimate experience so conceived is the reemergence
of all drops of water back into the single undifferentiated ocean. This
is how Shankara interprets the Upanishadic quest for ultimate knowledge.

But what are the essential components of a path designed to ac-
complish this ultimate feat? In the first section of this chapter we en-

countered the *Brihad Aranyaka Upanishad*'s creation myth, which recounts how the world of multiple forms came into being out of desire, a desire for another. The essential element in the story for Shankara is the unity that preceeds the diversity produced by desire. Since desire is associated with the creative force that divides the original oneness, eradicating desire is a necessary step toward the process of reunification. This brings us to the idea of renunciation. The highest spiritual path, according to Shankara, consists of a meditative practice designed to lead one to the insightful realization that "I am *brahman*." He calls the practice of meditating on and realizing the true self "*samadhi*." An important prerequisite to this practice, however, is a withdrawal from ordinary social and domestic activities and a retreat from our ordinary investment in the data of the senses. That is, one of the most prominent consequences of Shankara's theory is the move toward world renunciation. Shankara is credited with founding an important order of renouncers (*sannyasi*s) known as the Dashanamis. These are men who embark on the path by performing their own funeral rite, thereby indicating the end of their former identity and the beginning of full-time participation in a celibate religious community and meditation on *brahman* as the impersonal absolute.

Ramanuja's Vishishta Advaita Vedanta

Diametrically opposed to the views of Shankara is the perspective of those Hindus—especially the Vaishnavas (worshippers of God in the form of Lord Vishnu)—for whom the personal nature of the divine is an ultimate attitude and not an illusion to be transcended. One of Shankara's most determined and well-known opponents was Ramanuja (1017–1137), an important theologian and chief interpreter of Vedanta for the southern Indian devotional movement known as Shri Vaishnavism. His philosophical system is designated Vishishta Advaita ("Non-Dualism of the Differentiated"), since it takes differentiated things to be real, and understands them to be attributes of a nondual reality. Ramanuja's philosophy values both unity and multiplicity, a stance that results in a very different view of the nature of God, the world, and the self.

In his commentary on the *Brahma Sutra*, Ramanuja criticizes Shankara for his refusal to acknowledge any qualities or distinctions in the nondual reality of *brahman*. Like Shankara, Ramanuja accepts the Upanishadic assertion that *brahman* is the sole reality; however, for him, *brahman* means God, who is endowed with innumerable excellent qualities. "The word 'Brahman' primarily denotes that supreme Person who is the abode of all auspicious qualities to an infinite degree and is free from all worldly taint. This supreme Person is the only Being the knowledge of whose real nature results in liberation" (1.1.1, p. 1). Thus Ramanuja does not make a distinction between *brahman* and God, as does Shankara. Rather, Ramanuja interprets Upanishadic descriptions of *brahman* as "without qualities" to mean the absence of certain kinds of qualities: qualities that are negative or binding. In effect, he reverses Shankara's privileging of *brahman* without qualities (*nirguna*), arguing that *brahman* with qualities (*saguna*) is the higher form. Specifically, Ramanuja resists Shankara's conceptualization of *brahman* as pure undifferentiated consciousness, contending that if this were true, any knowledge of *brahman* would be impossible, since all knowledge depends on a differentiated "object." "Brahman cannot be, as the Advaitins say, nondifferentiated pure Consciousness, for no proof can be adduced to establish non-differentiated objects" (1.1.1, pp. 19–20).

The particular kind of experience for which we should aim, according to Ramanuja, is a blissful knowledge of *brahman* as the Lord with infinite and amazing qualities or, stated more simply, the love of God. But for this relationship to be possible, there must be a distinction between the knowing subject or the one who loves (the individual soul), and the known object or the beloved (the Lord). Many of the devotional theologians within Hinduism remark that they do not want to become sugar (Shankara's goal); instead, they want the blissful experience of tasting sugar (Ramanuja's goal). This means that difference must be taken seriously, and this implies a very different picture of the world of sense experience than the one we encountered in Shankara's Advaita system.

The world is real, for Ramanuja, and was created out of God's desire to become manifold. That is, the world is the result of a real transformation of *brahman*. The stock example used to explain this viewpoint is the transformation of curds from milk. Curds that are produced from processing milk are both different and nondifferent from their source. This view is more widely accepted by Hindus than is Shankara's view that the world is ultimately an illusion. It implies that the creative process that resulted in multiplicity is not finally to be overcome but rather is to be appreciated for what it truly is, the product of God's creative activity. Like Shankara, Ramanuja connects the desire of the one to become many with the concept of *maya*, but instead of conceptualizing *maya* as "illusion," as does Shankara, Ramanuja takes it to be the "creative power" of God. "The word Maya does not mean unreal or false but that power which is capable of producing wonderful effects" (1.1.1, p. 73). The world, then, is viewed in a much more positive light, and in fact Ramanuja goes on to characterize it as the "body of God." He maintains that *brahman* "is the creator, preserver, and destroyer of this universe, which It pervades and of which It is the inner Ruler. The entire world, sentient and insentient, forms its body" (1.1.1, p. 55). That is, the conditioned and transitory world is an attribute of the unconditioned and eternal God, as the transitory body is an attribute of the eternal soul. The world is therefore different from God, yet it is also inseparably connected to God, as an attribute is connected to its substance.

This is also the case with the individual soul (*jiva*). It, too, is considered to be part of the body of God, and it is in this manner that Ramanuja interprets the Upanishadic identity of *brahman* and the true self. Whereas Shankara ultimately characterized the individual soul as a false illusion, for in his view all distinction is obliterated in the final experience of *brahman*, Ramanuja maintains that it is real and eternal. As a part of *brahman*, the soul is both different and nondifferent from the whole (2.3.42, p. 298). The world of matter and individual souls enters into God at the time of dissolution and separates from God at the time of creation. Rejecting Shankara's claim that the true self is pure consciousness beyond experience, Ramanuja maintains that the true self is a special enjoyer of experience (2.3.20, p. 285). In its highest state, it is the eternal, blissful knower of *brahman*.

The path to freedom and the blissful experience of *brahman* is well represented in the following passage. "This bondage can be destroyed only through Knowledge, i.e., through the Knowledge that Brahman is the inner ruler different from souls and matter. This Knowledge is attained through the Grace of the Lord pleased by the due performance of the daily duties prescribed for different castes and stages of life, duties performed not with the idea of attaining any results but with the idea of propitiating the Lord" (1.1.1, p. 80). Far from renouncing the world of action, a very particular way of acting is indicated here that is linked to the *karma-yoga* of the *Bhagavad Gita*, the other major Vedanta text. *Bhagavad Gita* 2.47 states that one in pursuit of ultimate liberation should act in a manner that avoids both an attachment to the results of action and the abandonment of action. That is, as a path of action, *karma-yoga* is situated between two modes of behavior current in Hindu religion. On the one hand, the path of Vedic sacrifice—and ordinary action, for that matter—is a mode of action wherein the act is performed with a controlling concern for the outcome of the action. Why, after all, do we do anything if it is not for the result we expect to achieve by performing the act? Much religious activity follows the same logic; a religious act such as Vedic sacrifice is performed to obtain some desired result. In accord with the *Bhagavad Gita*, however, Ramanuja holds that such action reveals a fundamental ignorance and serves only to bind us further. Life, according to Ramanuja, is a cosmic play (*lila*), wherein God is the ultimate Playwright (2.1.33, p. 237). The ordinary human urge to control the outcome of all our actions is tantamount to an effort to usurp the role of the Playwright. Moreover, insisting on a particular outcome of action is like walking into an extraordinary store filled with an amazing assortment of candies with a fixed desire for a certain kind of candy bar, one that, as it turns out, happens not to be there. The result is suffering and bondage in a potentially wonderful situation. What, then, to do? The answer certainly does not lie in abandoning all action, for that is the other mode of behavior to be avoided. Following the *Bhagavad Gita*, Ramanuja insists that one should engage in the action that comes to one according to one's own life situation. World renunciation is simply another attempt to establish control and cannot lead us to the state of blissful enjoyment. Instead, Ramanuja advises us to surrender completely to God, for only then are we free to enjoy the marvelous show that is the world. Whereas Shankara renounces the world, Ramanuja demonstrates how to live freely in it.

Although Ramanuja has little to say about the worship of concrete forms of God in his commentary on the *Brahma Sutra*, he belongs to a devotional community in which this type of meditation is the central religious practice. Acts directed to pleasing the Lord instead of one's egoistic self are often enacted in the context of worship of concrete forms or bodies of God, either in a temple or at a home shrine. Informed by such texts as the *Brihad Aranyaka Upanishad*'s conversation wherein Vidagdha asked Yajnavalkya how many gods there are, these concrete forms are considered to be multiple forms of a single, nondual divinity. *Brahman* is understood to be fully present in these special bodies, which are limited forms of the infinite that God compassionately assumes for the purpose of granting accessibility to embodied beings with ordinary senses. The limited forms are like the defining frame placed around certain works of art that serve to allow focused perception of something that might have otherwise been missed. A great deal of Hindu practice involves the loving service of such concrete forms of God. Whereas Shankara saw these acts as preliminary to the higher business of *samadhi* meditation, for Ramanuja, loving acts directed toward God are supreme. Loving devotion implies a very different attitude toward human emotions than we observe in Shankara. Since the world is real for Ramanuja, everything in it—including human emotions—can be used as fuel for the spiritual life.

The goal of such devotional acts is a kind of union with God, wherein the liberated soul lives in the loving presence of the Lord but does not dissolve into undifferentiated oneness with Him. This is often conceived of in Vaishnavism as an eternal and blissful existence in God's heavenly abode of Vaikuntha. Here "the released self abides as an enjoyer of the supreme Brahman" (4.4.20, p. 493).

We observe, then, two radically different religious sensibilities arising from—or at least being justified by—the same Upanishadic texts. For Shankara the nondualism of the *Brihad Aranyaka Upanishad* means that the world of multiplicity and everything connected with it is, in the final analysis, an illusion. With the dawn of true consciousness, the world, the individual self, and even God are revealed to be unreal. Participation in the ordinary world, then, is viewed as a hindrance to the highest spiritual life. The consequence of this view is a religious life that values world renunciation and is suspicious of anything based on ordinary human senses. Ramanuja, on the other hand, interpreted the nondualism of the *Brihad Aranyaka Upanishad* to mean that there is a single cause to everything but that the multiple effects of that single cause are real. Ultimate reality is understood to be God as the Inner Controller of the manifold world and the individual soul. The consequence of this position is a religious life of devotional activity that views the world positively and uses the ordinary senses to pursue a blissful experience of the differentiated *brahman*. Although world-renouncers can still be found in almost all religious centers in India today, devotional practices in temples and home shrines dominate the Hindu tradition.

Critical Discussion

The Vedanta philosophy represented by Shankara and Ramanuja is a textual tradition. What this means specifically is that Vedanta philosophers—though they insist that the final proof of anything must be experience—rely heavily on scriptures such as the *Brihad Aranyaka Upanishad*, which they take to be authoritative. Many philosophers today would not accept scripture as a reliable source of truth. Moreover, Vedanta philosophy rests on the transcendental claims of the Upanishads, represented by the concept of *brahman*. Obviously, this too makes it suspect for secular philosophers, for whom the idea of transcendence is highly problematic. This is, after all, what makes Vedanta a "religious" philosophy. The philosophical traditions of India differ from many of those in the West on this exact point, for much of Hindu philosophy is intended to be of practical assistance to spiritual experience.

In contrast to many of the other theories represented in this book, Vedanta philosophy appears to have little to say about social and political struggles and reforms or about practical morality. Although some recent defenders of Vedanta philosophy have denied this accusation, it holds a certain amount of truth. The writings of Vedanta philosophers are preoccupied with achieving a higher knowledge and freedom and with metaphysical concerns regarding the nature of ultimate reality, the world, and the self. *Brahman* for Shankara, for example, has little to do with the ordinary world and transcends all normative distinctions, and the true self is beyond the categories of good and evil. It should be pointed out, however, that Shankara insists that there are moral consequences of all actions for people living in the conditioned world of *maya*. Selfless, compassionate acts erode false boundaries and lead to higher realization, whereas egoistic, violent acts reinforce false boundaries and lead to further bondage. Moreover, although in theory Ramanuja's system values the world, sometimes in practice it is the case that worldly particulars are valued only so far as they lead to the knowledge of God, and not in themselves.

Although women participate actively in the metaphysical discussions of the *Brihad Aranyaka Upanishad*, and although there is no textual evidence to suggest that they were in any way excluded from the higher goals expressed in that text, women are excluded from Shankara's order of renouncers and are never allowed to serve as temple priests in Ramaunja's tradition of Shri Vaishnavism. Although Ramanuja opened his tradition to women and the lower classes, Vedanta philosophy in general, and Shankara's school in particular, tends to be very elitist. It requires a knowledgeable religious practitioner who is well educated in scripture, at least in its expectations for the highest realization. In classical Indian society, this deters all but those who occupy the upper classes. Those denied such preparation by birth are likewise often denied the opportunity for the highest achievement—at least in this lifetime.

For Further Reading

Basic Text: *Brihad Aranyaka Upanishad* (many translations and editions). All quotations are from the recent translation by Patrick Olivelle, *Upanisads* (New York: Oxford University Press, 1996). This is a very readable and reliable text that includes a valuable introduction. Other readily available translations are those by Robert E. Hume, *The Thirteen Principal Upanishads* (New York: Oxford University Press, 1971), and by R. C. Zaehner in *Hindu Scriptures* (New York: Knopf, 1966).

Shankara's commentary on the *Brahma Sutra*: Few reliable translations exist. I have quoted from one of the most available English translations: Swami Gambhirananda, *Brahma-Sutra-Bhasya of Sri Shankaracarya* (Calcutta: Advaita Ashrama, 1977).

Ramanuja's commentary on the *Brahma Sutra*: Few reliable translations exist. I have quoted from one of the most available English translations: Swami Vireswarananda and Swami Adidevananda, *Brahma-Sutras, Sri Bhasya* (Calcutta: Advaita Ashrama, 1978).

For an overall introduction to Indian philosophy, see M. Hiriyanna, *Outlines of Indian Philosophy* (Bombay: George Allen & Unwin, 1973).

For more on the philosophy of the Upanishads, see Paul Deussen, *The Philosophy of the Upanishads* (New York: Dover, 1966).

For more on the *Brahma Sutra*, see S. Radhakrishnan, *The Brahma Sutra: The Philosophy of Spiritual Life* (London: George Allen & Unwin, 1960).

For more on Shankara's Advaita Vedanta, see Eliot Deutsch, *Advaita Vedanta: A Philosophical Reconstruction* (Honolulu: University Press of Hawaii, 1969).

For more on Ramanuja's Vishishta Advaita Vedanta, see John Carman, *The Theology of Ramanuja* (New Haven: Yale University Press, 1974).

For more on the worship of concrete forms of divinity within Hinduism, see Diana Eck, *Darsan: Seeing the Divine Image in India* (New York: Columbia University Press, 1996).

4

The Bible: Humanity in Relation to God

In the introductory chapter, we saw that Christianity contains a theory of the universe, a theory of human nature, a diagnosis, and a prescription, and we reviewed some of the standard objections and responses. In this chapter I look in more detail at the main ideas about human nature and destiny in the Bible. There is an obvious distinction between the Old Testament, which is recognized as the authoritative Word of God by both Jews and Christians, and the New Testament, which is distinctive of Christianity, so I treat these separately. (The third great monotheistic world religion of semitic origin is Islam, which started in the seventh century, recognizing Abraham, the Jewish prophets, and Jesus as forebears but claiming that Muhammed is the uniquely authoritative messenger of God. But it would take another chapter, and different expertise, to do justice to Islam.)

There are obvious problems in interpreting and assessing ideas from the Bible. On the one hand, believers have come (through one tradition or another) to treat it as sacred text, and many people earnestly expect to find in it guidance for their life. On the other hand, there has grown up over the past two centuries a great body of expertise in the ancient languages of Hebrew, Aramaic, and Greek and in the archeology, history, and sociology of the communities that produced the biblical texts over many centuries, and there is now a large industry of academic study and interpretation. The texts are of very different dates, written and edited by different hands, and produced and used for different purposes. To say there is a Judeo-Christian belief in X, an Old Testament conception of Y, or a New Testament view of Z is to generalize and risk oversimplification, but for introductory purposes this can hardly be avoided. It is impossible to please everyone—the scholars with their academic controversies, and the believers with their various faiths.

Obviously, Judaism and Christianity, like Confucianism and Hinduism, are hardly "theories" on a par with the others later in this book. The Jewish and Christian traditions are notoriously diverse. Christian doctrines have developed over two thousand years: within the three main divisions of Christianity (Roman Catholicism, Eastern Orthodoxy, and Protestantism), there are many more subdivisions and differences. Although all acknowledge their derivation from the Old and New Testaments and the credal statements of the early Church, there is disagreement about the relative authority of these sources. Some Protestants maintain the infallibility of the biblical texts as the inspired Word of God. (We should note, however, that there has been considerable disagreement about just *which* texts count as inspired— for example, the status of the Apocrypha remains disputed.) Catholicism and Orthodoxy emphasize the traditional authority of the Church in the interpretation of scripture and the formulation of creeds and practical guidance (Catholicism eventually proclaimed the doctrine of papal infallibility in the nineteenth century). Other believers say that people's religious experience is the ultimate basis for theology.

In this chapter I first take a brief look at the background theory of the universe that is common to Judaism and Christianity (and Islam)—namely, the monotheist conception of God as Creator, Ruler, and Judge. It is impossible to avoid touching on this eternally debated topic here, but I attempt only a brief review of the conception and some of its difficulties, for my main concern here is to examine the Judaic and Christian conceptions of *human* nature. I outline these in turn, under the headings of theory, diagnosis, and prescription. At the end I mention some of the philosophical diffficulties that face some of the distinctively Christian claims, in their traditional metaphysical interpretations.

Metaphysical Background: The Judaic-Christian Conception of God

First, then, let us consider the basic monotheist claim about the nature of the universe, that God exists. What *sort* of God is thus asserted to exist? Not, surely, a Being who is literally "up there," located somewhere in space. When the first Russian astronauts reported that they hadn't met God, this was not even weak evidence against His existence; it wasn't the right sort of evidence at all. The Christian God, although thought of as a Person, is not supposed to have a body. He is not one object among others in the universe; He does not occupy a position in space or last for a certain length of time. Nor is He to be identified with the whole universe, the sum total of everything that exists—that is pantheism, not monotheism. The God of the Bible is transcendent as well as immanent: although in some sense present everywhere and all the time, He is also beyond or outside the world of things in space and time (Psalm 90:2, Romans 1:20), for He is the Creator of the whole physical universe.

The transcendent existence of God is essential to biblical monotheism, then. But there are long-standing philosophical difficulties about the doctrine. How are we supposed to know that it is true? Different ways of knowing have been proposed. Some claim that there are valid arguments—or at least good evidence of a probabilistic sort—for the existence of God. These would have to be reasons that we can all appreciate by the use of our human rationality ("natural theology"). Others appeal to divine authority and say that God has revealed Himself to us in historical events, in the Bible, or through the Church, perhaps in miracles ("revealed theology"). Some say that there can be individual awares of God, which is a kind of direct knowledge of Him ("experiential theology"?). And some assert a combination of these alleged ways of knowing.

The claims of biblical or ecclesiastical authority and religious experience are obviously controversial. To put it mildly, not everyone finds the biblical texts or the claims of the churches overwhelmingly convincing. Not everyone reports religious experience, and those who do disagree about what it tells them. Severe doubt has been cast on the viability of natural theology since the eighteenth century, when Hume and Kant formulated their stringent criticisms of the ontological, cosmological, and design arguments for the existence of God (arguments that proceed respectively from the very concept of God, from the mere existence of the world, or from the apparent order in the world). Since Darwin's theory of evolution, modern biological science has undermined much of the force of the latter by giving scientific explanations of the marvelous adaptation of plants and animals to their environment.

Some theists try to counter those criticisms of natural theology and offer to refashion some of the traditional arguments (notably from the order in the universe found by modern physics), but the validity of those reformulated arguments is, of course, questioned by nonbelievers. There has been a recent movement to try to present a supposedly biblically based "creation science" as a rational alternative to geology and evolutionary biology, but its status is hotly disputed. Many Jews and Christians now agree that God's existence can be neither proved nor disproved by reason alone, that belief in Him is rather a matter for faith.

But what exactly is it that people believe when they say they have faith in God? A vital part of the Judeo-Christian doctrine of God is that He is the Creator of the world (Genesis 1:1, Job 38:4). This does not imply that the Creation was an event in time. Theism need not be contradicted if a cosmological theory says that the universe has an infinite past, and more recent theories of the "big bang" that began the physical universe should not be interpreted as scientific confirmation of the religious doctrine of Creation. But the question remains, just what is meant by saying that God is the Creator of the world? It seems to imply that if God did not exist, the world would not exist, or would not continue to exist and operate as it does. It also suggests that the world and everything in it is fundamentally in accordance with His purpose, that there is nothing that exists or happens save by His design—or at least by His permission.

If God is transcendent, He is not visible or tangible; nor, surely, is He like the unobservable entities (such as atoms, electrons, and magnetism) that scientific theory invokes to explain what we can observe through our senses: God is not a scientific postulate. Yet He is not a mere abstraction, like numbers and the other objects of mathematics. He is supposed to be a personal Being, who creates us, loves us, judges us, and redeems us. God, according to the Biblical conception, has immense human significance—He is not a mere architect who set things up and takes no further interest in the progress of human history. He is supposed to remain in ultimate control of everything that happens, to be supremely good and benevolent, and to have specific purposes for human existence. His significance is thus at least as much moral as cosmological: belief in Him is supposed to affect how we conceive of ourselves and how we ought to live.

The question remains, however, why anyone should believe in the existence of such a personal Creator and Lord. Many (though not all) people would *like* to believe some such thing, for it seems to offer an overall "meaning" to human history and to individual lives, but we are here seeking reasons for thinking it true, rather than motives for wanting it to be true. It has long been alleged that there is obvious evidence *against*, in the notorious "problem of evil." The suffering (both animal and human) and the evil in the world seem to count against there being an omniscient, omnipotent, and benevolent God. Yet, as we saw in Chapter 1, theists do not usually take this as disproving their claim, and various defences are proposed. It is sometimes suggested that out of suffering greater good can eventually come, or that the possibility of evil must be there if we are to be genuinely free to make moral choices. But the nonbeliever may still wonder why God did not make the world such that suffering was not the only way to produce goodness and such that human beings freely choose rightly. It seems that the theist does not take his or her belief in God to be falsifiable by evidence about the actual state of the world.

If empirical observation cannot count for or against God's existence, just what is being asserted? This is where the philosophical debate about meaningfulness and verifiability comes into play. Surely any factual statement, any claim about how things actually are in the universe, must somehow be testable by observation (see Chapter 1). If the assertion of God's existence is such that no conceivable evidence could count for or against it, then it is hard to see how it can be a factual claim. Some theists suggest that in certain human experiences—moral or religious or mystical—there is the possibility of empirical verification of God. But descriptions of such experiences are highly controversial, and nonbelievers will interpret them in other ways, not in terms of a transcendent God. It has also been suggested that in the life after death we shall be able to verify the existence and nature of God, by some sort of direct observation. But this is to meet one verifiability problem by posing another—for how can we *now* find evidence for the reality of life after death?

Some modernizing "theists" have suggested that all that people are doing when they say that God exists is to express and recommend a set of attitudes to life—perhaps that love is the most important thing in the world, that we should feel grateful for the good things in life, that we should acknowledge our finitude and our failings, or in general that we should behave *as if* the universe were ruled by a loving God. Yet an atheist might be sympathetic to such attitudes, while still disagreeing on the metaphysical question. Some theologians have offered to explain God as ultimate reality, the "ground of all being," or whatever concerns us ultimately: the first two phrases here may seem to retain some sort of metaphysical claim, but the latter seems quite compatible with atheism. The relation between attitudes to life and metaphysical beliefs remains a deep puzzle. If anything is to deserve the name of theism, must it involve *more* than an attitude?

Most believers will agree that their belief is not a scientific one, and many are attracted to the idea that science and religion give complementary accounts of the universe, describing the same ultimate reality from different sides, as it were. However, this still does not explain how religious statements can give knowledge of one particular aspect of reality, unless they are testable by some sort of experience. This remains one of the most basic philosophical problems about religious claims, and this is why so much of the contemporary discussion in the philosophy of religion centers around questions of meaning and epistemology. In this book I cannot pursue these questions further, for my chosen task is to concentrate on the understanding of human nature.

The Old Testament Theory of Human Nature

The opening chapters of Genesis, the first book of the Hebrew Bible, tell a story of the divine creation of the whole world, including human beings. The question immediately arises whether we should read these passages literally as narrating historical events or see them as a set of myths that may express important truths about the human condition, but not at the level of history or science. Two large difficulties face any attempt to see literal truth here. One is that the text itself displays internal inconsistencies, for there are two different creation stories in Genesis, at 1:1–2:4 and at 2:5–25, which give incompatible accounts at several points (notably on the creation of woman, discussed later). Old Testament scholars have concluded that the book of Genesis must have been put together by ancient editors from two sources (usually labeled P and J). The text we have, whatever people may believe about its ultimately divine inspiration, is surely a result of human editorial processes. The other difficulty for a literal reading is, of course, the inconsistency of such an interpretation with the results of modern cosmology, geology, and biology.

I propose that only symbolic readings of the creation stories can be taken seriously. It is now widely, if not universally, accepted that they are myths or parables expressing deep religious truths about the human condition, rather than history or science, so there need be no incompatibility with the theory of evolution. Anyone who asserts the historical existence of Adam and Eve as unique ancestors of all humanity is in my view insisting on an overliteral interpretation of scripture. But to interpret the stories as parables is not to imply that whatever they are thus interpreted as saying is true. In this discussion, I am not approaching the texts from the presupposition of faith, assuming that they *must* somehow have some vital lesson for us all. I am asking what they say, symbolically, about human nature, and I hope to examine what they say in an open-minded spirit.

God Himself can hardly be treated as a mere symbol in the Bible (as we noted earlier). Much else may be poetry, parable, symbol, allegory, or myth—but not God, who is obviously conceived of as the supreme Reality. The Hebrew conception of humanity sees us as existing primarily in relation to God, who has created us to occupy a special position in the universe. We have (for better or for worse) a certain degree of power over nature: we domesticate animals and grow most of our food by agriculture. As Genesis 1:26 puts it, mankind is made in the image of God, to have dominion over the rest of creation. Human beings are unique in that we have something of the rationality and personhood of God. We are rational beings, but we are also persons, we have self-consciousness, freedom of choice, and the capacity for personal relationships and love. God created us for fellowship with Himself, so we fulfil the purpose of our life only when we love and serve our Creator.

But although human beings are thus seen as having a special role compared to the rest of Creation, we are at the same time continuous with nature. We are made of "dust from the ground" (Genesis 2:7), that is, of the same matter that composes the rest of the world. It is a common and recurrent misinterpretation of the biblical doctrine of human nature that it involves a dualism between the material body and an immaterial soul or spirit. Such dualism is a Greek idea (it occurs in Plato), but it is not to be found in the Old Testament (or indeed in the New, as we shall see). We are persons: we are different both from inanimate matter and from the animals, but our personhood does not consist in the possession of an immaterial entity that is detachable from the body. The "breath of life" (Genesis 2:7) that God is described as breathing into Adam's nostrils is not a soul but the gift of life itself. There is no firm expectation of life after death in the Old Testament.

The relation of women to men in the Hebrew scheme of Creation is somewhat ambiguous from the start. One Creation story represents the whole human race as created together (Genesis 1:27); the other tells us of Eve being made out of Adam's rib (Genesis 2:21–23). One account suggests equality, whereas the other suggests dependence of woman on man. God Himself is almost always described in male terms, and there is a tremendous emphasis on the importance of producing male descendants. Genesis 3:16 is not the only place where the husband is described as "master" of the wife. (The devaluing of daughters and wives is not peculiar to Hebrew culture, either.)

Probably the most crucial point in the biblical understanding of human nature is the notion of freedom, conceived of as the choice between obedience to God's will, faith in Him, and love for Him— or disobedience, faithlessness, and pride. The necessity for choice between obedience and disobedience, good and evil, is presented early, in Genesis 2:16–17. Greek thought puts great store on the intellect, on our ability to attain rational knowledge of theoretical and moral truth; the highest fulfilment of human life was thought by Plato and Aristotle to be attainable only by those who are able to gain such knowledge. The Judeo-Christian tradition, in contrast, puts the emphasis on human goodness, and this is something that is open to all, and independent of intellectual power. There is thus a democratic impetus, an ideal of the equality of all finite human beings before God, implicit in the Bible—though it may be questioned just how well Jewish and Christian practice has lived up to this. The concern with human goodness is not just with right action: it is at least as much with the foundation in human character and personality from which such life will flow. And in a crucial way, it goes beyond the sophisticated conceptions of human virtue offered by Plato and Aristotle, for the biblical writers see the only firm foundation for human goodness as faith in the transcendent yet personal God.

There are various dramatic examples in the Old Testament of this ultimate requirement of obedient submission to God, rather than use of the intellect to reason things out and make one's own judgments about truth and morality. One is the story of Abraham's being told by God to sacrifice his only son, Isaac (Genesis 22). God rewards Abraham for his readiness to obey this terrible command, promising that he will be the patriarch of innumerable descendants. (A different response to the situation, clearly not approved of by the writer, would have been to reject any such killing of an innocent child as immoral, indeed, obscene, and to conclude that any such "command" could not really come from a good, loving God. Even if it were only given as "a test of faith," what sort of "god" would play such a trick?) Another famous case of faith's being preferred to reason is the resolution of the struggles of Job and his interlocutors with the problem of evil. No reasoned solution is offered; in the end, God just appears and asserts His power and authority, and Job humbly submits (Job 38–42).

Diagnosis

Given this doctrine of humanity as made by God, the diagnosis of what is basically wrong with human kind follows. We are infected with sin, we misuse our God-given free will, we choose evil rather than good, and we therefore disrupt our relationship to God (Isaiah 59:2). But this doctrine of "the Fall" needs disentangling from misinterpretation. The Fall is not a particular historical event: the story of the temptation of Adam and Eve to eat the forbidden fruit of the tree of knowledge (Genesis 3:1–24) should be also read as parable rather than history. It is a symbol of the fact that although we are free, we are all subject to sin; there is a fatal flaw in our nature.

It it is interesting to note that Genesis 3:14–19 represents certain familiar features of human life as the result of the Fall, as punishments imposed by God for disobedience. Examples are the painfulness of childbearing, women's desire for their husbands (and their submission to them!), the necessity for men to work hard to get food, and even death itself. Perhaps it is easy to wish for a life in which these things were not necessary, to idly imagine a primeval Eden or a heavenly Paradise in which there is no tension between inclination and necessity, or between desire and duty. It is quite another thing, however, to conceive of these features of life (except perhaps relations between the sexes) as the result of human moral failings.

Identifications and condemnations of human sinfulness recur throughout the Old Testament. Cain and Abel, the two sons of Adam and Eve, begin the fratricidal history of humanity when Cain murders his brother. In Genesis 6:5–7 God is even represented as bitterly regretting His creation of humankind and resolving to wipe out all living things—until Noah finds favor in His eyes and is allowed to save a representative sample of all species. In Genesis 11:1–9 the Lord is depicted as confusing the single language of humanity because people were growing too proud and had tried to build the tower of Babel up to the heavens. Throughout the subsequent history of the children of Israel, there are repeated prophetic denunciations of their sinfulness and unfaithfulness to God. Pride, selfishness, and injustice keep on manifesting themselves throughout the story.

Prescription

The Hebrew prescription for humankind is based on God, just as much as the theory and diagnosis is. If God has made us for fellowship with Himself, and if we have turned away and broken our relationship to Him, then we need God to forgive us and restore the relationship. Hence the idea of salvation, a regeneration of humanity made possible by the mercy, forgiveness, and love of God. In the

Old Testament we find the recurring theme of a "covenant," a quasi-legal agreement like that between a powerful conquerer and a subject state, made between God and His chosen people. One covenant was with Noah (Genesis 9:1–17), another with Abraham (Genesis 17); the third, most important one was with the "children of Israel" led by Moses, by which God redeemed them from their bondage in Egypt and promised that they would be His people if they kept His commandments (Exodus 19).

But none of these covenants seems to be totally effective in fulfilling God's will: sin does not disappear from the face of the earth (nor has it still, we may want to add!). There is even a danger of spiritual pride, if a certain group conceives of itself as "God's chosen people" and therefore feels justified in conquering and oppressing its neighbors. The Old Testament records genocide by the children of Israel and often seems to approve of it (see, e.g., Joshua, chs. 8–11). There is an obvious tension between the potentially universal tendencies (God as Father of *all* humankind) and an exclusive tribalism.

When the people fail to obey God's commandments and laws, there comes the idea of God's using the events of history, especially defeat by neighboring nations, to chastise them for their sin (a theme that recurs throughout the histories and prophets in the Old Testament). But there is also the prophetic promise of God's merciful forgiveness, His blotting out of human transgressions, and His regeneration of humanity and the whole of creation (Isaiah, chs. 40–66). And the hope begins to be expressed for some new Divine initiative of salvation, the idea of the coming of a Messiah, whom Christians (but not, of course, Jews) identify in the figure of Jesus.

The Christian Doctrine of Human Nature

There is a contrast made in the New Testament between what is often translated as "the spirit" and "the flesh." This is attributed to Jesus himself in John 3:5–6. It is obviously tempting to interpret this in philosophically dualist terms as meaning the distinction between incorporeal soul and physical body. But we have to beware of reading Greek ideas (or more recent ones) into the Bible. St. Paul's distinction between spirit and flesh (Romans 8:1–12) seems to be not so much between mind and matter but between regenerate and unregenerate humanity.

It is also tempting to identify "the flesh" with our biological nature—our bodily desires, especially sexuality—and to see the opposition between flesh and spirit as another version of Plato's conflict among Appetite, Spirit, and Reason (note the different uses of the term "spirit"). But it is surely a misinterpretation of the Christian conception of human nature to identify the distinction between good and evil with that between our mental and our physical natures. The view that our sexual desires are intrinsically evil is not now part of Christian theology, though it has to be admitted that such asceticism had a strong influence in the development and popularization of Christianity. We can find hints of it in St. Paul (see I Corinthians 7:25–40, where marriage is described as second best to celibacy), and it was made more influential by St. Augustine.

As for the relations between men and women, it is often remarked that in the gospel stories Jesus treats women with great respect. Nevertheless, he did not choose any to be his disciples: in that way he was presumably a man of his time, a Jewish rabbi. Although he says that in Christ there is neither Jew nor Gentile, male nor female, St. Paul also wrote that "man was not created for woman's sake, but woman for the sake of man" (referring back to the second creation story in Genesis). He also displays a curious obsession with women's hair (some say he was talking about veils), whose cultural context is obscure to contemporary readers (I Corinthians 11:2–16). It has to be admitted that much Christian thought has found females theologically problematic ever since—witness the continuing controversies about the ordination of women.

What about immortality? Here there is a clear difference between the Old and New Testaments. It is made very explicit in the latter that we are to expect some kind of survival of death. The phrase "eternal life" is used quite often, especially in the gospel of John, where Jesus is represented as offering eternal or "everlasting" life to whomever would believe in him (John 3:16). He is also described as proclaiming the coming of the "Kingdom of Heaven" or the "Kingdom of God"—see Matthew 4:17, 23. But perhaps we should not immediately jump to the conclusion that this phrase means the continuation of human life after death. Could it mean rather a new and better way of living in this life, a way that relates properly to the eternal? "Eternal life" surely does *at least* mean that in Christian thought, but it is impossible to ignore that Christianity has also laid great stress on the hope of resurrection for all believers, a transformation of our present embodied existence in this world into something radically new (see John 5:24–29 and, most explicit, St. Paul's account of the resurrection in I Corinthians 15). We explore some of the difficulties in this doctrine later.

The Christian Doctrine of Sin

The doctrine of "original sin" does not imply that we are totally and utterly depraved. It does imply that nothing we can do can be perfect by God's standards: "All have sinned, and fall short of the glory of God" (Romans 3:23). We find in ourselves a conflict. We often recognize what we ought to do, but somehow we do not do it. St. Paul expresses this vividly in Romans 7:14ff—so vigorously, in fact, that he personifies sin to the extent of saying that "it is not I who do wrong, but sin that dwelleth in me" (verse 17), which threatens to excuse the sinner from responsibility, which was surely not St. Paul's intention!

Sin is not basically sexual in nature: sexuality has its rightful place within our divinely created nature, in the institution of marriage. The true nature of sin is not essentially bodily; it is something mental or spiritual, consisting primarily in pride, in the assertion of our will against God's, and our consequent alienation from Him. Sin might be described as the misuse of self-assertiveness, but this surely does not mean that all self-assertion is sinful. Nietzsche notoriously characterized Christianity as recommending "slave morality," praising meekness and humility, even self-abasement, and discouraging vigorous human flourishing. A superficial reading of the "beatitudes" in Jesus' sermon on the mount (Matthew, ch. 5) may suggest this. "Blessed are the poor in spirit," he said—but how are we to understand those words? Some of the other stories of Jesus (for example, the expulsion of the moneychangers from the temple) and the writings of St. Paul suggest no inhibition on clear moral judgment, righteous anger, and resolute action.

The Fall of humanity somehow involves the whole creation in evil (Romans 8:22); everything is in some way "short of the glory of God." But it is not necessary for Christians to personify the power of evil in a conception of a Devil, or demonic powers, to express this idea of a cosmic Fall. And it is heresy to believe in twin and equal powers of good and evil; for Jew and Christian alike, God is ultimately in control of all that happens. But this belief runs directly into the problem of evil, which we have already noted.

Christian Salvation

It is in the New Testament, in the life, ministry, and death of Jesus, and in the writings of his followers (especially St. Paul) that we find the distinctively Christian idea of salvation. The central claim is that God was uniquely present in one particular human person, Jesus, and that God uses the life, death, and resurrection of Jesus to restore us to a right relationship with Himself.

Because of the enormous historical influence of Christianity in Western civilization, the words "Christian" and "Christianity" are often used in all sorts of vaguely honorific ways. Until recently, it was quite shocking or foolhardy to declare oneself not a Christian— and, in some circles, it still is. What *are* we to mean by the word? What criteria does someone have to satisfy to count as a Christian? And why is this question regarded as so important? It is surely because of a cultural inheritance that has, at least until recently, been widespread in the West, an assumption that "we" are somehow identified with Christianity and that it is therefore necessary to define what Christianity essentially is in order to distinguish "ourselves" from "others." Notoriously, further divisive distinctions are often insisted on, when various types of Christian define themselves in opposition to rival brands.

Whatever connotations the term "Christian" has come to have, it is at least connected in meaning with one particular historical figure, Jesus. To be a Christian, it is hardly enough to say that Jesus was a good man or a man of great religious insight, for an atheist, or a member of another faith, may say such things. The Jews, believing that God has acted in history by selecting them as his "chosen people" and hoping for a Messiah, have never accepted the Christian identification of Jesus as uniquely divine. Islam recognizes him as a great teacher but only a forerunner of a greater one, Muhammed.

The most central Christian claim is surely that of a unique action of God in one particular person, in one episode of human history. This is traditionally expressed in the doctrine of incarnation—that Jesus is the Son of God, both human and divine, the eternal Word made Flesh (John 1:1–18). The early philosophical formulations of this doctrine—two natures in one substance, and so on—are perhaps not essential. But the basic idea of incarnation, that God is *uniquely* present in Jesus, surely is. And equally important is the idea of atonement, that the particular historical events of the life, death, and resurrection of Jesus (and their continual representation by the Christian Church) are the means by which God reconciles His creation to Himself. It is not enough to say that Jesus' life and death are an example to us all: Christians claim that the resurrection of Jesus really happened (1 Corinthians 15:17), however flagrant the contradiction with all the known laws of nature. (The idea of the Virgin Birth is almost as miraculous, but perhaps less crucial.)

The Christian prescription is not quite complete, however, with the saving work of Jesus Christ. It remains for this salvation to be accepted and made effective in each individual person and to be spread throughout the world by the Christian Church. Love of God and life according to His will is open to all regardless of intellectual ability (1 Corinthians 1:20). "If I understand all mysteries and all knowledge . . . but have not love, I am nothing" (1 Corinthians 13:2). This love (for which the Greek word is *agape*, formerly translated rather misleadingly as "charity") is not to be identified with merely human affection. It is ultimately divine in nature and can be given only by God.

All people must accept the redemption that God has effected for them in Christ and become members of the Church, the community in which God's grace is active. Different Christian traditions have emphasized individual response or Church membership, but most agree that both are necessary. Thus, the regeneration of humanity and world takes effect: "if anyone is in Christ, he is a new creation" (2 Corinthians 5:17). There is not necessarily a single experience of conversion in each individual, nor does regeneration take place all at once; it must be a lifelong process, one that looks beyond to life after death for its completion and perfection (Phillipians 3:12).

Some Critical Points about Christianity

The doctrines of incarnation, atonement, and resurrection are a problem to human rationality, and indeed their formulation has provoked much disagreement within Christianity. How can one particular human being who lived and died in one episode in history be a member of the transcendent, eternal Godhead? The doctrine of the Trinity—that there are three persons in one God (Father, Son, and Holy Spirit)—multiplies the conceptual problems rather than solves them. The standard thing to say, of course, is that these are mysteries rather than contradictions, that human reason cannot expect to be able to understand the infinite mysteries of God, that we can only accept in faith what God has revealed of Himself to us. But this kind of statement from within the perspective of faith does nothing to answer the genuine difficulties of the unbeliever or the uncommitted. The same applies to atonement: not many Christians now interpret this as a propitiatory sacrifice, as if God requires blood to be shed (any blood, even that of the innocent) before He will be prepared to forgive sins, but it is still an enormous mystery how the crucifixion of a Jewish religious teacher at the hands of the Roman governor Pontius Pilate in Jerusalem in about the year 30 can effect a redemption of the whole world from sin.

Unlike the Old Testament, in which there is hardly a mention of immortality, Christianity developed a clear expectation of life after death. But this is thought of as "resurrection of the body," rather than the Greek idea of the survival of an incorporeal soul. The theologians of the early Church did begin to use ideas from Greek philosophy, and the conception of immaterial and immortal soul found its way into Christian thinking and has tended to stay there ever since. The Christian Creeds, however, explicitly express belief in the resurrection of the *body*, and the main scriptural warrant for this is in 1 Corinthians 15:35 ff., where St. Paul says that we die as physical bodies but are raised as "spiritual bodies." It is not clear what a spiritual body is supposed to be, but St. Paul does use the Greek word *soma*, which means body.

This belief in the resurrection of the body is another of the distinctive doctrines of Christianity. To interpret it as meaning only that the good or evil that men do lives after them, or to take the promise of eternal life (John 4:14) as only of a new way of life in this world, seems to evacuate the doctrine of some of its content. But this metaphysical content runs into philosophical difficulties. If bodies are resurrected, then, presumably, being *bodies* of some kind, they have to occupy space and time. It is surely not meant that they exist some-where in our physical universe—that at some large distance from the earth there exist the resurrected bodies of St. Paul, Napoleon, and Aunt Agatha! So it seems that what we have to try to make sense of is the idea that there is a space in which resurrrected bodies exist but that has no spatial relations to the space in which we live. But can we do that?

The question of time is at least as difficult. Perhaps it is not in-tended that there will be a time in the future of this world at which the resurrection will take place—although, when Paul says "we shall all be changed, in a moment, in the twinkling of an eye, at the last trumpet" (1 Corinthians 15:51–52), it does sound like that, if taken literally. Is it meant that there is somehow a system of events that has no temporal relation to the events of this world, or are the res-urrected bodies timeless, in which case what sense can be made of the idea of resurrected *life*—for life, as we understand it, is a process in time. Is a life that literally goes on *forever*, in unending time, even an attractive prospect? The answer is, I suggest, not as obvious as we tend to assume, because we do not usually think about what it would mean. But if it is a life that is not in time, what sense can we make of it? How can persons live a *personal* life in relation to other persons, but in a timeless state?

In the late middle ages (the thirteenth century), St. Thomas Aquinas made an impressive synthesis of Christian and Aristotelean ideas, which has since become Catholic orthodoxy. On the question of im-mortality, he retained (with dubious consistency) an element of Platonism, saying that although the resurrrection involves the recre-ation of a complete human being, a combination of body and soul, the soul nevertheless has a separate existence until the resurrection. This may seem to solve the problem of maintaining personal iden-tity, but at the cost of incurring the problems of dualism, in particu-lar that of the coherence of the notion of disembodied existence of any sort of personality.

A final conceptual problem (or mystery) arises over the parts played by human being and God in the drama of salvation. The fun-damental Christian conception is certainly that redemption can come only from God, through His offering of Himself in Christ. We are "justified" in the sight of God not by works, but simply by faith

(Romans 3:1–28), by our mere acceptance of what God does for us. If we are saved, we are saved by this free grace of God, not by anything that we can do ourselves (Ephesians 2:8). Yet, just as clearly, the Christian doctrine is that our will is free; it is by our own choice that we sin in the first place, and it must be by our own choice that we accept God's salvation and work out its regeneration in our lives. The New Testament is full of exhortations to repent and believe (e.g., Acts 3:19) and to live the life that God makes possible through the regenerating power of the Holy Spirit (Galatians 5:16).

There is thus a tension, if not a contradiction, between the view that salvation and grace are due to God and the insistence that so much depends on our individual, freely chosen responses to God. In a famous controversy in the fourth and fifth centuries, St. Augustine emphasized the former, and Pelagius the latter. Although Pelagius's ideas were condemned as heretical, the doctrine of human free will is surely an essential element in Christian belief, difficult as it may be to reconcile with the theory of the complete and utter sovereignty of God. The relation of human action and divine grace remains a crucial internal problem for theology.

Many thinking Christians may acknowledge that there are these conceptual problems in the distinctively Christian doctrines. But they would emphasize that Christianity is more than a theory; it is a way of life, though not a political, this-worldly ideology like Marxism. They remain practicing Christians and accept the basic theory despite its difficulties because of what they find in reading the Bible, in the worship and sacraments of the Church, in the practice of prayer—a certain growth in the inner or "spiritual" life. There can be no complete assessment of Christianity unless this is considered. But it has also to be realized that what counts as "spiritual growth" is itself not uncontroversial, and any claim that such growth is uniquely possible in one particular religious tradition is even more disputable.

For Further Reading

The basic text is obviously the Bible, of which there are many translations and editions. One excellent version for present purposes is the *Oxford Study Bible: Revised English Bible with the Apocrypha*, edited by M. J. Suggs et al. (Oxford: Oxford University Press, 1992). This edition contains helpful essays on the historical, sociological, literary, and religious background of the biblical texts.

For an introduction to Judaism, see N. de Lange, *Judaism* (Oxford: Oxford University Press, 1986). For an introduction to Islam, the third great monotheistic religion, see F. Rahman, *Islam*, 2d ed. (Chicago: Chicago University Press, 1979).

For more on Christian understandings of human nature, see Reinhold Niebuhr's classic *The Nature and Destiny of Man* (New York: Scribner's, 1964); E. L. Mascall, *The Importance of Being Human* (New York: Columbia University Press, 1958), which presents a neo-Thomist view; *Man: Fallen and Free*, edited by E. W. Kemp (London: Hodder & Stoughton, 1969), which presents an interesting variety of essays, including a notable summary by J. A. Baker of the Old Testament view; and J. Macquarrie, *In Search of Humanity* (London: SCM Press, 1982; New York: Crossroad, 1983), which presents a more existentialist view.

For a feminist critique of Christianity, while retaining theism, see Daphne Hampson, *After Christianity* (London: SCM Press, 1996).

Books on philosophy of religion are countless. One very comprehensive set of readings is *Philosophy of Religion: Selected Readings*, edited by M. Peterson et al. (Oxford: Oxford University Press, 1996).

P A R T

III

Five Philosophical Thinkers

5

Plato: The Rule of Reason

Let us start our examination of non-religious theories of human nature by considering the philosophy of Plato (427–347 B.C.). Although it dates back nearly two and a half millenia to the beginnings of Western thought in ancient Greece, Plato's pioneering thought is still of great contemporary relevance. He was one of the first to argue that the open-minded but systematic use of our reason can show us the best way to live. A clear conception of human virtue and happiness based on a true understanding of human nature is, in Plato's view, the only answer to individual and social problems.

A short sketch of Plato's background will help us understand the origin of his ideas. He was born into an influential family in the Greek city-state of Athens, which enjoyed economic prosperity through its empire and trade and at one stage developed a remarkably democratic system of government. We remember Athens above all as a center of unprecedented advances in intellectual inquiry, including drama and history, mathematics and science, and as the home of the great ethical philosopher Socrates, whose teaching so impressed Plato (and many others since). But Plato grew up in a politically disturbed period in Athens: the war with Sparta ended in disastrous defeat, and a period of tyranny ensued. When democracy (of an unstable sort) was restored, Socrates came under political suspicion; he was brought to trial and condemned to death in 399 B.C. on a charge of subverting the offical religion and corrupting the young.

Socrates' method of arguing and teaching was akin in some ways to that of the Sophists of his day. These were self-styled experts who offered (for a fee) to impart certain kinds of skill; in particular they taught the art of rhetoric, i.e., persuasion by public speaking, which was important for political advancement in Athens. (They might be described as the public relations consultants of their time!) They had thus to touch on questions of value, and one of the opinions most commonly expressed was a skepticism about whether morals, politics, or religions involved anything more than arbitrary conventions. The Athenians were aware of the variety of beliefs and practices that prevailed in other Greek city-states, and in other cultures around the Mediterranean, so they were confronted with the philosophical question of whether there is any nonarbitrary criterion of truth in these matters. What we now call "cultural relativism" was thus a tempting option even at this early stage of thought.

Unlike the Sophists, Socrates charged no fees, and he concerned himself with more fundamental philosophical and ethical questions. His great inspiring idea was that we can come to know the right way to live if only we use our reason properly. Socrates has been called "the grandfather of philosophy," not so much for any conclusions he reached but for pioneering the *method* of using rational argument and inquiry in an open-minded, nondogmatic way. Famously, Socrates claimed superiority to unthinking men only in that he was aware of his own ignorance, whereas they were not. Plato's early dialogues (especially the *Apology*) show this to have been for Socrates not a mere intellectual skill but a way of life, a vocation to make his fellow Athenians think about their lives in ways they would not otherwise have done, to convince them that "the unexamined life is not worth living." Socrates felt called with an almost religious intensity to do this, to disturb people's mental complacency whatever the consequences, so it is not surprising that in a period of political turbulence he found himself a focus of hostility, even to the point of death.

In all this, Socrates deeply influenced Plato, who was shocked at the execution of his inspirational teacher. Disillusioned with contemporary politics, Plato retained Socrates' faith in rational inquiry; he was convinced that it was possible to attain knowledge of deeply-lying truths about the world and about human nature and to apply this knowledge for the benefit of human life. Socrates did not leave any writings behind; his influence was entirely oral. Plato himself expressed some skepticism about the value of books, tending to agree with Socrates that actual dialogue was the best way to make people think for themselves and thus effect any real change in their minds. However, Plato did write very extensively, and often with great literary skill; his works are the first major treatises in the history of philosophy. They are in dialogue form, typically with Socrates taking a leading part. Many scholars think that in the early dialogues, such as the *Apology, Crito, Euthyphro*, and *Meno*, Plato was mainly expounding Socrates' ideas, whereas in the later dialogues (mostly longer and more technical) he was expressing his own distinctive theories. Plato founded the Academy in Athens, which can be described as the world's first university. The tradition of systematic philosophical inquiry was continued by his great successor Aristotle in the Lyceum in the following generation.

One of the most famous and widely studied of Plato's dialogues is the *Republic*. This is a lengthy, complex, and closely argued work, traditionally divided into ten "books" (which, however, do not always correspond to natural divisions of the argument). As the title suggests, one main theme is an outline of an ideal human society, but its central argument is at least as much about individual human nature and virtue. In the course of this work, Plato give us his views on many topics, including metaphysics, theory of knowledge, human psychology, morals, politics, education, and poetry. I concentrate on the *Republic* here although I make occasional reference to other works of Plato. I incorporate some critical points along with my exposition. (There is a traditional numbering system for the texts: my references are to the *Republic* unless otherwise stated.)

Metaphysical Background

Although Plato mentions God, or the gods, at various places, it is not clear how literally he takes such talk (he is certainly a long way from

the polytheism of Greek popular religion). When he does talk of
"God" in the singular, he does not mean the conception of God familiar from the Bible, a personal Being who relates to individual people and intervenes in human history. Plato has in mind a rather more
abstract ideal: in the *Philebus* and the *Laws*, God or the divine is
identified with reason in the universe. (The opening sentence of the
Gospel of John—"In the beginning was the word," i.e., *logos*—
displays the influence of this Platonic idea.) In the *Timaeus* Plato
gives a non-Biblical account of creation in which "divine wisdom"
struggles to organize preexistent matter.

What is most distinctive of Plato's metaphysics is his so-called
"theory" of "Forms" (the Greek word is *eidos*). But it is a matter of
great difficulty and controversy to say what this amounts to, for he
never presents it as an explicit "theory" or doctrine, nor does he argue
for it in any systematic way. It is taken for granted at crucial points
in various dialogues, though to Plato's credit we also find him
wrestling with difficulties in it, notably in the *Parmenides*. On this
topic especially we have to remember that he was a pioneer in philosophy, struggling to express and clarify fundamental but difficult
ideas for the first time in human thought.

One thing that we can note immediately is that Plato realizes that
human knowledge is not simply a matter of mere passive observation of things and events in the world around us. Our knowledge involves understanding, in that we actively interpret the data we receive
through our sense organs, we apply concepts to classify and mentally
organize what we perceive, using our rational powers (see the related
remarks on Kant in Chapter 6). Scholars dispute whether Plato's
Forms can be identified with concepts, yet this may be helpful as a
first approximation to understanding him. I present four main aspects
of the Forms here—logical or semantic (to do with meanings and
concepts), metaphysical (to do with what is ultimately real), epistemological (to do with what we can know), and moral or political (to
do with how we ought to live).

The logical aspect concerns Forms as principles of classification;
this relates to the meaning of general terms. What justifies our application of one word or concept such as "bed" or "table" to many
particular beds or tables? These are Plato's own examples at *Republic*
596, and part of his point there is that craftsmen who make beds and

tables must have a concept of what they are trying to make. But this "one over many" problem can be raised about any general concept, not just human artifacts. At 507 Plato distinguishes many different good things and beautiful things from the single Forms of Goodness and Beauty. The "nominalist" view is that there is nothing that all instances of a concept literally have in common—at best, there may be some similarities between them. The view traditionally labeled "Platonic realism" is that what makes particular things count as Fs is their resemblance to, or "participation in," the Form or Idea of F, which is an abstract entity, something different from all the individual instances. This may appear to be Plato's answer at *Republic* 596: the principle that for each general word there is one Form. But elsewhere he suggests that only some special kinds of word or concept, those that pick out genuine unities (or "natural kinds") express what he would call a Form. He is reluctant to accept, for example, that there are Forms corresponding to the terms "mud," "dirt," or "barbarian" (the latter was used for all non-Greeks, and its sense was like that of our term "foreigner").

An important metaphysical aspect of Forms is that Plato thinks of them as more real than material things, in that they do not change, decay, or cease to exist. Individual material things get damaged and destroyed, but the Forms are not in space or time, and they are knowable not by the senses, only by the human intellect or reason (485, 507, 526–27). Plato's grand metaphysical theory seems to have been that, beyond the world of changeable and destructible things, there is another world of unchanging eternal Forms. The things we can perceive are only somewhat distantly related to these ultimate realities, as he suggested by his famous and haunting image of the typical human condition as being like that of prisoners chained up facing the inner wall of a cave, in which all they can see are mere shadows cast on the wall, knowing nothing of the real world outside (515–17). (If Plato were alive today, he might be quick to point out how well his image applies to people who rely for their "knowledge" on watching television, movies, and computer screens!) Plato elaborates on his cave picture to make it fit the more detailed structure of his theory: his prisoners see the shadows cast from a fire by artifacts carried about within the cave, whereas outside there are other, more real objects that themselves cast shadows by the light of the sun.

The usual human condition may be ignorance, but Plato thought that, by a process of education, it is possible for human minds—the more able of them, at least—to attain knowledge of ultimate reality, the world of Forms. The epistemological aspect of his theory is that only this intellectual acquaintance with the Forms properly counts as knowledge. Plato discusses the nature of knowledge in several dialogues, but in the *Republic* we find the thesis that only what fully and really exists can be fully or really known: perception of impermanent objects and events in the physical world is only belief or "opinion," not knowledge (476–80).

One of the clearest illustrations of these aspects of the theory of Forms comes from the geometrical reasoning with which Plato was familiar and that Euclid was to systematize later. Consider how in doing geometry we think about lines, circles, and squares, although no physical object or diagram is *perfectly* straight, circular, or equal-sided. What we count as straight or equal for some practical purposes, to some degree of approximation, will not be so by a more precise standard; irregularities or differences can be always be found if things are examined closely enough. Yet theorems concerning geometical concepts—straight lines without thickness, perfect circles, exact squares—can be proved with certainty by deductive arguments. We thus seem to attain knowledge of exactly defined, unchangeable mathematical objects, which are the patterns or forms that material things imperfectly resemble. Like many other philosophers since his time, Plato was deeply impressed by the certainty and precision of mathematical knowledge and took this as an ideal to which all human knowledge should aspire. He therefore recommended mathematics as a vital educational means for detaching our minds from perceptible things.

It is the moral application of the theory of Forms that plays the most important role in Plato's theory of human nature and society. When we consider moral concepts such as "courage" and "justice," we can distinguish many particular courageous actions or just dealings from the general concepts Courage and Justice. In the early dialogues Plato depicts Socrates seeking an adequate general conception of the virtues and never being satisfied with mere examples or subclasses of them. We have to distinguish these ideals from the messy reality of human beings in actual situations. An action or a person may be right, just, or beautiful in one way, but not in other ways; for example, doing the best thing for one friend or relation may involve neglecting another. No individual is a paragon of virtue; neither is any human society ideal. Plato holds, nevertheless, that there are absolute standards of value set for us by the ethical Forms (472–73). And, for him, the Form of Goodness is preeminent: it plays an almost God-like role in his system, being described as the source of all reality, truth, and goodness. He compares the Good in the world of the Forms to the sun as the source of all light in the world of material things (508–9).

It is crucial to Plato's whole philosophy that we can, by the proper use of our faculty of reason, come to *know* what is good. In this he was following the lead of his teacher, Socrates. In some of the early dialogues (*Protagoras* and *Meno*), Plato portrays Socrates arguing for what seems to have been the historical Socrates' own doctrine, that to be virtuous, to be a good human being, it is enough to know what human virtue is. All the virtues are said to be identical at root, in that one cannot really possess any one of them without the others; this unique human goodness is identified with knowledge, in the wide sense of wisdom. Socrates is thus committed to the doctrine that nobody knowingly or willingly does what he or she thinks to be wrong. But this surely conflicts with all-too-obvious facts about human nature; don't we often know quite well what we ought to do and yet not actually do it? We see later how Plato attempts to cope with this difficulty.

The theory of Forms is the basis of Plato's answer to the intellectual and moral skepticism or relativism of his time. It is one of the first and greatest expressions of the hope that we can attain reliable knowledge about the world as a whole and about the goals and proper conduct of human life and society. Yet we may well think that Plato has overintellectualized the role of reason and knowledge. He makes a good case (which we are about to examine) that we all need *practical* wisdom; we need to use our reason in exercising prudent self-control, moderating our emotions and desires and their expression and fulfilment. But in the central sections of the *Republic* (Books V–VII) he insists on a highly *theoretical* conception of reason as consisting in a knowledge of the Forms that is open only to a specially trained intellectual elite. It is not so obvious that explicitly philo-

sophical thinking is either necessary or sufficient for human goodness.

Theory of Human Nature

Plato is one of the main sources for the "dualist" view, according to
which the human soul (or mind) is a nonmaterial entity that can exist
apart from the body. According to Plato, the soul exists before birth;
it is indestructible and will exist eternally after death. Plato's main
arguments for these doctrines are given in earlier dialogues. In the
Meno he tries to prove the preexistence of the soul, arguing that what
we call learning is really a kind of "recollection" of an acquaintance
our souls supposedly had with the Forms before birth (he here asserts a version of reincarnation). People of average intelligence can
be brought to understand mathematical theorems (some of the simpler ones, anyway!), and to realize why they must be true, by having their attention called to the steps of a proof. Plato says (plausibly
enough) that the ability to recognize the validity of the steps and the
necessity of the conclusion must be innate. But he makes the much
more disputable claim that such innate abilities can come only from
knowledge of the Forms in a previous life, whereas we might now
offer evolutionary explanations.

In the *Phaedo*, Plato presents a number of other arguments that the
human soul must persist after the death of the body. He tries to disprove the materialist theory of the earlier Greek atomists such as
Democritus, who held that the human soul is composed of tiny particles that dissipate into the air at death. He also argues against the
conception (which Aristotle later developed in more technical terms)
that the soul is a kind of "harmony" of the functioning body, like the
music made by an instrument when properly tuned and played. Plato's
arguments are always well worth careful study: even if one disagrees
with them, one can learn a lot by trying to specify where they go
wrong. He held, with something of the force of a religious belief, that
it is the immaterial soul, not the bodily senses, that attains knowledge of the Forms: he compares the soul to the divine, the rational,
the immortal, indissoluble and unchangeable. In his famous representation in the *Phaedo* of Socrates' last conversations before his

death, Plato presents his philosophical hero as looking forward to the release of his soul from all bodily cares and limitations.

The doctrines of the immateriality and immortality of the soul appear at the end of the *Republic* in "the myth of Er" in Book X (608–20), but this Book has seemed to many commentators to be a rather ill-fitting addition. What is really central to Plato's main moral discussion is his distinctive theory of the three parts of the soul (435–41). Although he presents this as an argument for parts within what he calls "the soul," we need not interpret it as dependent on a metaphysically dualist view: we can take it as a distinction among three different aspects of our human nature. We can recognize the existence of internal conflicting tendencies in ourselves even if we take a materialist, evolutionary view of human beings as one kind of animal with a well-developed brain. (For my introductory purposes here I concentrate on in Plato's tripartite theory, but we should note that in the *Philebus* and the *Laws* he sees human nature as divided two ways between reason and pleasure; he also says more about pleasure in the *Gorgias* and the *Protagoras*.) Echoes of Plato's threefold distinction can be found in the works of many thinkers since, such as Freud, as we see in Chapter 8.

At this point in Plato's thought, we can see him, to his credit, acknowledging the implausibility of the Socratic doctrine that nobody willingly does wrong. (When St. Paul says, "I do the very thing I hate," he reports a human experience we all recognize.) Plato wrestles with both the theoretical question of how such inner conflict is possible and the practical problem of how one can achieve inner harmony. Let us first examine his arguments for the tripartite structure.

Consider an example of mental conflict or inhibition, such as a person who is thirsty but does not drink the available water because he believes it is poisoned or because of some religious asceticism. Quite often we do not (or do not immediately) gratify our bodily urges, for various reasons. But, conversely, we sometimes find ourselves giving way to the temptations of the proffered cigarette, the second cream cake, the fifth glass of wine, or the seductive charmer, even though we know that the consequences are likely to be bad for us (or for others). Bad habits can notoriously become addictive—we recognize gluttony (or, these days, anorexia), alcoholism, drug dependence, the habitual seducer, or the man or woman who endlessly pursues impossible mates. Plato argues that where there is any kind of internal conflict, there must be two different elements in the person with contradictory tendencies or desires. In the case of the thirsty man, there must be one part that makes him want to drink and a second that forbids him; the first Plato calls "Appetite" (under which he includes all the physical urges, such as hunger, thirst, and sexual desire), and the second he calls "Reason."

So far, Plato bases his analysis on familiar ground. But he takes another step to postulate the existence of a third element in our nature. This is proved, he argues, by different cases of mental conflict. The first example he offers seems somewhat weird: a story of someone who feels a fascinated desire to look at a pile of corpses and yet is disgusted with himself for wanting to (440). Plato's claim is that to explain cases of internal conflict like this we need to recognize the existence in ourselves of a third element, which he calls "Spirit" or passion. His argument for this is not very explicit, but it seems to be that because there is an *emotion* of self-disgust involved, not just an intellectual recognition of the irrationality or undesirability of the desire, Spirit must be distinct from Reason.

We surely have to agree that emotion is something different both from bodily desires and from rational or moral judgment. Love is not the same thing as lust, nor is it merely a judgment about the admirable qualities of the beloved. Anger, indignation, ambition, aggression, and the desire for power are not bodily desires, nor are they mere judgments about the value or disvalue of things, although they involve such judgments. Plato goes on to remark that children (and even animals) show "Spirit" before they display reason; anyone who has dealt with children can confirm this from experience of their high spirits, self-assertivenesss, stubbornness, and (sometimes) aggression and bullying.

Plato asserts that Spirit is usually on the side of Reason when inner conflict occurs. But if it is a genuinely distinct element in the mind, there must presumably be cases where it can conflict with Reason. Plato quotes a line of Homer, "He smote his breast, and thus rebuked his heart," in brief confirmation of this. And we can surely add examples from our own experience, occasions when we have felt emotions of anger, jealousy, or love that we judge unreasonable, undesirable, or even immoral. Perhaps there can even be cases in which one is pulled in *three* directions by the different elements—for example, by lust, romantic love, and reasoned judgment about the best partner to live with!

Plato presents his threefold theory in vivid, if somewhat crude, images. In the *Phaedrus* at 253–54 (a dialogue mainly about love), he compares the soul to a chariot, pulled by a white horse (Spirit) and a dark horse (Appetite) and driven by a charioteer (Reason) who struggles to keep control. In Book IX of the *Republic* at 588, he describes a person as composed of a little man, a lion, and a many-headed beast. This obviously involves an infinite regress—a person within a person, and so on—but Plato was too good a philosopher not to notice this; he must have been offering the picture only as vivid imagery.

Is Plato's tripartite anatomy of the soul adequate? It can be seen as an interesting first approximation, distinguishing some elements in human nature that can conflict with each other. But it may not be a rigorous or exhaustive division, even if one relabels the parts in modern terms as intellect, emotion, and bodily desire. In particular, it is not very clear what Plato's middle element of Spirit amounts to. Emotions are one part of our human nature, certainly—but did Plato also have in mind human desires or drives that are not *bodily* appetites but not exactly emotions either, such as self-assertion, ambition, or desire for money, status, or power? And where does the will come into the story—doesn't Plato still have to accept that it is one thing to recognize or judge (with one's reason) what one ought to do and another actually to do it? A different tripartite distinction of mental faculties that has become standard, especially since the advent of Christianity, is reason, emotion, and *will*. Perhaps we will have to distinguish at least five factors in human nature—reason, will, nonbodily drives, emotions, and bodily appetites.

Much of Plato's discussion seems to be conducted with men rather than women in mind, but he had views about the similarities and differences between the sexes that were strikingly original, even subversive, in his time. In Greek society, women played almost no part in public life and were confined to household duties; the philosophical discussions of love in the Platonic dialogues are all about male homosexual love, which was socially approved of. Plato argues, however, that there is no function in society that need be restricted to either sex. He allows that some women are athletic, musical, philo-sophical, and even "high-spirited" (the mind boggles! However, he meant courageous, and therefore suitable for military service.) (see 445). He still patronizingly assumes that men are on average better than women at everything, but he thinks that the only absolute dis-tinction is the biological one that males beget children and females bear them and that any other differences are only matters of degree. He is therefore prepared to admit women of appopriate talent to the ruling class.

The remaining feature of Plato's theory of human nature is that we are ineradicably social: to live in society is natural to human beings. Human individuals are not self-sufficient; we each have many needs that we cannot meet by ourselves. Even food, shelter, and clothing can hardly be obtained without the help of others. An individual on a desert island would have to struggle for survival and would miss out on the distinctively human activities of friendship, play, art, pol-itics, learning, and reasoning. Manifestly, different people have dif-ferent aptitudes and interests; there are farmers, craftsmen, soldiers, administrators, and so on, each fitted by nature, training, and expe-rience to specialize in one kind of task; division of labor is essential (369–70).

Diagnosis

Reason, Spirit, and Appetite are present to some degree in every per-son. Depending on which element is dominant, there are three kinds of people whose main desire is knowledge, reputation, or material gain: Plato describes them respectively as philosophic, victory-loving, and profit-loving (581). He has a very clear view about which of the three elements should rule: Reason ought to control both Spirit and Appetite (590). But each has its proper role to play; there should ideally be harmonious agreement among the three aspects of our na-ture, with Reason in overall command. Plato expresss this in the fol-lowing eloquent passage at 443:

> Justice . . . isn't concerned with external actions, but with a man's in-ward self. The just man will not allow the three elements which make

up his inward self to trespass on each other's functions or interfere with each other, but by keeping all three in tune, like the notes of a scale . . . will in the truest sense set his house in order, and be his own lord and master, and at peace with himself. When he has bound these elements into a single controlled and orderly whole, and so unified himself, he will be ready for action of any kind. . . .

Just as the reasoning part of the individual soul ought to direct and control the other parts, so those people—men or women—with the most highly developed "reason" (which includes moral wisdom, as we have seen) ought to rule society in the interests of everyone. A well-ordered, "just" society is one in which each class of person plays a distinctive role, in harmony with the other classes (434).

Plato describes this ideal condition of human beings and society by the Greek word *dikaiosune*, which has traditionally been translated as "justice." But when applied to individuals, this term does not have its modern legal or political connotation. Perhaps there can be no exact English translation: "virtue," "morality," "right living," "well-being," or "mental health" may help to convey what Plato had in mind. At 444 he actually says that virtue is a kind of mental health or beauty or fitness, and vice a sort of illness or deformity or weakness. His fundamental point is that what is good or bad for us depends on our human nature, the complex of factors in our psychological makeup.

The theory of the parts of the soul (with the background theory of Forms as objects of knowledge) thus defines Plato's ideals for individual and social well-being, and when he looked at the facts of his own day he found that they were very far from ideal. Would his judgment of our present condition be any less harsh, one wonders? Many people do not show much "inward harmony" or controlled coordination of their desires and mental powers. And many human societies do not manifest the orderliness and stability that Plato sought.

The problems of human individuals that Plato diagnoses are intimately related to the defects in human societies. One cannot attribute to him either the simple moralistic view that social problems are due to individual wrong-doing or the merely sociological view that the social order produces the faults in individual people. Plato would say, I think, that the two are interdependent. An imperfect society tends to produce flawed individuals, and troubled or poorly educated individuals contribute to social problems.

Plato devotes Book VIII of the *Republic* (543–76) to a systematic classification of five kinds of society, beginning with the ideal outlined earlier, which he calls an "aristocracy" (meaning an aristocracy of talent, rather than birth). He goes on to diagnose four types of imperfect society, which he calls "timarchy," "oligarchy," "democracy," and "tyranny." He also describes a kind of defective individual supposedly typical of each society. He offers an account of how each kind of social order can arise by degeneration from its predecessor and how each individual character may be formed as a result of problems in the previous generation (concentrating, as a male Greek, on the relations between fathers and sons).

In a "timarchic" society such as that of Sparta, honor and fame, especially in warfare and hunting, are valued above all. Reason and philosophical understanding are neglected, and Spirit plays the dominant role in society and in members of the ruling class (545–49). This is something like an "aristocratic" society in our sense of the word, for example, European societies of former centuries, now almost extinct.

In an "oligarchy," the older class divisions break down, money making become the dominant activity, and political power comes to reside with the wealthy. Plato expresses disgust for the resulting type of character, who

> establishes his appetitive and money-making part on the throne, setting it up as a king within himself, . . . and makes the rational and spirited parts sit on the ground beneath appetite, one on either side, reducing them to slaves. . . . He won't allow the first to reason about or examine anything except how a little money can be made into great wealth. And he won't allow the second to value or admire anything but wealth and wealthy people or to have any ambition other than the acquisition of wealth or whatever might contribute to getting it. (553)

"Democracy" might arise by the oppressed majority's seizing power. In the *Republic* Plato took a very jaundiced view of democracy as he understood it, influenced no doubt by his experience of the arbitrariness and instability of Athenian democracy, in which every adult male citizen (but not women or slaves) could vote in the meetings that decided policy, and government positions were often filled by lot (555–57). Plato thought it absurd to give every person an equal say, when most people, in his view, do not know what is best. He criticizes what he labels the "democratic" type of person as lacking in discipline, pursuing mere pleasures of the moment, indulging "unnecessary, spendthrift" desires. (The successful money-maker, for all his faults, at least exerts some self-control.)

> A young man . . . associates with wild and dangerous creatures who can provide every variety of multicolored pleasure in every sort of way.
>
> . . . seeing the citadel of the young man's soul empty of knowledge, fine ways of living, and words of truth . . . [these desires] finally occupy that citadel themselves.
>
> . . . and he doesn't admit any word of truth into the guardhouse, for if someone tells him that some pleasures belong to fine and good desires and others to evil ones and that he must pursue and value the former and restrain and enslave the latter, he denies all this and declares that all pleasures are equal and must be valued equally. (559–61)

Anarchy, Plato thinks, is the sequel to the chaotic and unbridled liberty of democracy: permissiveness spreads, fathers and teachers lose authority. (He displays horror at the idea of liberating women and slaves.) There then arises a desire for restoration of some sort of order, and typically some forceful, unscrupulous individual emerges, wins absolute power, and becomes a tyrant (565–69). The tyrannical character, as Plato diagnoses it, is not so much the tyrant himself (who has, after all, to exercise some intelligence and self-control to maintain his power) but the person who is completely dominated ("tyrannized") by his own appetites, especially sexual desires. He will stop at nothing; he will sacrifice possessions and money, family relations and friends in the frenzied pursuit of his lusts (572–76).

In this series of social diagnoses and character sketches, one may feel that the analogies between individual and society are sometimes overstretched. But each sketch shows notable sociological and psychological insight, and their contemporary applications are obvious. Plato concludes that each type of person and society departs further from the ideal, reaching a deeper level of degradation and unhappiness. He is clear that the money-making, pleasure-seeking, and lust-dominated people are far from happy, and this is part of his case for why "justice" is in the interests of the individual.

Prescription

Plato has said that "justice" is essentially the same thing in both individual and society—a smooth working together of the parts within the soul or of the classes in the state (435); the lack of such harmony is injustice. But there is some ambiguity in the *Republic* about how far individuals can change themselves without institutional reform, or whether social change must come from individual improvement. (This is a problem that is still very much with us.) One main purpose of Plato's argument is to answer the challenge of the cynical Thrasymachus (presented in Book I) by showing that it is in the interest of the individual to be just. Plato does this by reconceptualizing what justice is, insisting that it is a harmony of the three elements in the soul (Book IV), which is bound to make each one of us a happier, more fulfilled human being (Book IX).

But how can such harmony be attained? Plato remarks at 444 that virtue and vice are the result of one's actions, good or bad: so it seems that what we make of ourselves is, at least to some extent, up to us (an existentialist theme; see Chapter 9 on Sartre). However, mere intellectual recognition or moral judgment hardly seems enough, it is one thing to recognize the attractiveness of mental harmony but quite another thing to *achieve* it in oneself.

Here the social element comes into Plato's story: he lays great stress on appropriate education as the most important way to produce virtuous, harmonious, well-balanced, "just" people (376–412 and 521–41). Plato was one of the first to see education as the key to constructing a better society. By education he means not just formal schooling but all the social influences on one's development—though he largely ignores the period of infancy and early childhood, which more recent psychology has recognized as crucial (see Chapter 8 on Freud, and Chapter 10 on Skinner). Plato goes into considerable detail about the kind of education he envisages, and formal academic study is by no means at the center—that is something reserved for an elite subgroup at an appropriately mature age. What Plato sees as vital for everyone is a training of the whole person—Reason, Spirit, and Appetite together. He therefore recommends gymnastics, poetry, and music as elements of the common curriculum. We may find the details of his educational proposals amusingly archaic, but the general principle that "character-forming" foundations are even more important than academic superstructures remains as realistic as ever.

But how is education to be instituted? It requires a clear conception of what is being aimed at—a whole theory of human nature and human knowledge, in fact. Morever, it needs elaborate social organization and resources. This is one main reason why in the *Republic* Plato offers a prescription that is radically political:

> There will be no end to the troubles of states, or of humanity itself, till philosophers become kings in this world, or till those we now call kings and rulers really and truly become philosophers, and political power and philosophy thus come into the same hands. (473)

He is well aware that this sounds absurdly unrealistic, but, given his understanding of the Forms, human knowledge, and human nature, we can see his rationale for it. If there is such a thing as the truth about how we ought to live, then those who have such knowledge are the only people who are properly qualified to govern society. Philosophers are, by Plato's definition, those who have come to know the Forms; if they were to govern society, the problems of human nature could be solved.

In order to produce lovers of wisdom, fit to be philosopher-kings or "Guardians," Plato proposes that the higher stages of education be open only to those mentally able to undertake them. At an appropriate age, they would study mathematics and then philosophy, the disciplines that lead the mind toward knowledge of the Forms and a love of truth for its own sake. The élite thus produced would prefer to go on with intellectual studies, but Plato expects them to respond to the call of social duty (one wonders why?) and apply their expertise to the running of society. After experience in subordinate offices, some of them would be ready for supreme power. Only such lovers of wisdom and truth would be impervious to the usual temptations to misuse power, for they would value the happiness of a right and rational life more than material riches (521).

The way of life of these Guardians would be spartan, in something like the modern sense of the word (Plato must have derived some of his ideas from the historical Sparta). They would have no personal property, and no family life; women and children would be held in common. The state would select which Guardians were suitable for breeding, and organize occasional "mating festivals." The resulting children would be brought up communally by nurses, and precautions would be taken to ensure that no parent recognized his or her own child (457–61). Here Plato goes flatly against the psychological need for strong emotional bonds between children and the adults who bring them up (normally their parents). As a high-born Greek male, he obviously had no experience of childcare and children's needs!

Plato's view that his trained Guardians would be such lovers of truth and goodness that they could be trusted never to misuse their power seems naively optimistic. We surely need constitutional checks to guard against exploitation or tyranny. Plato asks, "Who is qualified to wield absolute power?" but should we not rather ask, "How can we ensure that nobody has absolute power?" What if even well-educated people disagree about questions of morals and politics, as we know that they often do? Is there any way of showing which is the right view? Plato hopes to use rational argument, and he is one of the great philosophical pioneers in doing so. But when someone thinks he or she knows the ultimate truth about some important question, the person may be intolerant of those who disagree and may feel justified in forcing his or her view on others (as the history of political and religious controversies bears witness).

What of the rest of society—the nonélite? Many different economic and social functions need to be performed, and a division of labor is the natural and efficient way of organizing this. Plato makes a three-fold division of society (412–27), parallel to his theory of the soul. Besides the Guardians, there would be a class, traditionally called the "Auxiliaries," that would play the roles of soldiers, police, and civil servants: they would put the directions of the Guardians into effect. The third class would contain the workers of all kinds—farmers, craftsmen, traders, and all those who produce and distribute the material necessities of life. The division among these three classes would be very strict; Plato says that the "justice" or well-being of the society depends on each person performing his or her own proper function and not interfering with others (432–34).

> The object of our legislation is not the welfare of any particular class, but of the whole community. It uses persuasion or force to unite all citizens and make them share together the benefits which each individually can confer on the community; and its purpose in fostering the attitude is not to enable everyone to please himself, but to make each man a link in the unity of the whole. (519–20)

Plato here seems more concerned with the harmony and stability of the whole society than with the well-being of the individuals in it. We may be in favor of "community spirit," of each person's contributing something to the well-being of society. But Plato seems to envisage rather more than this in his strict class division and his insistence that each person fulfil his or her allotted function and that alone. This is what he calls "justice" in the state, but it is plainly not what we mean by the term, which implies equality before the law and something like fair shares for all. If a worker is not content to be a worker, to accept a certain strictly limited share of economic goods, and to have no say in politics, then Plato's state would forcibly compel him to remain in his station. But what is the point of a stable society unless it serves the interests of the individuals in it?

Plato's republic has a distinctly authoritarian, somewhat totalitarian, character. For example, he has no compunction about censorship; he proposes to exclude poets and other artists, on the grounds that they appeal to the lower, nonrational parts of our nature (605). Plato would surely be horrified at the pervasive influence of what we now call "the media" on everyone from early childhood on. We may not like his solution of state censorship, but he calls our attention to the continuing problem of how truth and goodness can be presented amid a welter of competing cultural and economic influences.

In the *Republic* Plato dismisses democratic constitutions rather quickly and, we may wish to say, unfairly. Admittedly, he was thinking of Athenian-type democracy, in which every citizen had a vote on major decisions. Even if electronic voting systems might make this technically feasible in modern states, it would surely result in unstable government, subject to the changing whims of an enormous electorate influenced by collective emotion and "rhetoric" or clever advertising—which was Plato's criticism of Athenian democracy. He would surely be scathing about the manipulation by the mass media in contemporary political campaigns! However, the most essential feature of modern parliamentary democracies—that a government must submit itself for reelection within a fixed period of time— provides a means for peaceful change of government that is absent from Plato's *Republic*. It should be noted, however, that, in the *Statesman* and the *Laws*, he offers a substantially different political prescription: he there advocates the rule of law and endorses democracy, for all its imperfections, as the best kind of constitution, given human nature as it is.

The *Republic* is one of the most influential books of all times. The sketch in this chapter offers a sample of the richness of the ideas it contains but can be no adequate substitute for a study of the text itself. In this chapter I have concentrated on this one dialogue; the reader should remember that Plato wrote much else, developing and changing his views. Socrates and Plato started a tradition of rational inquiry into how we should live; this was taken further by Aristotle (with a less other-worldly metaphysics). Nothing, I suspect, would please Plato more than to know that some of us still carry on this ethical inquiry.

For Further Reading

Basic text: Plato's *Republic*. There are many translations, but the one that has recently earned most praise for readability and liveliness is by G. M. A. Grube, revised by C. D. C. Reeve (Indianapolis: Hackett, 1992). The *Republic* is a lengthy and complex work; some readers may prefer to approach Plato via his shorter dialogues, such as the *Euthyphro*, *Apology*, *Crito*, *Phaedo*, *Meno*, or *Protagoras*.

For a general introduction to the whole of Plato's thought, see, in the Past Masters series, R. M. Hare, *Plato* (Oxford: Oxford University Press, 1982). This is also available as the first part of a trilogy entitled *Founders of Thought* (Oxford: Oxford University Press, 1991), which contains equally masterful introductions to Aristotle by Jonathan Barnes and to Augustine by Henry Chadwick.

For a deep philosophical discussion of the *Republic*, see Julia Annas, *An Introduction to Plato's Republic* (Oxford: Oxford University Press, 1981). This manages to combine scholarship (and technical difficulty, where necessary) with clear-sighted attention to the main moral argument, its foundation in claims about human nature, and its continuing contemporary relevance (see especially the summing up in Ch. 13).

For a classic attack on Plato's political program (which overinfluenced earlier versions of this chapter), see K. R. Popper, *The Open Society and its Enemies*, 4th ed. (London: Routledge, 1962).

For a very full scholarly treatment of Plato's moral philosophy, see Terence Irwin, *Plato's Ethics* (Oxford: Oxford University Press, 1995).

6

Kant: Reason and Freedom, History and Grace

We are jumping over a long historical gap from the ancient world of Greece, Rome, and early Christianity to the thought of Immanuel Kant (1724–1804), who is generally recognized as the greatest philosopher since Plato and Aristotle. Much had happened in between. After the fall of the Roman empire, Christianity became the dominant ideology in Europe. Its theological formulations were influenced by Greek philosophy; in the case of St. Augustine, by Plato and neo-Platonism. The rise of Islam in the near East from the seventh century on led to a flowering of Islamic theology, philosophy, science, and medicine in North Africa and Spain. For a while there was some fruitful contact between the rival civilizations, before intolerance and conflict took over; some of the thought of the classical world was transmitted to the West via Arab scholars. St. Thomas Aquinas's great Christian systematization in the thirteenth century was based on Aristotle's philosophy. The fall of Byzantium (the heir to the Eastern half of the Roman Empire) to the Moslems in 1453 brought a further influx of classical texts to the West.

Three movements of worldwide historical importance then developed in Europe. In the Renaissance of the fifteenth and sixteenth centuries, the literature, arts, and philosophy of the ancient world exerted a new influence on Western thought. When the religious Reformation started in the sixteenth century, led by Luther and Calvin, the unity of the Catholic Church was shattered, and a number of Protestant churches, movements, and sects developed that appealed to the authority of the Bible or to individual religious experience rather than to the tradition of the institutional Church. The rise of modern physical science in the seventeenth century—the combination of experimental method and systematic theory exemplified in the works of Galileo and Newton—demonstrated how new knowledge about the world could be solidly established on the basis of observation.

There were manifold new developments in thought about human nature in this period, too numerous to survey here. From the seventeenth century on, philosophers sought to apply the methods of science to the study of human beings; this was expressed in different ways in the thought of Hobbes, Spinoza, Hume, and many others. In the movement of ideas called the Enlightenment, this became a dominant theme. Locke's political thought strongly influenced the drafting of the new American constitution after 1776. The French *philosophes*—socially progressive thinkers such as Voltaire, Diderot, and Condorcet—laid the intellectual foundations of the French Revolution of 1789. The great hope of the Enlightenment was that scientific rationality could be applied to human affairs, that humanity could leave behind the authority of traditional beliefs and inherited rank and improve the conditions of human life by the use of reason.

Although he spent all his life in the small Prussian city of Königsberg (the modern Kaliningrad), which was then at the eastern margin of European culture, Kant received a wide-ranging education and attained a thorough knowledge of the science of his day. He well understood the system of Newton and always treated it with enormous respect. He himself contributed to science at one point, when he developed the nebular hypothesis, which was the first naturalistic (nontheological) account of the origin of the solar system. In the late eighteenth century, the second main stage of scientific development—the chemical revolution—was under way, and Kant was aware of that development, too. He predated the nineteenth-century Darwinian revolution in biology, of course, so some of his writing about design in nature ("teleology") looks antiquated.

Kant also had a very well-grounded humanistic education that embraced both classical philosophy and literature and European philosophy, theology, and political theory since the seventeenth century. One writer who made an especially deep impression on his ethical and social thought was Rousseau, the maverick of the French Enlightenment. Rousseau's ideas on human nature, culture, education, and history (especially in his two *Discourses* and in *Emile*) were transformed by Kant into his own philosophizing about human nature.

The works of Kant's "critical philosophy" were published in the final two decades of the eighteenth century. His major writings are the *Critique of Pure Reason* (1781), the *Groundwork* (or *Foundations*) *of the Metaphysics of Morals* (1785), the *Critique of Practical Reason* (1788), the *Critique of Judgment* (1790), *Religion within the Boundaries of Mere Reason* (1793), and *Anthropology from a Pragmatic Point of View* (1798). None of these is easy reading, but the *Groundwork* is relatively short and is widely used as an undergraduate text (the *Prolegomena* is a rather less successful introduction to Kant's theoretical philosophy). Kant also wrote shorter, stylish essays for the educated public on such topics as "What Is Enlightenment?," "What Does It Mean to Orient Oneself in Thinking?," "Idea for a Universal History with Cosmopolitan Intent," and "Perpetual Peace." He wanted to be not just an academic philosopher— which he certainly was in every sense of the term—but also a socially influential and progressive thinker. He gained reputations as both in his own time and has since been revered as the deepest thinker of the Enlightenment.

Kant repeatedly expressed his faith in the free, democratic use of reason to examine everything, however traditional, authoritative, or sacred. Reason should appeal only to the uncompelled assent of anyone capable of rational judgment. Human reason thus has to provide its own self-discipline: we can scrutinize the pretensions and limitations of reason itself by our "higher judicial reason." It is ironic, then, that in his old age, when his reputation was already well assured, Kant got into trouble with his government. For most of his life he had benefited from the comparatively liberal rule of Frederick the

Great in Prussia, but after that monarch's death a more conservative
regime took over. Its censors detected an unorthodox strain in Kant's
Religion within the Boundaries of Mere Reason and forbade him to
publish further on the topic. (There was no question of drinking hem-
lock, Socratic fashion, but it is interesting to note that it was an alleged subversion of state-approved religion that got both philosophers
into conflict with their political masters. There are still countries
where such things can happen.) Kant's response was wily, if not con-
spicuously courageous—he gave a promise to obey but worded it in
such a way that he felt bound to it only for the lifetime of Frederick
William II, whom, in the event, he managed to outlive.

Metaphysics and Epistemology

Kant is typical of his age (and indeed of much Western thought even
now) in inheriting the twin influences of Christianity and science and
in seeing the most fundamental problems of philosophy in how to
combine the two. In his case, the Christian influence was partly the
traditional theological conceptions—God as ominiscient, omnipotent,
and benevolent; an immortal human soul; and human free will—but
partly also the moral ideas of an extreme form of Protestantism, the
Pietism of his parents, which emphasized the importance of right living above all dogma and ritual. We see later in this chapter that the
latter influence became subversive of the former.

The impact of science on Kant is equally obvious. One fundamental objective of his philosophy was to explain how scientific
knowledge is possible. He developed a systematic theory of knowledge and human cognitive faculties to show how both the empirical
methods of physical science and the method of proof in mathematics depend on a priori presuppositions. He claimed that these cannot
themselves be proved by experience (observation of the world); nor
are they mere logical truths ("analytic"). Such principles can, however, be seen by philosophical reflection, specifically by "transcendental arguments," to be necessary conditions of any empirical
experience of the world. In his *Critique of Pure Reason*, Kant sets
out an elaborate theory of our forms of perception, thought, and judgment and offers an account of how we can have some knowledge

that is a priori and yet "synthetic" in that it is not just a matter of definition or analysis of concepts.

Kant's "Copernican revolution" was his doctrine that "objects must conform to our knowledge," which seems to mean that certain basic features of the objects of our knowledge are due to the nature of our human cognitive faculties. We can know the world only "as it appears" to us; we cannot know it "as it is in itself." The world as we experience it, the world of "appearances," is thoroughly imbued with the forms of our perception (space and time) and the forms of our thought (the categories—the logical forms of judgments). The world as it is in itself may not be spatial or temporal (indeed, Kant slips—with questionable justification—into the stronger assertion that it is definitely *not* in space or time). This "transcendental idealism" shook the foundations of all previous philosophy, and the reverberations have been felt ever since, not least in contemporary philosophical debates about realism and idealism.

Kant argued (in the "Second Analogy" in his first *Critique*) that universal determinism—the principle that every event has a preceding cause, a state of affairs that makes that event necessarily happen—is a presupposition of science and, indeed, of any empirical knowledge of the world. He struggled to reconcile this with his equally strongly held belief in human free will. He never withdrew his claim that every event in the physical world is causally determined; the problem for him (as for many other thinkers) was an "Antinomy" between two apparently inconsistent metaphysical beliefs. He did not foresee twentieth-century quantum mechanics, of course, with its undetermined events at the subatomic level, but the advent of an indeterministic physical theory does not in itself solve the free will problem, for we still need to understand how people can justly be held responsible for their actions.

Kant inherited and supported the general scientific methodology of his age: he believed that sufficient causes for all material events can always be found among other material events. He did not accept Descartes's dualism, according to which our minds are nonmaterial entities that causally interact with our brains. In his "First Analogy," he argued that all events in the world (which must include mental processes) have to be seen as changes in persisting "substance," which here seems to mean matter. In the "Third Analogy," he said that everything in the world must be part of a single, interacting system of reality. But his attitude to materialism about human nature was mixed, as we see later.

In the second main section of the *Critique of Pure Reason*, the "Dialectic," Kant claims to diagnose how and why we tend to claim illusory metaphysical knowledge of things as they are in themselves (the soul, the universe as a whole, uncaused "free" events, and God or "necessary being"). Such claims have long been central to Christian theology, and hence to much Western philosophy, but they go beyond the bounds of knowledge Kant set out in the preceding section, the "Analytic." Kant's view is that we *can neither prove nor disprove* these traditional metaphysical assertions. In one respect he makes a decisive break with the tradition of rationalist philosophy and natural theology (still by no means dead), which tries to offer proofs (whether logical or empirical) about God and the soul. But there has long been a "fideist" tradition in religious thinking as well, exemplified especially in Augustine, Pascal, and Kierkegaard, which emphasizes that faith must go beyond reason. At first sight, Kant seems to fit into that tradition, retaining theological concepts in their traditional meanings but saying that they are a matter for faith rather than knowledge. Whether this is the whole story, we shall have to see.

Theory of Human Nature

The overarching problem of Kant's philosophy was to reconcile the claims of morality and religion (as he saw them) with scientific knowledge (as he understood it). He thus hoped to relate physical nature and human nature in one big picture. In this he remains a central and characteristic figure of the whole "modern" age since the rise of science in the seventeenth century.

Let us begin with Kant's acount of human cognitive faculties. Early in the first *Critique* he writes:

> Our knowledge springs from two fundamental sources of the mind;
> the first is the capacity for receiving representations (receptivity for
> impressions), the second is the power of knowing an object through
> these representations (spontaneity in the production of concepts).

> Through the first an object is *given* to us, through the second the object is *thought.* . . . To neither of these powers may a preference be given over the other. Without sensibility no object would be given to us, without understanding no object would be thought. Thoughts without content are empty, intuitions without concepts are blind. (A50–1/B74–5)

Kant developed an epistemological theory that reconciles the one-sided views of his rationalist and empiricist predecessors. Knowledge depends on the interaction of two factors—on the one hand, what is given in perception, namely, sensory states passively caused by objects outside the mind, and, on the other, the way the mind actively ("spontaneously") organizes these data under concepts and thus makes judgments that are expressible in propositions. Animals have the first capacity ("sensibility"), but they lack "understanding"; they do not make judgments or assertions. (But there is an interesting question how far some of the higher animals, such as primates or dolphins, may approximate to human thought.) Animals perceive food, prey, predators, mates, and offspring very effectively, but they do not think *that* anything is the case. They can feel pain, bodily pleasures, warmth, or cold, and they can be in states of emotional arousal such as fear and aggression, but they do not have *concepts* of sensations or emotions—an animal cannot think *that* it, or another animal, is in pain, or is afraid. (In this, Kant can be seen as building on Aristotle's distinctions among plants, animals, and humans.)

In some of his writing, Kant adds to this dualism of "sensibility" and "understanding" a third faculty, which he calls the "imagination." Anticipating modern psychology and cognitive science, Kant saw that there must be some sort of mental processing that leads from the raw data in our sense organs to our conceptual recognitions and judgments. His general label for this process is "synthesis." He realizes that synthesis is almost entirely unconscious, and he attributes it to the "imagination." The reason for the latter appellation is that this mental power sometimes operates to produce merely imaginary or illusory results, for example, when one "sees" a face in the fire or thinks one sees a person lurking in the bushes where there is in fact only a shadow. Kant holds that it is the same faculty of imagination that also operates in veridical perception, as when one sees that there

really is someone there or, indeed, when one recognizes the person
as a known individual: the imagination is similarly involved when
one sees a newspaper cartoon as representing a particular individual.
The imagination is a necessary ingredient of everyday perception, but
Kant claims that it also operates in aesthetic awareness, where it can
exercise "free play" and give us a sense of delight, as for example,
when we appreciate music or visual patterns as in abstract art.

There is a further depth in Kant's account of human cognitive faculties, for he lays enormous stress on "reason" (the term that figures
in the titles of his first two *Critiques*). Sometimes it seems that this
is just another name for the understanding, the power of conceptual
thought that distinguishes us from other animals. But it emerges that
Kant has in mind a yet higher role for reason. He insists that we do
not just make lots of particular judgments about the world; we try to
integrate all these bits of knowledge into a unified system. We often
want to know not merely what is the case but *why* it is so; we try to
explain one fact in terms of others. In the "Antinomies" section of
his first *Critique*, Kant offers an elaborate theory of how our faculty
of "reason" leads us towards an ever-increasing unification of our
knowledge under general laws or principles. He here expresses something crucial about scientific method, but it is not just a point about
the specialized theories of science; it applies to everyone's conception of reality—we accept that any one fact must cohere with all
others.

There is a vital practical dimension to Kant's conception of reason (echoing Aristotle on "practical reason"). He points out that we
are not merely perceiving, judging, and theorizing beings; we are also
agents—we do things, we affect the world by our actions as well as
being affected by the world in perception. In this respect, too, we
transcend the animals. Obviously, they "do" things; they can "act"
very effectively, in one sense of these words. But they do not have
concepts of what they are trying to achieve, so we cannot ascribe to
them intentions to make it the case *that* such-and-such a state of affairs obtains. There are causes for their behavior in internal desires
and external perceptions, but since animals cannot *give reasons* for
their actions, they cannot really be said to *have* reasons for them. In
this sense, they do not *act*; they only behave.

Kant further distinguishes among human reasons for actions. Some of our reasons appeal only to the agent's own desires (and factual beliefs)—I am doing A because I want to achieve B, and I believe that in the present circumstances A will be the most effective way to bring about B. This is what Kant calls a "hypothetical imperative." But he insists that not all reasons for action take this form, which involves only the rational selection of means to ends, which are the satisfaction of one's own wants. Sometimes we accept an obligation, a moral "ought," a reason for action that holds irrespective of one's self-interested desires and may even go against them. A simple example is any situation where one admits the claims of elementary justice, "fair shares for all," as when cutting the available cake. In such cases, Kant says that we recognize the validity of what he calls a "categorical imperative" of the form "I ought to do C, whatever my own desires and inclinations on the matter may be." This is what Kant calls "pure practical reason" operating in us. He gives some highly abstract formulations of this in his theoretical works on ethics, but at bottom his appeal is to the common experience of moral obligation.

Kant's analysis of human cognitive faculties seems to me basically correct. But the large question that arises is what metaphysics or ontology of human beings makes these distinctive faculties possible. Here the going gets more difficult and controversial. Kant's official line on the issue of dualism or materialism about human nature was that we *cannot know* what we are "in ourselves." The traditional metaphysical arguments of what he called "rational psychology" (e.g., in Plato and Descartes) cannot, he claims, prove the existence of an incorporeal soul. We can only know ourselves "as we appear" to ourselves in introspection ("inner sense") and to each other as embodied human beings acting in the world (observed by "outer sense"). But Kant insisted that we cannot prove that we are ultimately *material* beings, either: in his view, we simply cannot know either way. In his characteristic fashion, he leaves the metaphysical question open, as a matter for faith rather than knowledge. His own preference comes out when he rejects "a soulless materialism" and suggests that there are reasons of a moral kind for believing that we can survive death and live on into an infinite future.

Kant was a rock-solid believer in human freedom and moral responsibility. He sees us as free, rational beings who can act for moral reasons, not just on selfish desires. Probably his single greatest philosophical problem, to which he devoted some of his most obscure and controversial theorizing, was how to reconcile free will with physical determinism. He famously, but obscurely, offers his distinction between appearances and things in themselves as the key to this conundrum. In his solution to the Third Antinomy in the first *Critique*, he suggests that if appearances are "viewed not as things in themselves, but merely as representations," they can have both empirical causes and "intelligible causes" or "grounds":

> Man knows himself also through pure apperception . . . in acts and inner determinations which he cannot regard as impressions of the senses. He is thus to himself, on the one hand, phenomenon, and on the other hand, in respect of certain faculties the action of which cannot be ascribed to the receptivity of sensibility, a purely intelligible object. We entitle these faculties understanding and reason. (A546–7/B574–5)

A natural interpretation of this statement is that we can be aware of the reasons (the "intelligible causes") for our actions—and indeed for our beliefs—in a way that is different from our perception of the external world and even from our passive introspective awareness of sensations, bodily desires, and emotions. (In Kant's technical terminology, "apperception" is different from both "outer" and "inner" sense.)

So far, so good—perhaps! But how can this solve the free will problem? In Chapter 3 of the *Groundwork*, Kant distinguished two points of view, by which we can regard ourselves as belonging either to the sensible world of perceptible appearances or to the intelligible world of laws and reasons. He says that our reason has causality with respect to appearances (or at least we represent it as doing so). This presumably means that our recognition of rational and moral norms has perceptible effects on what we do. Yet, according to his theory of the limitation of the category of causality to perceptible experience, we should not be able to *know* of this causality of reason. Kant seems to be caught in an antinomy of his own making here—between the truism that people's reasons or intentions are mental states occurring in time, and knowable by our usual ways of understanding each other, and his own insistence on the unknowability and nontemporality of the noumenal world, including ourselves "as we are in ourselves," our "intelligible character."

Is it true that we can know nothing whatever about people's reasons, including their moral motivations? In some places, Kant seems to bite this bullet, claiming that the real morality of actions, even our own conduct, is entirely hidden from us and that "our imputations can refer only to the empirical character" (A551/B579, note). This implies not merely that we can never make any *perfectly* just judgment (as he wisely acknowledges) but that we can never make even a reasonably well-justified judgment about the moral aspects of an action. Such skepticism hardly fits with Kant's insistence that the ordinary person has as good a moral judgment in practice as the philosopher. Nor does it fit with his saying that however much we know about the influences that induce someone to lie, we nonetheless blame the agent and hold that he could have resisted those influences.

Kant, like most of us, is pulled in two directions here. We think that we can and should continue our practice of holding people responsible for their actions, praising and blaming them, sometimes rewarding or punishing—and not in a merely manipulative, string-pulling, causally calculating way. But, on the other hand, we want, when we think about the matter, to be properly sensitive to the causal influences on people's character formation and emotional states and to be appropriately cautious in our interpretations and judgments about people's motivations for action.

In the *Groundwork*, Kant offers a distinctively practical defense of freedom. In any situation where one is making up one's mind how to act, reviewing the reasons for and against various possible courses of action, one cannot simultaneously think of one's decision as already determined: however much one might be impressed by theoretical arguments for determinism, there is no escaping the necessity to make up one's mind what to do here and now. As Kant puts it, we have always to act "under the idea of freedom"—so from the practical point of view we are already free. Whether this is enough of an answer to the philosophical problem about free will is still much debated.

Diagnosis

We have seen how Kant emphasizes the distinction between self-interested and moral reasons, inclinations and duty. He contrasts our human nature with the animals, on one side, and with the conception of a "holy will," on the other. Animals do not have any tension between desires and duty, for they do not have the concept of duty or, indeed, of any sort of reasons for action, although they have desires, of course. A hypothetical rational being who was without desires (an angel?) would also not experience any tension between duty and inclination, but for the opposite reason: such a being would not be subject to the temptation of desires and would always do the right thing. But we human beings are mixed creatures, midway between animals and angels. We are finite beings with our individual needs (not merely physical desires, but emotional needs or drives for love, approval, status, and power); yet we are also rational beings—and for Kant that includes "pure practical reason," the recognition of moral obligations. The tension between these two sides of our nature is an inescapable feature of the human condition.

A basic philosophical problem here is how people can be motivated to do their duty, to fulfill a moral obligation when it goes against their own self-interested desires. "Why be moral?" the skeptical philosopher asks. On that question Kant offers some very abstruse theorizing that has kept his interpreters busy ever since, but I think that at root he is appealing to what he takes to be the universal and necessary fact that we all accept the validity of some moral obligations or other (although we sometimes disagree about what they are in particular cases).

It is relevant here to point out here a distinction—which Kant occasionally recognizes—*within* the class of self-interested reasons, between desires for immediate satisfaction and considerations of prudent, longer-term self-interest. One can resist the allure of a second cream cake, an expensive car or dress, or a seductive tempter, in the interest of one's own health, wealth, or happiness. So our mixed nature—more than the animal level, but less than perfectly rational—is also manifested in our capacity to recognize prudential reasons and our ability to act on them—at least sometimes! We all need to be able to postpone the satisfaction of immediate desires in the interest of longer-term goals. To be unable to do this is not to be fully human, to be reduced to an almost animal level (like Plato's "tyrannical" man). Any child needs to start learning at an early age to postpone some gratifications (Freud makes interesting comments on this, as we see in Chapter 8). We all have to negotiate a balance between short-term and long-term satisfaction.

On the moral question, there is a very practical problem for parents, teachers, social workers, legislators, and social reformers: namely, how people can acquire the motivation to do the right thing. Kant has quite a lot to say about such practical questions; not all his writing is at the level of abstruse metaphysical theory. An obvious response is to offer rewards or threaten punishment. That may help solve the practical question, but it does not answer the philosophical problem of how anyone can be motivated by anything other than self-interest. Setting up a system of rewards and punishment amounts only to putting new self-interested reasons in place. That may (or may not!) induce external conformity to legal or moral rules, but it cannot create the truly virtuous inner attitude, the will to do the right action *just because it is right* (and recognized by the agent as such). Such a good "will" is, Kant insists, the only thing that is really good in itself.

Kant does not look on moral praise and blame as just more external incentives for people to comply with ethical duties. They are, instead, ways of "sharing in the reason of one another." My blaming you for neglecting an ethical duty is not like my slapping you on the wrist. Moral praise and blame should induce you to act accordingly only if you are rationally convinced that they are appropriate. If they are designed to operate on you only by appealing merely to your interest in avoiding the displeasure and bad opinion of others, they lose their moral content. All external rewards and punishments for Kant concern only "the realm of law," not the realm of ethics. No ethical duties can be enforced through rewards and punishments of any sort without violating the rights of free beings. This is an important Kantian ethical doctrine that separates him from a lot of moral theory (especially in the utilitarian tradition).

In his works of ethical theory, Kant tends to present his view in an apparently morally severe guise, which suggests that the only motivation of which he really approves is the grim determination to do one's duty irrespective of one's own inclinations. He almost seems to imply that if one is spontaneously inclined to look after one's children, to tell the truth, or to help someone in distress, that does not make the actions admirable and might even *detract* from their moral value! Wider and more careful reading of Kant dispels this common misinterpretation. Of course, he is concerned to approve of and encourage virtues as traits of human character (aren't we all?)—the more that people develop mental dispositions to do the right things, the better. Kant's point is that, as rational beings, we are not just bundles of innately given or socially trained inclinations; we have reasons for our actions, and those reasons are always implicitly general, so they can be made explicit as "maxims" and rationally and morally assessed. It is not enough for us to effect appropriate results in the world: distinctively human virtue involves having morally good reasons and intentions.

How, then, are right actions and virtuous dispositions to be achieved and encouraged? It is not sufficient just to formulate a philosophical theory of what pure practical reason requires, by way of universalizing the "maxims" behind our actions, applying to all rational beings and treating each person as an end "in himself." Nor is it enough to state more specific moral rules or to describe their application in particular cases. For, as Plato and St. Paul saw, it is one thing to recognize an "ought" and another thing to do it. Philosophizing and moralizing notoriously have limited effect on human conduct.

In his late work *Religion within the Boundaries of Mere Reason*, Kant continued to wrestle with the most profound problems of human nature, and he suggested some new insights, or new versions of old ones. He talks of the "radical evil" in human nature, using almost biblical language. He quotes or paraphrases the Bible frequently and suggests how these sacred scriptures of Christian tradition should be interpreted as expressing fundamental moral truths about the eternal human condition, even if this is not their literal or historical meaning. He acknowledges what he calls the "frailty" of human nature, our difficulty in doing what we know we ought to do, and our "impurity"—our tendency to confuse or adulterate moral reasons with other motives. For Kant, what is (radically) evil is not our naturally given desires; nor is it the tension between these desires and duty. It is, rather, what he calls the "depravity" of human nature, or the human heart—the freely chosen *subordination* of duty to inclination, the deliberate preference for own's own happiness (as one conceives of it) over obligations to other people, insofar as the two conflict.

This is another place where Kant, along with so many other thinkers, is pulled in two directions. On the one hand, he insists very strongly that the evil in us is a result of our own choice, our wrong use of our freedom. But, on the other hand, in his own version of the doctrine of original sin, he wants to say that evil is "radical" or innate in us, a universal and unavoidable feature of our condition as needy but rational beings:

> There is in the human being a natural propensity to evil; and this propensity itself is morally evil, since it must ultimately be sought in a free power of choice, and hence is imputable. This evil is *radical*, since it corrupts the ground of all maxims; as natural propensity, it is also not to be *extirpated* through human forces. . . . Yet it must equally be possible to *overcome* this evil, for it is found in the human being as acting freely. (*Religion* 6:37)

Kant's position is not that radical evil must attach to every rational but finite creature of needs (he envisages an ideal of "humanity well-pleasing to God" and free of this evil, while retaining the same needs and inclinations as ourselves). Our needs as finite beings involve our animal nature, which Kant regards as innocent in itself. Nor does he think it coherent to attribute a predisposition to evil to our rational nature, which would make us devilish beings. He thinks that radical evil attaches to our predisposition to humanity (to rational self-love), not as an inevitable consequence of this predisposition but as a result of its development under social conditions. This is the Rousseauian aspect of Kant's doctrine—the "unsocial sociability" of human beings—our need and inclination to be members of society, combined with our tendency to be selfish and competitive. Paradoxically, Kant's thesis that we are by nature evil amounts to much the same thing as Rousseau's famous assertion that we are by nature good (there was a related debate within the Confucian tradition; see the end of Chapter 2). The phrase "by nature" is used by the two philosophers in opposed ways. Rousseau means by it "prior to the social condition," and he argues that social development has corrupted original human nature. Kant, in contrast, thinks that our nature develops properly only in society, but he doesn't believe there is such a thing as a pre-social *human* condition.

Prescription

Kant's answer to the problems of human nature shares the ambiguity of his diagnosis. The quotation from his *Religion* strongly suggests that only a religious answer will suffice. If the evil in us cannot be "extirpated through human forces," yet needs to be "overcome" somehow, believers of one stripe or another will be quick to jump in and say that only God's salvation (in their recommended version) can do the trick. Much of Kant's mature work, including the later sections of all three *Critiques*, touches on religious themes. A first glance may suggest that this is mere conventional piety, artificially tacked on to his serious philosophical work (some readers have thus put it down to Kant's senility, or to his desire to please his manservant, his public, or his political masters). But more careful reading shows his understanding of the legitimate role of religious belief to be far from Christian orthodoxy, so it is not surprising, if hardly admirable, that Prussian censors tried to hinder the publication of his thought.

Chapter 3 of the Dialectic of the *Critique of Pure Reason* opens with remarks about the inspiration to be gained from ideals of divine perfection and wisdom, which transcend all experience (even depiction in a"romance"!). Kant then classifies all possible theoretical arguments for the existence of God into three—ontological, cosmological, and "physico-theological" (design) arguments—and criticizes each in turn. His arguments are clearly and vigorously expressed; these are classics of philosophical criticism of natural theology (along with Hume's *Dialogues Concerning Natural Religion*). An original aspect is Kant's claim that the argument from design presupposes that from cosmology, which in turn depends on the ontological argument. So, if he is right, demolishing the latter brings down the whole house of cards.

But Kant destroys only to try to rebuild on a different, practical basis. Although propositions about God, immortality, and free will cannot be proved (or disproved) by the theoretical use of reason, Kant thinks they can be justified from the "practical" point of view. When we are thinking of how to *act*, different considerations arise. The idea of freedom is involved most directly in our deliberations about what to do. But what about God and immortality—where do they come in, or do they have to come in at all? Kant offers various versions of his "moral theology"—in the Method section of the *Critique of Pure Reason*, in the Dialectic of the *Critique of Practical Reason*, in sections 86–91 of the *Critique of Judgment* (where he emphasizes the importance of the feelings of gratitude for well-being, of obligation to sacrifice desire to duty, and of answerability to judgment), and, of course, in the *Religion*.

In various places, Kant distinguishes three questions that sum up "all the interests of reason, speculative as well as practical":

1. What can I know?
2. What ought I to do?
3. What may I hope?

The first question is discussed in depth in the first *Critique*. The second, about moral duty, is treated in the *Groundwork*, the second *Critique*, and other ethical works. The third ("If I do what I ought to do, what may I then hope?") is a new topic, comparitively neglected in philosophy, asking a question that is somehow both theoretical and practical. In the Dialectic of the second *Critique*, Kant gives one of his fullest expositions of his "practical" argument for belief in immortality and God, but in later work, such as the *Religion*, the force of these arguments and the interpretation of the metaphysical claims themselves seem to get somewhat attenuated.

Kant is deeply concerned about the relation between virtue and happiness. He argues, as we have seen, that there is more to morality than the performance of right actions: he also puts forward the idea that there must be a final end of all moral striving—the "highest good"—which is a combination of virtue and happiness for all rational beings. However, it is all too obvious that virtuous actions are not necessarily rewarded with happiness in the world as we know it. It seems an obvious step—and one that millions of people have taken—to say that justice requires there to be a "Supreme Reason" underlying nature who governs according to moral rules and who will reward everyone appropriately in a future life beyond this world.

It may seem that, in invoking God and immortality, Kant is doing no more than repeating the common human hope for justice and reward in a life after death. But it is fundamental to his moral philosophy that our motive for doing our duty should *not* be to reap benefit thereby; it would therefore be utterly inconsistent for him to postulate rewards beyond death in order to motivate right action. And yet, he says, we need to have ground to hope that virtue will eventually be rewarded. His case seems to be that our very motivation for moral action will be undermined unless we can at least believe that the highest good, the ultimate combination of virtue and happiness, is *possible*. One is not supposed to aim directly at it for oneself, but one needs to have *hope*—one has to assume that doing the right thing here and now is not utterly pointless. But does moral resolution really require belief in the traditional theological claims about the survival of individual persons into an infinite future, or about the existence of an omnipotent, omniscient, and benevolent God? This remains far from obvious.

In the *Religion*, Kant sometimes backs off, as when he says of the conventional notions of heaven and hell that they are "representations powerful enough . . . without any necessity to presuppose dogmatically, as an item of doctrine, that an eternity of good or evil is the human lot also objectively" (6:69). And "this faith needs only *the idea of God* . . . without pretending to secure objective reality for it through theoretical cognition" (6:154, footnote). Again, speaking of the struggle between "the good and the evil principles":

> It is easy to see, once we divest of its mystical cover this vivid mode of representing things, apparently also the only at the time *suited to the common people*, why it (its spirit and rational meaning) has been valid and binding practically, for the whole world and at all times: because it lies near enough to every human being for each to recognize his duty in it. Its meaning is that there is absolutely no salvation for human beings except in the innermost adoption of genuine moral principles in their disposition. . . . (*Religion* 6:83)

No wonder that such "demythologizing" language worried religious conservatives two centuries ago in Prussia; it unsettles Christian orthodoxy even today, perhaps especially now that we are less inclined than Kant and Plato to distinguish what is believable by an elite and by "the common people."

For all his use of religious and specifically Christian language, Kant also entertained more this-worldly hopes, expressed especially in his essays on history, which paved the way for the more explicitly historical philosophies of Hegel and Marx in the following century. He envisioned the possibility of progress in human history through the gradual emancipation of people from poverty, war, ignorance, and deference to traditional authorities. He was a supporter of the French Revolution, though aware of its excesses. In his essay *Perpetual Peace*, he sketches a future world order of peaceful cooperation between nations with democratic constitutions. (He would surely be delighted with the achievements of the European Economic Union in the second half of the twentieth century, for all its faults.) At the end of his *Anthropology*, his hope took an explicitly worldly form—for the progress of humanity in history, despite its propensities for evil. Kant was in all this an Enlightenment thinker, but, unlike many others, he had a vivid and realistic sense of the dark side of human nature, our potentiality for evil—which has been only too amply confirmed since his time. His social optimism is not naive: how realistic it is, we must judge for ourselves, when we have tried to take the measure of his thought.

Kant's practical philosophy leaves with this fundamental, thought-provoking ambiguity between the hope for gradual social amelioration, with the corresponding resolution to contribute to it, and a more religious viewpoint that sees our only ultimate hope in divine grace, given to us in so far as we acknowledge our finitude and our faults and resolve to be better human beings as best we imperfectly can.

For Further Reading

For a short introduction to Kant's central ideas, see Roger Scruton, *Kant* (Oxford: Oxford University Press, 1982), in the Past Master Series, a little gem of compressed insight.

For a more comprehensive, but still digestible, introduction to the whole of Kant's thought, see Otfried Hoeffe, *Kant* (Albany: State University of New York Press, 1994).

For a clear account of the ethics, see Roger J. Sullivan, *An Introduction to Kant's Ethics* (Cambridge: Cambridge University Press, 1994).

Allen Wood, in *Kant's Moral Religion* (Ithaca: Cornell University Press, 1970), gives an excellent defense of Kant's theory of religion. This is unfortunately out of print now, but Wood has contributed a chapter on this topic in *The Cambridge Companion to Kant*, ed. Paul Guyer (Cambridge: Cambridge University Press, 1992).

For those brave enough to start reading Kant for themselves, the conventional starting points are his two formidably titled shorter works, *Groundwork for the Metaphysics of Morals* and *Prolegomena to Any Future Metaphysics*, of which there are various translations.

Easier reading for those more interested in the practical side of Kant's thought can be found in *Kant on History*, ed. L. W. Beck (Indianapolis: Bobbs-Merrill, 1963) or *Kant's Political Writings*, 2d ed., ed. H. Reiss (Cambridge: Cambridge Unversity Press, 1991). Some may like to look at Kant's *Religion within the Bounds of Reason Alone.* There is a translation by T. M. Greene and H. H. Hudson (New York: Harper & Row, 1960) and a newer one in the multivolume *Cambridge Edition of the Works of Immanuel Kant.*

7

Marx: The Economic Basis of Human Nature

In comparing Marxism to Christianity in Chapter 1, I mentioned the most basic ideas of Marxism and some of the standard objections. In this chapter I go a little deeper into Marx's theories. Our contemporary view of Marxism is, of course, strongly colored by our knowledge of the rise and fall of communism in the twentieth century, but I propose to concentrate here on the nineteenth-century thought of Karl Marx himself (including the works he wrote in collaboration with Engels). Though his ideas were enormously influential, he cannot be held totally responsible for the failings of later communist regimes.

If Kant was the deepest philosopher of the Enlightenment, Marx was the great theorist of the industrial revolution, the development of the contemporary capitalist economic system. Although hostile to religion, Marx (with most of Western civilization) inherited an ideal of human equality from Christianity, and he shared the Enlightenment hope that scientific method could diagnose and solve the problems of human society. Behind all his elaborate social and economic theorizing, he had a prophetic zeal to point the way towards a secular form of redemption.

Life and Work

Karl Marx was born in 1818 in the German Rhineland, of a Jewish family who became Christian; he was brought up as a Protestant but soon abandoned religion. He displayed his intellectual ability early, and in 1836 he entered the University of Berlin as a student in the Faculty of Law. There was a ferment of philosophical, aesthetic, and social ideas in the "Romantic" movement of that time, into which the young Marx eagerly plunged. He wrote poetry and worked on an academic dissertation on ancient Greek metaphysics, while also being earnestly concerned with social reform. His early writing has a vigorous philosophical and poetic style, expressing the passionate intensity of his thought. The dominant intellectual influence in Germany at that time was the philosophy of Hegel, and Marx became immersed in studying and discussing Hegel's ideas, so much so that he abandoned his legal studies and devoted himself to philosophy (in a broad sense of the term).

The leading inspiration in Hegel's thought was the idea of progress in human history. Hegel argued that each culture or nation has a kind of personality of its own and that its historical development is to be explained in terms of its particular character. He applied this personification to the whole world and identified reality with what he called *Geist*, i.e., Mind or Spirit (this may sound vaguely theological, but it seems to be closer to pantheism than to the biblical conception of God). He interpreted human history as the progressive self-realization of *Geist*, seeing this as the fundamental spiritual movement behind all history. Successive stages of human social life express increasingly adequate ideas of freedom, but each stage is subject to conflicting tendencies; its demise lays the foundation for the next stage of freedom. Hegel developed an influential conception of "alienation" in which the knowing subject is confronted with an object other than ("alien to") him- or herself; this distinction between subject and object is supposed somehow to be overcome in the process by which Spirit gradually realizes itself in the world.

The followers of Hegel split into two camps over how his ideas applied to politics and religion. The "Right" Hegelians held that the processes of history could be relied on to lead to the best possible results and saw the contemporary Prussian state as the culmination of all preceding historical development. They thus held conservative political views, and they tended to emphasize the religious elements in Hegel's thought. In contrast, the "Left" or "Young" Hegelians held that the best form of freedom had yet to be realized, that the nation-states of the time were very far from ideal, and that it was up to people to help change the old order and bring about the next stage of human history. Accordingly, they held radical views in politics and religion.

One of the most important thinkers in the radical group was Feuerbach, whose *Essence of Christianity* was published in 1841. Feuerbach held that Hegel had got everything upside-down, that far from God's progressively realizing Himself in history, religious beliefs are produced by human beings as a pale reflection of this world, which is the only reality. It is because people are unfulfilled in their actual, practical life that they need to believe in such illusory ideas, and thus become "alienated," projecting their own higher potential into theological fantasies and undervaluing their real human relationships. Feuerbach diagnosed metaphysics as "esoteric psychology," the expression of feelings within ourselves rather than truths about the universe. Religion is a symptom of alienation, from which we must free ourselves by realizing our purely human destiny in this world. Feuerbach was a forerunner of modern humanism and of the sociological or psychological explanations of religion offered by Marx, Durkheim, and Freud.

This, then, was the intellectual atmosphere that prevailed during Marx's formative years. His reading of Feuerbach broke the spell that Hegel had cast on him, but he retained the assumption that Hegel's philosophy of historical development contained truths about human nature and society in an inverted form. Marx wrote a critique of Hegel's *Philosophy of Right* in 1842–43 and became editor of a radical journal called the *Rheinische Zeitung*. This publication was soon suppressed by the Prussian government, and Marx escaped to Paris. In 1845 he was in turn expelled from Paris and moved to Brussels. During these formative years Marx encountered the other great intellectual influences of his life: his wide reading included the work of the British economist Adam Smith and the French socialist Saint-Simon, and he met other socialist and communist thinkers such as Proudhon and Bakunin and began his lifelong collaboration with Friedrich Engels.

In the 1840s Marx and Engels began to formulate the so-called materialist conception of history. By inverting Hegel's view as Feuerbach had suggested, Marx came to see the driving force of historical change as material rather than spiritual. Not in mere *ideas*, and certainly not in any cosmic Spirit, but in the *economic* conditions of life lay the key to all history. Alienation, he believed, is at root neither metaphysical nor religious but social and economic. Under the capitalist system, labor is something alien to the laborer; he works not for himself but for someone else who directs the process and owns the product as private property. This conception of alienation is expressed in the *Economic and Philosophical Manuscripts*, which Marx wrote in Paris in 1844 but which remained unpublished for a century. The materialist conception of history is expressed in other works of this period, notably the *German Ideology* of 1846 (written with Engels) and *The Poverty of Philosophy* of 1847.

Marx became involved with the practical organization of the socialist and communist movements, for he saw the purpose of his work as "not just to interpret the world, but to change it" (as he famously put it in his *Theses on Feuerbach* in 1845). Convinced that history was moving toward the revolution by which capitalism would give way to communism, he tried to educate and organize the "proletariat"—the class of industrial workers who had to sell their labor in order to survive and to whom he thought victory must eventually go. He was asked to write a definitive statement of the aims of the international communist movement, so (again with Engels) he produced the *Manifesto of the Communist Party* in 1848. Later in that year (although hardly as a result of the *Manifesto)* there were abortive revolutions in many European countries. After their failure, Marx found exile in Britain, where he remained for the rest of his life.

In London Marx lived a life of comparative poverty, existing on income from journalistic efforts and on gifts from Engels. He began research in the Reading Room of the British Museum, where he found extensive documentation on social conditions. In 1857–58 he wrote another set of manuscripts, the *Grundrisse*, in which he sketched a plan of his total theory of history and society; the complete text of these did not become available in English until the 1970s. In 1859 he published his *Critique of Political Economy* and, in 1867, the first volume of his magnum opus, *Capital*. These last two works contain much detailed economic and social history, reflecting Marx's work in the British Museum. Although now making much less use of Hegelian philosophy, Marx was still trying to apply his materialist interpretation of history to show the inevitability and the desirability of the surpassing of capitalism by communism.

It is these later works, from the *Communist Manifesto* on, that have become best known and have formed the basis of most subsequent communist theory and practice. In them we find German philosophy, French socialism, and British political economy, the three main influences on Marx, welded into an all-embracing theory of history, economics, sociology, and politics. This is what Engels came to call "scientific socialism": for Marx and Engels thought they had discovered the correct *scientific* method for the study of human society and could thus establish the objective truth about the present workings and future development of the society in which they lived.

However, the publication in this century of Marx's earlier works, particularly the *German Ideology* and the *Economic and Philosophical Manuscripts* of 1844, has shown us much about the origin of his ideas in Hegelian ideas. So the question has been raised whether there were two distinct periods in his thought—an early phase, which has been called humanist or even existentialist, and the later "scientific socialism." I think it is fair to say that the consensus is that there is a continuity between the two phases—that the theme of human alienation and the hope for salvation from it is still there in the later work; the contents of the *Grundrisse* confirm this. My discussion of Marx is therefore based on the assumption that his thought is basically a unity. As I expound his metaphysical background, his theory of human nature, his diagnosis, and his prescription, I include some critical comments on each point in turn.

Theory of History

Marx was an atheist, and in the general trend of his thought was materialist and determinist. As a would-be social scientist, he proposed to explain all human phenomenona by the methods of science, as he understood them. But all this is in no way peculiar to him: much the same description applies to most of the thinkers of the eighteenth-century Enlightenment, including Voltaire, de la Mettrie, and Hume.

What is distinctively new in Marx's understanding is his claim to have found the truly scientific method for studying the *historical development* of human societies. In his programmatic early philosophizing, he looked forward to the day when there would be a single science, including the science of mankind along with natural science. But that "single science" would surely include many levels—physics, chemistry, biology, psychology, sociology. Marx was not a reductionist, and he did not think that everything could be explained in terms of physics. He held that there are general socioeconomic laws that operate in human history, and that the major social and political changes can be explained by applying these laws to the prevailing conditions. In the preface to the first edition of *Capital*, he did compare his method to physics, saying that "the ultimate aim of this work is to lay bare the economic law of motion of modern society," and he also talked of the natural laws of capitalist production "working with iron necessity towards inevitable results." These famous rhetorical phrases suggest a very strict historical determinism, but let us examine whether Marx really meant this.

The most distinctive feature of Marx's view is his so-called materialist conception of history. Like Hegel, he held that each epoch has a definite character of its own and that the only universal laws in history concern the processes of development by which one stage gives rise to the next. Marx's theory, however, is that these laws are not mental but *economic* in nature. As he put it in his most-quoted formulation, in the preface to the *Critique of Political Economy*:

> In the social production which men carry on they enter into definite relations that are indispensable and independent of their will; these relations of production correspond to a definite stage of development of their material powers of production. The totality of these relations of production constitutes the economic structure of society—the real foundation, on which legal and political superstructures arise and to which definite forms of social consciousness correspond. The mode of production of material life determines the general character of the social, political, and spiritual processes of life. It is not the consciousness of men that determines their being, but, on the contrary, their social being determines their consciousness.

In popular expositions of "Marxism," this passage is sometimes taken to mean that the economic basis of a society determines *everything* else about it, down to the last detail. But Marx's own considered statements are vaguer than this and need not commit him to such an implausibly rigid determinism.

It is undeniable that economic factors are hugely important and that no serious study of history or social science can ignore them. Marx can take much of the credit for the fact that we now recognize this so readily. But does the economic base of a society *determine* its ideological superstructure? What Marx says about this is difficult to interpret, for it is not clear where the dividing line between foundation and superstructure should run. He talks of "the material powers of production," which presumably include natural resources (land, climate, plants, animals, minerals); tools and machinery; and perhaps the knowledge and skills embodied in human beings ("human resources"). But he also talks of the "economic structure" as including "relations of production," which presumably means the way in which work is organized (e.g., the division of labor, hierarchies of authority in the workplace, the legal rights and powers of ownership, systems of rewards and payments). The description of the latter, at least in modern societies, must surely use concepts like ownership, property, and money.

It seems that Marx (in the quoted passage, at least) is distinguishing *three* levels rather than two—material powers of production, relations of production, and ideological superstructure (ideas, beliefs, morals and laws, politics, religion, and philosophy). What, then, did he mean by "basis"? What determines what, exactly? If the basis includes only the strictly material powers of production, then he is committed to a rather implausible "technological determinism"—but can't the same natural resources and technologies be used in societies with different ideologies (e.g., Christian, Islamic, or secular)? If the basis includes also the relations of production, then the distinction between basis and superstructure is blurred. It seemed at first that Marx meant to count legal concepts like property as part of the ideological superstructure, but if the same technologies can be used in capitalist and socialist systems with different property relations, there would seem to be little economic determinism left. Small wonder that debate continues about what Marx meant and what might be true!

Marx applied his materialist conception of society in two ways—

synchronically and diachronically. At any one time, the economic base (whatever that is, exactly) is supposed to determine the ideological superstructure characteristic of that stage of society. But over time, there are changes: economic systems may be stable for some time, but they allow processes of technological and economic development that eventually result in large-scale social change. Marx divided history, very roughly, into epochs identified by their different economic systems—the Asiatic, the ancient, the feudal, and the "bourgeois" or capitalist phases—and he held that each phase had to give way to the next when the economic conditions were ripe. He expected capitalism to give way, just as inevitably, to communism.

Just how much determinism did Marx wish to assert, synchronically or diachronically? It is undeniable that any society has to produce enough of the necessities of life to provide for survival and reproduction. We have to eat if we are to think, but it does not follow that what we eat, or how we produce what we eat, determines what we think. Not every aspect of culture, politics, and religion is completely determined by economic factors. Marx himself did not assert this—in analyzing particular episodes in history, he allowed for the influence of cultural factors such as religion and nationalism. Quite plausibly, he compared the status of his own theory with that of Darwin's theory of evolution, which also outlines a general mechanism in terms of which changes can be explained but which does not offer a method of predicting them, because that would need an almost infinitely detailed knowledge of particular conjunctions of conditions.

It emerges, then, that the most plausible thing to say—and it seems to be what Marx himself did say, when he was careful—is that the economic basis has a very significant influence on everything else: it sets limits within which the other factors play their parts. The way in which a society produces the necessities of life at any one stage of economic development will have an important influence on how people in that kind of society characteristically think. But this is vague—what counts as "very significant" or "important"? It amounts only to a recommendation to seek out the economic factors in any particular case and examine how far they may influence the rest. However, that has proved an immensely fruitful methodology in the study of history, anthropology, sociology, and politics.

History is an *empirical* study in that its propositions must be tested by evidence of what actually happened. But it does not follow that it is a *science*, in the sense that a science can formulate *laws of nature*, generalizations of unrestricted universality. For history is, after all, the study of what has happened to human beings on our planet, in a finite period of time. The subject matter is wide, but it is one *particular* series of events; we know of no similar events elsewhere in the universe. For any particular set of events, even the fall of an apple from a tree, there is no clear limit to the number of different laws and contingent facts that may be involved in its causation—the laws of gravity and mechanics, the wind pressure and the weather, the decay of wood and the elasticity of twigs, and tweaking by human fingers. If there is no determinism governing even the fall of Newton's apple, how much more implausible it is to say that the course of history is predetermined. There may be some long-term and large-scale *trends* to be found, such as the increase in the human population since the Middle Ages. But a trend is not a law; its continuation is not inevitable but may depend on conditions that can change. (It is obvious, for example, that population cannot increase indefinitely—and its growth may be quite suddenly reversed by war, disease, or famine.)

On the basis of his general theory of history, Marx expected that capitalism would become more and more unstable economically, that the class struggle between the bourgeois owners of capital and the members of the proletariat, who have to sell their labor, would increase, with the proletariat getting both poorer and larger in number, until in a major social revolution the workers would take power and institute the new, communist phase of history. However, Marx did not, contrary to common interpretation, confidently predict that the revolution would take place first in the countries where capitalism was most developed—Britain, France, and the United States. In the *Communist Manifesto*, he pointed to Germany, which was still semifeudal at the time, as the place where he expected a bourgeois revolution to be followed shortly by a proletarian one. In some of his journalistic writing, he suggested that communism might first be achieved in China. He saw that world capitalist development enables the import of socialist ideas into countries where a relatively small proletariat, allied with an impoverished peasantry, could seize power from the traditional ruling class. All this clearly applies to the two revolutions in Russia in 1917.

About Russia and China Marx seems to have been roughly right in predicting the revolution, if not its subsequent vicissitudes (we can hardly count the imposition of communism in Eastern Europe by the Red Army after 1945 as a proletarian revolution in Marx's sense). In the advanced capitalist countries, however, the economic system has (on the whole, with notable exceptions, such as the great depression of the 1930s) become more stable, conditions of life for most people have improved vastly over what they were in Marx's time, and class divisions have been blurred rather than intensified (consider the large numbers of "white-collar" workers—office and managerial staff, civil servants, teachers, and so on—who are neither manual laborers nor industrial owners). This is a major refutation of Marx's prediction. It cannot be explained away by saying that the proletariat has been "bought off" by concessions of higher wages—for Marx predicted their lot would get worse. Nor is it enough to say that colonies have served as the proletariat for the industrialized countries—for some capitalist countries, such as those in Scandinavia, had no colonies. It may be suggested, however, that capitalism *as Marx knew it* has ceased to exist, that peaceful, gradual reforms have radically changed the nature of our economic system. I examine this idea later, in the "Prescription" section.

Theory of Human Nature

Except in his early study of Hegel and the Greeks, Marx was not interested in questions of "pure" or academic philosophy, which he would later have dismissed as idle speculation compared to the vital task of changing the world. So if he is labeled a materialist, this refers more to his materialist theory of history than to his position on the relation of mental states to the brain. According to a strict interpretation of Marx's theory, consciousness would be determined by the material conditions of life. But this could still be taken as an "epiphenomenalist" position—that the contents of consciousness, although ontologically nonphysical, are entirely determined by material events. Marx felt entitled to dismiss many people's ideas as "false consciousness," not properly supported by the "rationalizations" they offer for them but rather a reflection of their socioeconomic roles, arrived at through an unconscious mental process of which the subjects are not aware. Marx need not be committed to a metaphysically materialist view that consciousness is to be literally identified with brain processes.

What is most distinctive of Marx's concept of humanity is his view of our essentially *social* nature: "the real nature of man is the totality of social relations." Apart from the existence of obvious biological facts such as the need to eat and reproduce, Marx believed that there is no such thing as a fixed, individual human nature, that what is true of people in one society or period may not be true of them in another place or time: "All history is nothing but a continuous transformation of human nature." Whatever a person does is an essentially social act, which presupposes the existence of other people standing in certain relations to him or her. Even the ways in which we produce our food and bring up our children are socially learned. This is true of all economic production, which is typically a social activity requiring cooperation in one way or another. We should not conceive of society as an abstract entity that mysteriously affects the individual; rather, what kind of individual one is and what kind of things one does are determined by what kind of society one lives in. What seems "instinctual" or "natural" in one society or epoch—for example, a certain role for women—may be quite different in another.

In modern terms, we can summarize this crucial point by saying that sociology is not reducible to psychology. Not everything about human beings can be explained in terms of facts about individuals; the kind of society they live in must be considered, too. This methodological point is one of Marx's most distinctive contributions, and one of the most widely accepted. For this reason alone, he must be recognized as one of the founding fathers of sociology. And the *method* can be accepted whether or not one agrees with the particular *conclusions* he came to.

But there is at least one universal generalization that Marx is prepared to make about human nature. This is that we are *active*, productive beings; we are different by nature from the other animals because we *produce* our means of subsistence—and not just like bees producing honey, for we make conscious plans for our livelihood. It is natural for human beings to work for their living. No doubt there is a truth here, but (as with many assertions about human nature)

Marx also draws a value judgment out of this, namely, that the kind of life that is *appropriate* for human beings involves purposive productive activity. As we shall see, this is implicit in his diagnosis of alienation as a lack of fulfilment in industrial labor and in his prescription for a future communist society in which everyone can be free to cultivate his or her own talents in every direction. Because of this point, which is clearest in his early writings, Marx has been called a humanist.

What does Marx's theory imply about women and the question of feminism? If there is a truth in his insistence on the importance of production, there is surely also a truth about the necessity for *reproduction*. But we must think of reproduction as including not just sexual intercourse, pregnancy, and childbirth but the longer process of childcare, education, and socialization. Obviously, no society can survive unless it can produce new members to carry it on. In some places Marx acknowledged this (e.g., in the *German Ideology*), and Engels later addressed such questions more systematically. In *The Origin of the Family, Private Propety and the State*, Engels argued that social production determines both kinds of production: labor and the family. But, on the whole, Marx was a man of his time in his assumption that the traditional sexual division of labor in the family, with women being almost toally responsible for childcare, has a "purely physiological foundation" (*German Ideology*, pp. 51–52). It seems he did not realize that even what we may have thought of as biologically determined differences between the sexes may be affected by socioeconomic factors. Technical developments like reliable contraception and formula milk for babies and an economic structure that requires mental skills more than heavy manual labor have transformed the question of male and female "nature" in ways that Marx himself did not foresee but that his theory has the resources to accommodate.

Diagnosis

Marx's theory of what was wrong with people and society in the early capitalist era in which he lived involves his concept of "alienation" or "estrangement," which is a descendant of the concept used by

Hegel and Feuerbach. For Marx, "alienation" comprises both a description of certain features of capitalist society and a value judgment that they are fundamentally wrong. But the notion is so vague that it is often difficult to decide exactly *which* features of capitalism Marx is criticizing. He did not, after all, totally condemn capitalism: he acknowledged that it allows great increases in economic productivity. He believed that capitalism is a necessary stage of economic and social development, but he thought that it would be and ought to be surpassed.

Logically, alienation is a relation, that is, it must be *from* somebody or something; one cannot be just "alienated," any more that one can be married without being married to someone. Marx says that alienation is "from man himself and from Nature." But it is not clear how one can be alienated from oneself; the concept of Nature involved here has obscure Hegelian roots in the distinction between subject and supposedly alien object. For Marx, Nature seems to mean the humanly made world, so we can take him as saying that people are not what they should be because they are alienated from the objects and social relations that they create. People without capital have to sell their labor in order to survive and are therefore dominated in their working lives by the interests of the owners of capital. And the competitiveness of life under capitalism conflicts with the ideal of solidarity with other human beings (which Feuerbach emphasized). The general idea that emerges is that capitalist society is not in accordance with basic human nature.

Often it seems to be the institution of private property that Marx primarily condemns: in one place he boldly asserts that "the abolition of private property is the abolition of alienation." But elsewhere he says that "although private property appears to be the basis and cause of alienated labor, it is rather a consequence of the latter." Marx describes this alienation of labor as consisting in the fact that the work is not part of the worker's nature; he does not fulfil himself in his work but feels miserable, physically exhausted, and mentally debased. His work is forced on him as a means for satisfying other needs, and at work he does not "belong to himself"; he is under the control of other people. Even the materials he uses and the objects he produces are alien to him, because they are owned by someone else. Sometimes Marx seems to be blaming alienation on the institution of money as a means of exchange that reduces all social relationships to a common commercial denominator ("callous 'cash payment,' " as he put in the *Manifesto*). Why should cash payment be "callous," one wonders? In that context Marx was making a contrast with feudal society, in which there were nonmonetary economic relationships—but perhaps they could be callous in their own way. Elsewhere he suggests that it is the division of labor that makes people's work into an alien power, preventing them from switching from one activity to another at will.

What, then, *is* Marx diagnosing as the basic cause of alienation? It is hard to believe that anyone can seriously advocate the abolition of money (and a return to a system of barter?), the end of all specialization in work, or the communal control of everything (even toothbrushes, clothes, and books?). It is the private or public ownership of *industry*—the means of production and exchange—that is usually taken as the defining feature of capitalism or socialism. Among the main points in the practical program of the *Manifesto* are the nationalization of land, factories, transport, and banks. But it seems most implausible that state control of these can cure the alienation of labor that Marx describes in such psychological terms in his early works. If it is the *state* that is the basis of social evils, nationalization might well make things worse by increasing the power of the state, as the history of communist regimes in the twentieth century strongly suggests.

Perhaps we should understand Marx as saying (at least in his early phase?) that alienation consists in a lack of *community*, so people cannot see their work as contributing to a group of which they are members, since the state is not a real community. Such a diagnosis might suggest a prescription not so much for nationalization but for decentralization into "communes" (in which the abolition of money, specialization, and private property might begin to look more realistic). But the feasibility and desirability of this is obviously contentious on Marxist economic grounds; how can the kind of high-technology worldwide production and distribution on which we have now come to depend be organized in a society of independent communes?

There is, however, a more general diagnosis implicit in Marx, which would perhaps command universal assent: that it is wrong to treat any human being as only a means to an economic end (cf. Kant's formulation of the moral law as a requirement that we always treat rational beings as ends in themselves). Such exploitation did take place in the unrestrained capitalism of the early nineteenth century, when children worked long hours in filthy conditions and workers died early deaths after miserably unfulfilled lives. Something like this still happens in some countries; and even in the advanced nations where capitalism is trumpeted as a stunning success story, there is a constant tendency for the managers of corporations to try to beat the competition by extracting the greatest possible profit from the labor of their employees, by driving down wages, cutting the workforce, or extending working hours. The state may put restrictions on these practices, but as soon as the regulations are relaxed, each business naturally makes the most of its competitive opportunities.

Perhaps we can express Marx's main point in a paraphrase of Jesus' saying about the sabbath: production is intended for man, not man for production. This must mean *all* the people involved (men and women, of course)—employers, employees, consumers, and anyone affected by such side effects of industry as pollution. But it is difficult to agree on how to give social effect to this general value judgment.

Prescription

"If man is formed by circumstances, these circumstances must be humanly formed." If alienation is a social problem caused by the nature of the capitalist economic system, then the solution is to abolish that system and replace it with a better one. Marx thought that this was bound to happen anyway, that capitalism would burst asunder because of its inner contradictions, and the ensuing communist revolution would usher in the new order of things. Rather in the way that Christianity claims that God's salvation has been enacted for us, so Marx claimed that the resolution of the problems of capitalism is already on the way in the movement of history.

Marx's view on the metaphysical question of free will is rather ambiguous. His overall view obviously sounds determinist, with his theory of the seemingly inevitable progress of history through economic stages. And yet, just as with the Augustinian-Pelagian controversy within Christianity, there seems to be an irreducible element of human freedom left in the theory. Marx and his followers constantly appealed to people to realize the direction in which history is moving and to *act* accordingly, to help bring about the communist revolution. Within the Marxist movements, there were controversies between those who emphasized the need to wait for the appropriate stage of economic development before expecting the revolution and those (like Lenin) who asserted the need to *act* decisively to bring the revolution about. But perhaps there is no contradiction here, for Marx can say that although the revolution is bound to occur sooner or later, it is possible for prescient individuals and organized groups to assist its coming and "ease its birth pangs," acting as the midwives of history. He would probably condemn further philosophical inquiry into determinism and free will as idle speculation.

Marx held that only a complete revolution of the economic system will properly solve its problems. Limited reforms of capitalism, such as higher wages, shorter hours, and pension schemes may be welcome ameliorations of the harshnesses of the system, but they do not alter its basic nature. Hence the radical difference between the Communist Party, on one hand, and most trade unions and social democratic or democratic socialist parties, on the other. But, again, followers of Marx have disagreed about practical political strategy. Some have feared that working to reform the system would distract attention from the really important task of overthrowing it. Others have said, with support from Marx, that the very process of arousing workers to combine together to work for reform would "raise their consciousness," create "class solidarity," enable them to realize their power, and thus hasten more revolutionary changes.

Piecemeal reforms *have* significantly modified the economic system of capitalism, beginning with the British Factory Acts, which limited the worst exploitation of workers and children, and continuing with National Insurance, unemployment benefits, the National Health Services (in Europe, though not in the United States), and steady progress by trade unions in increasing real wages and decreasing working hours. In fact, many of the specific measures proposed in the *Communist Manifesto* have long since come into effect in the so-called capitalist countries—graduated income tax, consolidation of much economic control in the hands of the state, nationalization of some major industries in some countries, free education in state schools. The unrestrained capitalist system as Marx knew it in the mid-nineteenth century has ceased to exist in the most developed countries—and this has happened by step-by-step reform, not by once-for-all revolution. This is not to say that the existing system is perfect—far from it. But it is to suggest that the rejection of gradualist programs of reform by some Marxists (if not by Marx himself) is mistaken; reflection on the suffering and violence involved in revolutions elsewhere may confirm this.

Like Christians, Marx envisaged a total regeneration of humanity, but he expected it within the secular world. Communism is "the solution to the riddle of history," for the abolition of private property is supposed to ensure the disappearance of alienation and the coming of a genuinely classless society. Marx is extremely vague on how all this will be achieved, but he was realistic enough to say that there will be an intermediate period before the transition can take place and that this will require "the dictatorship of the proletariat." Alienation cannot be overcome on the day after the revolution. In a phrase that sounds very ominous in the light of twentieth-century history, he wrote that "the alteration of men on a mass scale is necessary"—but in his defense it may be said that he had in mind an alteration of consciousness, not the forcible social engineering methods of Soviet Russia. In the higher phase of communist society, the state is supposed to wither away, and the true realm of freedom will begin. Then human potential can develop for its own sake, and the guiding principle can be "From each according to his ability, to each according to his needs."

Some of this utopian vision must surely be judged unrealistic. Marx gives us no good reason to believe that communist society will be genuinely classless or that those who exercise the dictatorship of the proletariat will not form a new governing class with many opportunities to abuse their power, as the history of countries with communist regimes obviously suggests. There is no ground for expecting any set of economic changes to eliminate *all* conflicts of interest. States have not withered away; they have become more powerful—though we must also recognize the power of huge corporations and the increasingly global nature of the market, which limits the power of any one government.

Yet, with other elements in Marx's vision we can surely agree. The application of science and technology to produce enough for all; the shortening of the working day; the provision of universal education so that all human beings can develop their potential; the vision of a decentralized society in which people cooperate in communities for the common good and of a society in balance with nature—all these are ideals that almost everyone will share, though it is no easy matter to work out how they can be compatibly realized. No doubt, it is because Marxism has offered this kind of hopeful vision of a human future that it has been able to win and retain the allegiance of so many people. Like Christianity, Marx's thought is more than a theory; it has for many been a secular faith, a vison of social salvation.

Even now, although some of Marx's theoretical assertions in their more extreme formulations remain highly debatable, and despite the failings of the so-called communist regimes of the twentieth century, Marx's ideas are far from dead. Although social reforms and technical and economic developments have altered the face of capitalism, some thinkers see the need for a further transformation of the socioeconomic system and look to Marx for inspiration for such a change. However, the Marxist emphasis on *economic* factors directs our attention to only one of the obstacles in the way of human fulfilment. We must look elsewhere—for instance, to Freud, Sartre, and religious conceptions—for deeper insights into the nature and problems of human *individuals*.

For Further Reading

There is no one major text by Marx that one can recommend as basic. The *Communist Manifesto* is a natural starting point (though its third section is dated); the *German Ideology* is longer, but fairly readable.

There are various useful selections from Marx's writing, including *Karl Marx: Selected Writings in Sociology and Social Philosophy*, trans. T. B. Bottomore, ed. T. B. Bottomore and M. Rubel (London: Penguin, 1963; New York: McGraw-Hill, 1964), helpfully organized under themes; there is also *Marx and Engels: Basic Writings on Politics and Philosophy*, ed. L. S. Feuer (New York: Anchor Books, 1959).

For a biography of Marx, see Sir Isaiah Berlin, *Karl Marx: His Life and Environment*, 3d ed. (Oxford: Oxford University Press, 1963).

For a classic criticism of Marxism, see Karl Popper, *The Open Society and its Enemies*, Vol. I, 5th ed. (London: Routledge, 1966).

For a deeper discussion of Marx on human nature, see J. Plamenatz, *Karl Marx's Theory of Man* (Oxford: Oxford University Press, 1975).

For an encyclopediac and critical guide to the many varieties of Marxism, see L. Kolakowski, *Main Currents of Marxism*, 3 vols. (Oxford: Oxford University Press, 1975).

For a sophisticated defense of Marx in the light of analytical philosophy, see G. A. Cohen, *Karl Marx's Theory of History: A Defence* (Oxford: Oxford University Press, 1978).

To begin addressing the question how far Marxist theory needs amending to take account of feminism, see Engels, *Origin of the Family, Private Property and the State* (New York: International Publishers, 1972); and A. Jaggar, *Feminist Politics and Human Nature* (Totowa: Rowman & Littlefield, 1983), Ch. 4.

For a recent postcommunist defense of Marx's ideas, see Keith Graham, *Karl Marx Our Contemporary: Social Theory for a Post-Leninist World* (Toronto: University of Toronto Press, 1992).

8

Freud: The Unconscious
Basis of Mind

The next theory I consider is that of Freud, who in the twentieth century revolutionized our understanding of human nature. Freud spent nearly fifty years developing and modifying his theories, writing so vast an amount of material that only a specialist could hope to digest it all. No adequate discussion of human nature can fail to grapple with his thought, but this is a difficult task to attempt in a single short chapter, even if we concentrate on Freud himself, not on the many later developments in psychoanalytic theory and practice. I sketch his life and work, expound the most fundamental features of his theory, diagnosis, and prescription, and then make some critical points.

Life and Work

Sigmund Freud was born in Moravia in 1856, but in 1860 his family moved to Vienna, where he lived and worked until the last year of his life. Even in his school days, his precocious interests extended to the whole of human life, and when he entered the University of Vienna as a medical student he did not confine himself to medicine, attending other lectures, such as those of the influential philosopher of mind Franz Brentano. Freud became most deeply interested in biology and spent six years doing research in the laboratory of the great physiologist Brücke, writing papers on such technical topics as the nervous systems of fishes. He almost made a controversial reputation for himelf in pioneering the medical use of cocaine. In order to marry his fiancée, Martha Bernays, he needed a career that offered more secure financial rewards, so he somewhat reluctantly began work as a doctor in the Vienna General Hospital. In 1886 he set up his private practice in "nervous diseases." Most of his early patients were well-off Viennese women suffering from what was then called "hysteria," and he continued to treat a variety of psychological problems for the rest of his life.

Freud's career from then on can be divided into three main phases. In the first of these he arrived at his original hypotheses about the nature of neurotic problems and developed his distinctive theory and method of treatment, both of which have come to be known as "psychoanalysis." His interest in human psychology and mental problems had been fired by a visit to Paris in 1885–86 to study under Charcot, a French neurologist who was using hypnotism to treat "hysterics." Typically these were women who had mysterious paralyses, loss of speech, or loss of sensation in bodily regions that bore no relation to neurological deficit or injury but only to the ordinary concepts of bodily parts, for example, "hand" or "arm." Etymologically, the word "hysteria" relates to ancient explanations of such symptoms as due to disturbances of the womb—and nowadays the word simply means a state of irrational emotion—but in Freud's time it referred to a recognized yet puzzling syndrome that orthodox medicine found almost impossible to treat. (One wonders, of course, if its prevalence in late-nineteenth-century bourgeois women had something to do with their repressed social situation.) Freud was impressed, at least initially, by how Charcot's purely psychological method of hypnotism seemed to induce dramatic cures.

Faced with similar symptoms in his own patients, Freud first experimented with both electrotherapy and hypnotic suggestion but found them unsatisfactory, so he began to try another method derived from that of Breuer, a senior Viennese consultant who was a friend of his. Breuer's approach was based on the assumption that hysteria was caused by some intense emotional experience (a "trauma") that the patient had forgotten; his treatment was to induce the recall of the experience and a "discharge" of the corresponding emotion. The hypothesis that people could suffer from an "idea," a memory or emotion of which they were not consciously aware of but from which they could be relieved by bringing it into consciousness, is the basis from which Freud's psychoanalysis developed.

Freud found that the relevant ideas in his patients typically had some definite sexual content, and (ever ready to hazard a generalization) he speculated that neuroses *always* have a sexual origin. In many cases, his patients came up with reports of "infantile seduction"—what we now call child sexual abuse. At first he believed these stories, but then, in a dramatic change of theoretical tack that he later regarded as a crucial discovery, he came to think that they were largely based on fantasy, reflecting unconscious desires in the subject, rather than memories of what actually happened. (In view of recent debates and controversies, we have to wonder whether his first thoughts on this difficult matter may not have been nearer the truth.) In 1895 he published *Studies on Hysteria* jointly with Breuer, but soon afterward the collaboration broke up, and Freud went on his own theoretical way. (This was the first of many intense disputes with colleagues.)

In the closing years of the nineteenth century, Freud began to formulate his controversial theories about infantile sexuality and the interpretion of dreams, both of which are central to psychoanalytic theory. He also attempted to psychoanalyze himself. He introduced his distinctive theoretical concepts of resistance, repression, and transference. At this time he was writing (in correspondence with Fliess, another medical friend given to unorthodox speculations and who influenced him strongly in this period) the *Project for a Scientific Psychology*. In this work Freud tried to relate the psychological theory he was then developing to a physical basis in the nerve cells in the brain, a topic he had studied in his physiological work. Although much excited by this project, he came to think it too much ahead of its time and did not attempt to publish it. The manuscript was lost and was not rediscovered and published until 1950.

The second phase of Freud's work, in which the great works expounding his mature theory appeared, can conveniently be dated from the publication in 1900 of *The Interpretation of Dreams*, the book that he himself regarded as his best. There followed, in 1901, *The Psychopathology of Everyday Life*, in which he analyzed the unconscious causation of everyday errors such as slips of the tongue, and, in 1905, his *Three Essays on the Theory of Sexuality*. These works applied psychoanalytic theory to the whole of normal mental life, not just to neurotic cases. International recognition and the spread of psychoanalysis began: in 1909 Freud was invited to America, where he gave the *Five Lectures on Psycho-Analysis*, the first of his short, popular expositions of his ideas. In 1915–17 he delivered the much longer *Introductory Lectures on Psycho-Analysis* at the University of Vienna, in which he expounded the complete theory as it had developed up to then.

From after the end of World War I until his death, he engaged in the third phase of his work, making some important changes in his fundamental theories and undertaking wide-ranging speculative attempts to apply his ideas to social questions. In 1920 came *Beyond the Pleasure Principle*, in which he first introduced the concept of the "death instinct" (to explain aggression and self-destruction) as well as the "life instincts" (self-preservation and sexuality). Another late development was the tripartite structure of the mind—id, ego, and superego—which he first presented in *The Ego and the Id* (1923). In a popular work, *The Question of Lay Analysis* (1926), so called because he there discusses whether medical qualification is necessary to practice psychoanalysis, he expounded his basic ideas in terms of this new three-part structure.

Most of Freud's last years were devoted to social theorizing. (In 1913, he had already tried to apply his theories to anthropology in *Totem and Taboo*.) In *The Future of an Illusion* (1927), he treated religion as a system of false beliefs whose deep root in our minds must be explained psychoanalytically. In *Civilization and Its Discontents* (1930), he discussed the conflict between the demands of civilized society and human instincts, and in *Moses and Monotheism* (1939) he offered a controversial psychoanalytic interpretation of Jewish history. In 1938 the Nazis annexed Austria, and Jews were in danger, but because of his huge international fame Freud was allowed to flee to London, where he spent the last year of his life writing a brief final *Outline of Psycho-Analysis*.

Background Theory

What is distinctive in Freud's thought is his theory of the human mind, but we should take note of his background assumptions and how they differ from those of the theories discussed so far. Freud started his career as a physiologist and claimed to remain a scientist throughout: his constant hope was to explain all the phenomena of human life scientifically. He made no assumptions about theology, transcendent metaphysics, or the progress of history. Relying on his wide knowledge of biological science as it had developed up to his day and his thorough training in physiological research, he assumed that all phenomena are determined by the laws of physics, chemistry, and biology and that human beings, too, are subject to these. He was a man steeped in the confidence of late-nineteenth-century biological science, after the advent of Darwin's theory of evolution, accepting that human beings are one species of animal (albeit of a very special sort), and he accordingly proposed that our problems could be diagnosed and ameliorated by the methods of science. He has recently been described as a "biologist of the mind," but we shall see how far he moved away from physiological methods of explanation and treatment.

Theory of Human Nature

I expound Freud's approach to human nature under five main topics. His first basic assumption is *materialism*. Freud acknowledged a distinction between mental states and physiological states of the nervous system, but this was for him only a difference in language, not a dualism of two substances (mind and body). Many (though not all) philosophers would now agree that, in talking of states of consciousness (thoughts, wishes, and emotions), we are not committed to metaphysical dualism, and there is no reason to suppose that the case is any different for the *unconscious* mental states that Freud postulates. After his bold early attempt to identify a physiological basis for all mental states (in his *Project for a Scientific Psychology*), Freud came to think such theorizing too far ahead of the knowledge of the time. For the rest of his life he was content to leave the physical basis of psychology to the future development of science—and research in this area has indeed made enormous progress in recent years. But that all the complicated mental states and processes he postulated had *some* physiological basis, he did not doubt.

The second point is a strict application of *determinism*—the principle that every event has preceding causes—to the realm of the mental. Thoughts and behavior that had formerly been assumed to be of no significance for understanding a person—such as slips of the tongue, faulty actions, dreams, and neurotic symptoms—Freud assumed must be determined by hidden causes in a person's mind. He thought these could be highly significant, revealing in disguised form what would otherwise remain unknown. Nothing that a person thinks or does or says is really haphazard or accidental; everything can in principle be explained by something in the person's mind. This might seem to imply a denial of free will, for, even when we think we are choosing perfectly freely (even arbitrarily), Freud would claim that there are unknown causes that determine our choice. There is an interesting parallel with Marx here, in that he and Freud both believed that the contents of our consciousness, far from being perfectly "free" and uniquely "rational," are determined by causes of which we are not normally aware. But whereas Marx said that these causes are social and economic in nature, Freud claimed that they are individual and psychological, rooted in our biological drives.

The third and perhaps most distinctive feature of Freud's theorizing—the postulation of *unconscious mental states*—thus arises out of the second. But we must be careful to understand his concept of the unconscious correctly. There are lots of mental states, for instance, memories of particular experiences or facts, of which we are not continually conscious but that can be recalled when appropriate. These Freud calls "preconscious" (meaning that they can readily become conscious); he reserves the term "unconscious" for states that *cannot* become conscious under normal circumstances. His crucial assertion is that our minds are not co-extensive with what is available to conscious attention but include items of which we can have no ordinary knowledge. To use a familiar analogy, the mind is like an iceberg, with only a small proportion of it visible above the surface but with a vast hidden bulk exerting its influence on the rest. Freud would be happy to accept the findings of recent cognitive science that much information-processing is involved in the recognition of objects; we are unaware of these processes in our own minds, but psychologists can infer them as the best explanation of the facts of perception (and misperception).

So far, this gives us what has been called a *descriptive* account of the unconscious, but Freud's concept is also *dynamic* in nature. To explain puzzling human phenomena such as hysterical paralyses, neurotic behavior, obsessional thoughts, and dreams, Freud postulated the existence of emotionally charged ideas in the unconscious part of the mind, which actively yet mysteriously exert influences on what a person thinks, feels, and does. Unconscious desires or memories can cause people to do things that they cannot explain rationally, to others or even to themselves. Some unconscious states may previously have been conscious (e.g., traumatic emotional experiences) but have been repressed because they became too painful to acknowledge. But the ultimate driving forces of our mental life are innate and operate unconsciously from infancy.

Freud introduced a new *structural* concept of the mind into his theory in the 1920s, which does not coincide with the distinction among conscious, preconscious, and unconscious that he had used until then. In this late phase he distinguished three systems within the "mental apparatus." The *id* is said to contain all the instinctual drives that seek immediate satisfaction like a small child (they are said to operate on "the pleasure principle"); the *ego* contains the conscious mental states, and its function is to perceive the real world and to decide how to act, mediating between the world and the id (it is governed by "the reality principle"). Whatever can become conscious is in the ego (although it also contains elements that remain unconscious), whereas everything in the id is permanently unconscious. The *superego* is identified as a special part of the mind that contains the conscience, the moral norms acquired from parents and others who were influential in one's early childhood; though it belongs to the ego and shares its kind of psychological organization, the superego is also said to have an intimate connection with the id, for it can confront the ego with rules and prohibitions like a strict parent. The forces of repression are located in the ego and the superego, and they typically operate unconsciously. The poor old ego has the difficult job of trying to reconcile the conflicting demands of id and superego, given the often unhelpful facts of the real world. This is Freud's dramatic picture of the human condition, forever beset by external problems and internal conflict.

There are interesting, if partial, parallels with Plato in Freud's late theory of the tripartite structure of the mind. The id obviously corresponds closely to Appetite or desire, but it is not so clear how ego and superego correspond to Plato's Reason and Spirit. In its reality-knowing function, the ego seems to be akin to Reason, but Reason for Plato has also a moral function, which Freud would give to the superego. And yet Plato's spirited element seems to be performing a moralistic function in the situation of feeling disgusted with one's own desires (see Chapter 5).

The *instincts* or "drives" form the fourth main feature of Freud's theory. They are the motivating forces within the mental apparatus, and all the "energy" in our minds comes from them alone. Freud used such mechanical or electrical language in an almost literal way, influenced by his scientific training and the psychophysical theory of his early *Project*, in which he presciently wrote about flows of electrical charge through the neurons in the brain. His model for the mental drives tends to be pent-up charges, or pressure seeking discharge. His psychological classification of instincts is, however, one of the most speculative, variable, and uncertain parts of his theory. Although he admitted that we can distinguish an indeterminate number of instincts, he thought that they could all be derived from a few basic ones, which can combine or even replace each other in multifarious ways.

Of course, Freud held that one instinct is sexual in nature, and he notoriously traced much human behavior back to sexual thoughts and desires, often repressed into the unconscious. It is, however, a vulgar misinterpretation to say that he tried to explain *all* human phenomena in terms of sex. What is true is that he gave sexuality a much wider scope in human life than had formerly been recognized. He claimed that the beginnings of sexuality exist in children from birth and that sexual factors play a crucial role in adult neuroses. But Freud always held that there was at least one other basic instinct, or group of instincts. In his early phase he distinguished what he called the "self-preservation" instincts, such as hunger, from the erotic instinct ("libido"). He treated sadism as a perversely aggressive manifestation of sexuality. But in his later work he changed his classification, putting libido and hunger together in one basic "Life" instinct (Eros) and referring sadism, aggression, and self-destruction to a "Death" instinct (Thanatos). In popular language, his duality of love and hunger was replaced by love and hate.

The fifth main point in Freud's theory is his *developmental account* of individual human character. This is not just the obvious truism that personality depends on experience as well as on hereditary endowment. Freud started from Breuer's discovery that particular "traumatic" experiences could, although apparently forgotten, continue to exercise a baneful influence on a person's mental health. The fully fledged theory of psychoanalysis generalizes from this and asserts the crucial importance, for adult character, of the experiences of infancy and early childhood. The first five years are held to be the time in which the basis of each individual personality is laid down. So one cannot fully understand a person until one comes to know the psychologically crucial facts about his or her early childhood.

Freud produced detailed theories about the psychosexual stages of development through which every child is supposed to grow. These particular theories are more easily tested by observation than is the rest of his theorizing. Freud proposed to widen the concept of sexuality to include any kind of pleasure that involves parts of the body. He suggested that infants first obtain pleasure from the mouth (the oral stage) and then from the other end of the alimentary tract (the anal stage). Both boys and girls then become interested in the male sexual organ (the phallic stage). The little boy is alleged to feel sexual desires for his mother and to fear castration by his father (the "Oedipus complex"). Both the desire for mother and the hostility to father are then normally repressed. From age five until puberty (the "latency" period), sexuality is much less apparent. It then reappears and—if all goes well, which it all too frequently does not—attains its full "genital" expression in adulthood. Freud suggested that around the time of the Oedipus complex in boys, little girls develop "penis envy," but for some mysterious reason he never treated feminine sexuality as thoroughly as he did male sexuality. Quite late in his career, he made a statement that is astonishing, coming from someone whose professional practice consisted largely in treating the psychological problems of women: he wrote that "the sexual life of adult women is a dark continent for psychology"!

Diagnosis

Like Plato, Freud says that individual well-being or mental health depends on a harmonious relationship among the various parts of the mind and between the person and the external social world in which he or she has to live. The ego has to reconcile id, superego, and external world, choosing opportunities for satisfying the instinctual demands without transgressing the moral standards required by the superego, the internal representative of society. If the world does not supply enough opportunities for fulfilment, suffering will result, but even when the environment is reasonably favorable, there will be mental disturbance if there is too much inner conflict among the parts of the mind. Neurotic illnesses result from the frustration of the sexual instinct, either because of external obstacles or because of internal mental imbalance.

There is one particular mental process that Freud thought to be of crucial importance in the causation of neurotic illnesses, and this is what he called *repression*. In a situation of extreme mental conflict, in which someone experiences an instinctual impulse that is sharply incompatible with the standards the person feels he or she must adhere to, it is likely that he or she will repress it, that is, put it out of consciousness, flee from it, pretend that it does not exist. Repression is one of the "defense mechanisms" by which a person attempts to avoid inner conflicts. But it is essentially an escape, a pretense, a withdrawal from reality, and as such is doomed to failure. For what is repressed does not go out of existence but remains in the unconscious portion of the mind. It retains all its instinctual energy and exerts its influence by sending into consciousness a disguised substitute for itself—a neurotic symptom. Thus, people can find themselves behaving in ways that they may admit are irrational, yet feel compelled to continue without knowing why. For, by repressing something out of consciousness, they have given up effective control over it; they can neither get rid of the symptoms it is causing nor voluntarily lift the repression and recall it to consciousness.

As we should expect from his developmental approach to the individual, Freud locates the decisive repressions in early childhood, and he held that they are basically sexual. It is essential for the future mental health of the adult that the child successfully pass through the normal stages of development of sexuality. But this does not always proceed smoothly, and any hitch leaves a predisposition to future problems; the various forms of sexual perversion can be traced to such a cause. One typical kind of neurosis consists in what Freud called "regression," the return to one of the stages at which childish satisfaction was obtained. He even identified certain adult character types as "oral" and "anal," referring to the childhood stages in which he thought they originated.

There is much more detail in Freud's theories of the neuroses into which we cannot enter here, but he attributes part of the blame for them on the external world, and we should note this social aspect of his diagnosis. For the standards to which people feel they must conform are one of the crucial factors in mental problems, and these standards are in Freud's view a product of each person's social environment—primarily the parents, but also anyone who has exerted emotional influence and authority on the growing child. The instillation of such standards is the essence of education, making children into members of society; as Freud sees it, civilization requires a certain self-control, a sacrifice of individual instinctual satisfaction in order to make cultural achievements possible.

The standards instilled in any particular family or culture are not automatically the "best" or the most rational or the most conducive to happiness. People vary widely, and maladjusted parents are notoriously likely to produce maladjusted children. Freud was prepared to entertain the broader speculation that the whole relationship between society and the individual has gotten out of balance, perhaps making our whole civilized life neurotic. This theme came to prominence in his late work, *Civilization and Its Discontents*, but as early as the *Five Lectures* of 1909 he had suggested that our civilized standards make life too difficult for most people and that we should not deny a certain amount of satisfaction to our instinctual impulses. So there is a basis in the writings of Freud himself for those neo-Freudians, such as Erich Fromm, who would diagnose our troubles as lying at least as much in society as in the individual.

Prescription

Freud's hope was to restore a harmonious balance between the parts of the mind and, ideally, to suggest ways to improve individual adjustment to the world. The latter might involve programs of social reform, but Freud never specified these in any detail; his own professional practice to the end of his life was the treatment of neurotic patients. He was realistic about the limits of therapeutic influence— he famously described the aim of psychoanalysis as only to replace neurotic unhappiness by ordinary unhappiness. (The word "psychoanalysis" refers at least as much to Freud's method of treatment as to the theories on which that treatment is based.) It is this therapy that we must now examine.

The method developed gradually out of Breuer's discovery that one particular hysterical patient could be helped merely by being encouraged to *talk* about the thoughts and fantasies that had been filling her mind and that she could apparently be cured if she could be induced to remember the "traumatic" experiences that had induced her problems in the first place. Freud started using this "talking cure," assuming that the pathogenic memories were still somehow in the person's mind; he asked his patients to talk uninhibitedly, hoping that he could interpret the unconscious forces behind what they said. He required them to say whatever came into their mind, however absurd or embarrassing it might be (the method of "free association"). But he often found that the flow would dry up; the patient would claim to have nothing more to say and might even object to further inquiry. When such "resistance" happened, Freud took it as a sign that the conversation was getting near the repressed complex. He thought that the patient's unconscious mind was somehow realizing this and trying to prevent the painful truth being brought into consciousness, just as someone with a painful region in their body may flinch from examination. Yet, if the repressed material could be brought back into consciousness, the ego could be given back the power over the id that it had lost, and the patient could be cured of neurosis.

To achieve this happy result can require a long process, involving perhaps weekly sessions over a period of years. The analyst must try to arrive at the correct interpretations of the patient's unconscious mental states and present them at such a time and in such a way that the patient can accept them. Dreams provide very fruitful material for interpretation, for, according to Freud's theory, the "manifest" content of a dream is the disguised fulfillment of the unconscious wishes that are its real or "latent" content. Errors and faulty actions can also be interpreted to reveal their unconscious causation. As one would expect, the interpretations very often refer to a person's sexual life, childhood experiences, infantile sexuality, and relationships to parents. Clearly, all this demands a relationship of peculiar confidence between patient and analyst, but Freud found that much more than this developed; in fact, his patients often manifested a degree of emotion toward him that could be called love—or sometimes hate. This phenomenon he labelled "transference," on the assumption that the emotion was somehow projected onto the analyst either from the real-life situations in which it was once present or from the unconscious fantasies of the patient. The handling of such transference is of crucial importance for the success of the therapy, if it itself can be analyzed and traced back to its sources in the patient's unconscious.

The goal of psychoanalytic treatment can be summarized as self-knowledge. What the supposedly cured neurotic does with the new self-understanding is an individual decision, and various outcomes are possible. The patient may replace the unhealthy repression of instincts by a rational, conscious control of them (suppression rather than repression), or may be able to divert the instincts and desires into acceptable channels (sublimation), or may decide to satisfy them after all. But, according to Freud, there is no need to fear that primitive instincts will take over the subject, for their power is actually *reduced* when they are brought into consciousness.

Freud never thought that psychoanalysis is the answer to every human problem. When speculating about the problems of civilization and society, he was realistic enough to realize their extreme complexity and to abstain from offering any general social program. But he did suggest that psychoanalysis had much wider applications than just the treatment of neurotics. He said, "Our civilization imposes an almost intolerable pressure on us" and speculated that psychoanalysis might help to prepare a corrective. At the end of *Civilization and Its Discontents*, he cautiously proposed an analogy between cultures and individuals, suggesting that cultures might also be "neurotic" and in need of some sort of therapy. But he recognized the precariousness of this analogy and refused to "rise up before his fellow-men as a prophet."

Critical Discussion

The position of psychoanalysis on the intellectual map has been a matter of dispute ever since its inception. Psychoanalysts with Freudian and neo-Freudian orientations continue to practice, and a great variety of non-Freudian psychotherapeutic theories and methods have developed. Many academic psychologists have condemned Freud's theories as unscientific, either too vague to be testable or unsupported by the evidence when the claims are testable. Psychoanalytic therapy has been criticized for working by the power of suggestion, more akin to brainwashing or witchcraft than to scientific medicine. Some critics have fastened on the cult-like orthodoxy that has often been imposed by institutes of psychoanalysis and the "indoctrination" that all aspiring analysts are required to go through by themselves being analyzed. The theory and practice of psychoanalysis has even been likened to a quasi-religious faith.

Freudian theory obviously has a readily available method by which to analyze disparagingly the motivations of its critics. Any questioning of its truth can be alleged by its defenders to be based on unconscious resistance. So if, as has often been claimed, Freudian theory also has a built-in method of explaining away any evidence that appears to falsify it, then it will indeed be a closed system as defined in Chapter 1. And since belief in the theory is a requirement of membership of psychoanalytic societies, it might even be said to be the ideology of those groups. However, we should look more closely at the matter before we pass judgment.

We should first distinguish two independent questions: the truth of Freud's theories and the effectiveness of treatment based on them. Any doubts about psychoanalytic theory naturally extend to the therapy. But given that psychoanalytic treatment has by now been quite widely applied, we should be able to form some estimate of its success. This would in principle be a test of the theory, since, if the theoretical claims were true, we might expect the treatment to be effective. However, matters are not easy here. For one thing, understanding the causes of a condition does not necessarily give us the power to change it (e.g., the effects of a traumatic childhood, however well understood by a therapist, might be impossible to undo). Second, a true theory might be ineptly applied in clinical practice.

Third, there is considerable vagueness about what constitutes "cure" from neurotic illness. Who is to make such a judgment, and on what basis? A two-thirds recovery rate has been claimed for patients who persist with psychoanalytic therapy. This may sound reasonably favorable, but it must, of course, be compared with control groups of similar cases who have not been treated at all (or who have been treated by other methods, such as behavioral therapy or other, non-analytic kinds of psychotherapy). The proportion of spontaneous recovery from neurosis without treatment has also been estimated at about two thirds, so on those figures there is no clear proof of any therapeutic effectiveness.

On the question of the truth of the theories, the crucial problem is whether they are empirically testable. Freud put forward his theories as scientific hypotheses based on the observable evidence, and we have seen in Chapter 1 that testability by observation is a necessary condition for scientific status. But for some of the central propositions of Freudian theory, it is not clear whether or how they are testable. Let me illustrate this with examples from different levels of Freud's theorizing.

In applying his general postulate of psychic determinism, Freud arrives at some very specific claims, such as that all dreams are wish fulfillments, often in disguised form. But even if we accept that every dream must have a cause of some sort, it does not follow that the cause (or causes) must be mental rather than physical (e.g., a reaction to what one has eaten in the evening or a neurophysiological need for a sort of "cleaning out" process for information in the brain). And even if the cause is mental, it does not follow that it is unconscious, or deeply significant; could the dream be an outgrowth of a trivial experience of the previous day or a quite ordinary concern about the morrow? So, can Freud's general claim that the cause of every dream is a wish (often unconscious, and often disguised) be tested? Where an interpretation in terms of an independently established wish of the dreamer is made plausible, well and good. But what if no such interpretation is found? A convinced Freudian will assert that there must be a wish whose disguise has not yet been seen through. But this would make it impossible to show that a dream is *not* a disguised wish fulfillment and would threaten to evacuate the claim of any genuine empirical content, leaving only the suggestion that we should always *look* for a relevant wish. Freud's claim can be supported only if we can have independent evidence for the existence of the wish and the correct interpretation of its disguise. It is a tall order to maintain that this can be found for every single dream. (Similar doubts arise about the postulation of unconscious causes for everyday errors and slips of the tongue.)

Consider next the fundamental postulate of the unconscious mental states. We must ask ourselves whether this offers any good explanation of what we know about human beings. We should not dismiss them just because they are unobservable, for scientific theory often postulates entities that are not perceptible by the senses—for example, atoms, electrons, magnetic fields, and radio waves. But in these cases there are clear rules connecting the theoretical entities with observable phenomena; we can, for instance, infer the presence or absence of a magnetic field from the visible behavior of a compass needle or iron filings. In explaining human action and behavior in everyday terms, we appeal to beliefs, perceptions, sensations, desires, and intentions—and none of these are literally observable states. Some of Freud's theorizing goes only a little way beyond this everyday and relatively uncontroversial sort of explanation. Under hypnotic suggestion, subjects may very deliberately perform unusual or "silly" actions that the hypnotist has told them beforehand to do; if asked why they are doing these absurd things, they do not seem to remember the hypnotist's instructions but tries to offer rather lame "rationalizations" for their actions. In this case it seems plausible to explain the subjects' behavior (and rationalizations) in terms of an unconscious memory of the hypnotist's instructions. Some of the symptoms of Freud's hysterical patients invited similar explanations. But how are we to test whether such explanations, however intuitively plausible, are actually true?

It has been suggested that psychoanalysis is not primarily a set of scientific hypotheses to be tested empirically but rather a way of understanding people, of seeing a *meaning* in their actions, mistakes, jokes, dreams, and neurotic symptoms. Since people, as conscious and rational beings, are so different from the entities studied by physics and chemistry, why should we criticize psychoanalysis for failing to meet criteria for scientific status that have been taken from the physical sciences? Perhaps the psychoanalytic account of a dream or a symptom is more akin to the interpretation of a work of art such as a poem or painting, in which there may be good reasons, but of an inconclusive kind, for a variety of interpretations. Many of Freud's conceptions can be seen as extensions of our ordinary ways of understanding each other in terms of everyday concepts such as love, hate, fear, anxiety, rivalry, and so on. And the experienced psychoanalyst can be seen as someone who has acquired a deep intuitive understanding of the springs of human motivation and a skill in interpreting the multifarious complexities of how they work out in particular situations, regardless of the theoretical views he or she may espouse.

Such a view of psychoanalysis has been given philosophical backing by the distinction between *reasons* and *causes*. Scientific explanation in terms of causes has often been contrasted with the explanation of human actions in terms of reasons—the beliefs and desires that made it rational for the agent to do what he or she did. (See Chapter 9 for what Sartre has to say on this.) And it has even been suggested that Freud misunderstood the nature of his own theories, presenting them as offering scientific discoveries about the causes of human behavior. However, the sharpness of this dichotomy has been questioned by those who argue that conscious beliefs and desires can act both as reasons *and* as causes and, hence, that *unconscious* beliefs and desires may well play this dual role, too. There are deep philosophical issues here about how far the methods of scientific investigation and explanation are applicable to human beliefs and actions, but I cannot pursue them here (I advert to them again in Chapter 12).

Even if we accept that unconscious mental states can explain hypnosis and certain kinds of neurosis, success in these rather special cases is far from proving the whole of Freud's theorizing. The trouble with many of the Freudian unconscious states is the unclarity of the criteria for inferring their presence or absence in any particular person (as in the discussion of dreaming). If stamp collecting is asserted to be a sign of unconscious "anal retentiveness," how could one show that such an unconscious trait is *not* present in someone? Freud put forward very general theories that go a long way beyond our everyday explanations in terms of reasons. In particular, he appealed to the concept of repression, as a postulated process of pushing mental ideas into the unconscious and keeping them there by force. Here he is in danger of talking of persons within the person, internal "homunculi" with knowledge and purposes of their own. What exactly is it that does the repressing, and how does it know which items to select for repression? As we see in Chapter 9, Sartre makes an apposite criticism at just this point.

Freud's theory of instincts or drives is particularly unclear in its status, as is suggested by his vacillations on the subject. One can describe as instinctive any form of behavior that is not learned in the lifetime of the individual (although it may often be difficult to *show* that it has not been learned in some way or other). But is anything added by referring instinctive behavior to *an* instinct as its cause? If it is claimed that there are only a certain *number* of basic instincts, how can we could decide which are basic, and how they are to be distinguished and counted? If the sexual drive is alleged to be behind behavior that we do not at first recognize as sexual, such as artistic creation or the pursuit of political power, how are we to decide who is right about this? A similar question arises if an aggressive or "death" instinct is put forward to explain depression and self-destructive behavior. Could any evidence settle whether either of Freud's main instinct theories is right as against, say, an Adlerian theory of a basic instinct of self-assertion or a Jungian theory of an instinctual need for God? There are conceptual problems of definition here, as well as the need for perceptible tests for postulated unobservables.

Freud's account of instincts or drives seems unduly reductionist and physiological: "What, then, do these instincts want? Satisfaction—that is, the establishment of situations in which the bodily needs can be extinguished. A lowering of the tension of need is felt by our organ of consciousness as pleasurable, an increase of it is soon felt as unpleasure." Obviously, he had sexuality in mind in such passages, perhaps primarily *male* orgasm—though his talk of pleasurable satisfaction of bodily needs can also be applied to eating and drinking. But is it remotely plausible to say that *all* human behavior is driven, directly or indirectly, by short-term bodily needs? This is not true even of many animals. Consider parental behavior. Many creatures expend tremendous energy on the feeding and defense of their young, and it seems that such behavior is instinctual, but with a different drive from that for copulation. Humans also show (however imperfectly) parental behavior that surely has an intinctive, biological component. Consider also our need to work, to try to do something difficult that serves some meaningful end. If our desires for food and sex are plentifully fulfilled but there is nothing else to do, we rapidly get bored. We see in Chapter 11 how theories of drives or instincts were modified by Lorenz.

The developmental approach to individual character and the theory of the stages of infantile sexual development are rather more easily tested by observation. In this area, some of Freud's propositions seem to be confirmed by the evidence; others are not clearly supported, while others are very difficult to test. The *existence* of what Freud called the oral and anal characters has been confirmed by the discovery that certain traits of character (for instance, parsimony, orderliness, and obstinacy—the anal traits) do tend to go together. But the claim that these types of character *arise* from certain kinds of infant-rearing procedures has not been so well supported. There are practical difficulties in establishing correlations between infantile experience and adult character, so the theory is hard to refute decisively. Other parts of Freud's psychosexual theories present conceptual difficulties about testing. How, for example, could one test whether infants get distinctively *erotic* pleasure from sucking? Freud's claims about infantile sexuality obviously require extremely careful investigation, in view of his now notorious change of mind, first accepting his patients' stories of child sexual abuse, then deciding that such ostensible memories could largely be due to fantasy.

This treatment of a few examples suggests why there is serious doubt about the scientific status of some of Freud's key theoretical assertions. Some seem untestable because of conceptual unclarities, and among those that *can* be tested, only some have received empirical support. Even now, no unambiguous verdict can be passed on Freud's theories as a whole. His imaginative genius in suggesting new psychological hypotheses is obvious. Freud was also blessed with considerable literary gifts, and one can be carried along by the stylishness of his prose. But however influential and persuasive someone's thought and writing may be, we should never excuse ourselves the task of critical evaluation. Freud wrote so much, of such human importance, that the critical elucidation of it will occupy us for many years to come.

For Further Reading

An excellent starting point for reading Freud himself is his "Five Lectures on Psycho-Analysis," reprinted in *Two Short Accounts of Psycho-Analysis* (London: Penguin, 1962) and in *A General Selection from the Works of Sigmund Freud*, ed. by J. Rickman (New York: Doubleday Anchor, 1957). There is also Freud's second "short account," "The Question of Lay-Analysis," which introduces the later theory of id, ego, and superego. Further exploration of Freud's thought could continue with his *Introductory Lectures on Psycho-Analysis* of 1915–17, reprinted in the Pelican Freud library.

For a brief survey of Freud's work, see Anthony Storr, *Freud* (Oxford: Oxford University Press, 1989), in the Past Masters series. Richard Wollheim, *Freud* (London: Fontana, 1971), in the Modern Masters series, provides an introduction by a philosopher who is a Freudian.

Biographical studies started with the classic, if somewhat hero-worshipping three-volume work by Ernest Jones, *The Life and Work of Sigmund Freud*, abridged version by L. Trilling and S. Marcus (London: Penguin, 1964; New York: Basic Books, 1961). Among many recent books there have been Frank J. Sulloway, *Freud: Biologist of the Mind* (New York: Basic Books, 1979; London: Fontana, 1980), and the controversial study by Jeffey Masson, *The Assault on Truth: Freud's Suppression of the Seduction Theory* (New York: Farrar, Straus & Giroux, 1987), which questions Freud's integrity.

Among many general evaluations of Freud's work, B. A. Farrell, *The Standing of Psycho-Analysis* (Oxford: Oxford University Press, 1981) gives a clear, balanced survey, and R. Webster, *Why Freud Was Wrong: Sin, Science and Psychoanalysis* (London: Harper/Collins, 1995) offers a more hostile view in light of recent work.

For survey of post-Freudian psychoanalytical theory, see Morris N. Eagle, *Recent Developments in Psychoanalysis: A Critical Evaluation* (New York: McGraw-Hill, 1984).

For discussion of philosophical issues arising from Freud's theorizing, see R. Wollheim and J. Hopkins (eds.), *Philosophical Essays on Freud* (Cambridge: Cambridge University Press, 1982).

9

Sartre: Radical Freedom

⊰━━━⧱⧱⧱⧱━━━⊱

In moving from Freud to Sartre we go from biology, medicine, and pychopathology to an academic philosophical system that Sartre also expressed in novels and plays and applied to social and political issues. Yet there is a common concern with the nature of human minds and consciousness, and with the problems of the human individual. To understand Sartre, it is helpful first to locate him in the context of the historical development of existentialist thought.

Many different writers, philosophers, and theologians have been called "existentialist." Insofar as any common core can be discerned, there are three main concerns that are central to existentialism. The first related to *individual* human beings. Existentialists think that would-be general theories about human nature leave out precisely what is most important—the uniqueness of each individual and his or her life situation. Second, there is a concern with the *meaning* or purpose of human lives, rather than with scientific or metaphysical truths, even if the latter are about human beings. Inner or "subjective" experience is regarded as more important than "objective" truth. Third, there is a strong emphasis on the *freedom* of human beings, on each individual's ability to choose his or her attitudes, purposes, values, and actions. Existentialists not only maintain this as a truth but try to persuade people to act on it, to exercise their freedom and to be aware that they are doing so. In the typical existentialist view, the only truly admirable, "authentic" way of life is the one freely chosen by each person.

This common core of existentialism can be found in a wide variety of contexts. It is naturally expressed in descriptions of the concrete detail of particular characters and situations, whether in real life or in imaginative literature. It is also characteristic of religious accounts of the human condition that they do not merely assert metaphysical propositions but present them as having vital significance for individual human lives; the free, response of each person is sought. However, someone can count as an existentialist *philosopher* only if he or she offers some general analysis of the human condition. Existentialist philosophies come in various forms, the most radical division being between religious and atheist.

The Danish Christian thinker Søren Kierkegaard (1813–55) is generally recognized as the first modern existentialist, though there is of course an existential dimension to most Christian thought, notably that of St. Paul, St. Augustine, and Pascal. Like his contemporary Karl Marx, Kierkegaard reacted against Hegel's philosophy, but in a very different way. He rejected the Hegelian abstract theoretical system, likening it to a vast mansion in which one does not actually live, and maintained the supreme importance of the individual and his or her life choices. Kierkegaard distinguished three basic ways of life, which he called the aesthetic, the ethical, and the religious, and he required people to choose between them. He held that the religious (more specifically, the Christian) way is the "highest," although it can be reached only by a free, nonrational "leap into the arms of God."

The other great nineteenth-century existentialist was a crusading atheist. The German writer Friedrich Nietszche (1844–1900) argued that since "God is dead" (i.e., the illusions of religious belief have now been seen through), we will have to rethink the whole foundations of our lives and find our meaning and purpose in human terms alone. In this, he had much in common with his earlier compatriot Feuerbach, whose humanistic atheism we mentioned when introducing Marx. What is most distinctive of Nietzsche is his emphasis on our radical, unsettling freedom to change the basis of our values. As in other existentialist thinkers, there is a tension between a "relativist" thesis that there is no objective basis for valuing one way of life more than another and what seems to be a recommendation of a particular choice. In Nietzsche's case, this is suggested by his vision of the "Superman," who rejects our present meek religion-based values and replaces them by the "will to power" (a phrase that, in the light of subsequent history, has acquired sinister connotations).

In the twentieth century also, existentialists have included both religious believers and atheists, but existentialism has certainly been a major force in theology. Existentialist philosophy has been centered in contintental Europe and has had less influence in the English-speaking countries. Although influenced partly by Kierkegaard and Nietzsche, it became in the hands of Heidegger and Sartre a more academic and, indeed jargon-ridden style of philosophizing. One main influence behind this is "phenomenology": the German philosopher Husserl hoped to find a new starting point for philosophy, describing not so much the objective world but "phenomena" as they are given in human experience.

This concern with the subjective, with how things appear in human consciousness, rather than with scientific truth about the physical world is characteristic of twentieth-century existentialist philosophers. The most original and influential of these is undoubtedly Martin Heidegger (1889–1976), whose major early work, *Being and Time*, appeared in 1927. Heidegger's language is strange and difficult: in rejecting the problems and concepts of traditional metaphysics, he invents hyphenated neologisms in the German language to try to express his distinctive insights. He has a central existential concern with "Being" and the meaning of human existence and with the possibility of "authentic" life achieved by facing up to one's real situation in the world and, in particular, to the inevitability of one's own death. "Being" in Heidegger's writing begins to sound rather like God, or at least an impersonal substitute for the biblical God—an ultimate reality of which we can become aware if we attend in the right sort of way (in quasi-mystical kinds of experience) and that may be expressed in poetry or music but that cannot be adequately formulated in scientific or philosophical statements.

Sartre's Life and Work

The most famous French existentialist is Jean-Paul Sartre (1905–1980). Sartre's philosophy is deeply indebted to Heidegger, but his writing (some of it, at least) is rather more accessible. In a brilliant academic career, Sartre absorbed, among much else, the thought of the great European philosophers, especially Hegel, Husserl, and Heidegger. Many of the obscurities of his philosophy can be traced to the influence of these three writers of ponderous German abstractions. Themes from Husserl's phenomenology can be detected in Sartre's first books—the remarkable philosophical novel *Nausea* of 1938 and his four short studies of psychological topics, *The Transcendence of the Ego* (1936–37), *Imagination* (1936), *Sketch for a Theory of the Emotions* (1939), and *The Psychology of the Imagination* (1940). His central work, expounding at great length his philosophy of human existence, is the celebrated *Being and Nothingness*, written while he was a prisoner of war and published in 1943.

During World War II Sartre was sympathetic to the French Resistance to Nazi occupation, and some of the atmosphere of that time can be found in his work. The choice that confronted all Frenchmen and women—collaboration with the Germans, resistance, or quiet self-preservation—was a very obvious instance of what existentialists see as the ever-present necessity for individual choice. These themes are expressed in Sartre's trilogy of novels, *Roads to Freedom*, and in his plays, such as *No Exit* and *Flies*. Sartre gave a short, stylish account of atheistic existentialism in *Existentialism and Humanism*, a lecture delivered, to much public acclaim, in Paris after the city was liberated from the Germans in 1945, but his treatment there is more popular and does not give an adequate account of his thought.

Sartre became a very public French intellectual for the rest of his life. As time went on, he modified the very individualistic approach of his early writings and gave much more attention to social, economic, and political realities. He came to espouse a form of Marxism, which he described as "the inescapable philosophy of our time," though needing refertilization by existentialism. This change is expressed in his *Search for a Method* (1957) and in his second obscure magnum opus, *Critique of Dialectical Reason* (1960). He was politically active on the left, joining the Communist Party for a few years but resigning at the time of the Hungarian Revolution in 1956. He supported Algeria's struggle for liberation from French rule and opposed the American war in Vietnam. Toward the end of his life he applied his method of "existential psychoanalysis" in major biographies of the French writers Baudelaire and Flaubert. I do not attempt to deal with the later developments in Sartre's thought in this chapter; I consider only the existentialist philosophy of *Being and Nothingness* (and the other early works), and make page references to the English translation.

Being and Nothingness, it is only fair to warn the reader, is probably the most unreadable of the texts referred to in this book. This is a matter not just of length and repetitiousness but of a word-spinning delight in the technical term, the abstract noun, the elusive metaphor, and the unresolved paradox. The influence of Hegel, Husserl, and Heidegger may explain this but can hardly excuse it. One does wonder whether Sartre could not have said what he had to say more clearly, and a lot more briefly. He had an extraordinarily self-confident ability to pour philosophical verbiage onto pages (usually in cafés, at the dead of night, so the story goes), but he does not seem to have been so good at self-criticism or editorial revision (legend has it that his manuscripts were taken from the café table straight to the printers). It is all the more tantalizing when one finds passages of relative lucidity and insight within the conglomeration of verbiage. However, a reader who makes the effort to understand him will begin to find a view of human nature that has a certain compelling fascination.

Theory of the Universe

Sartre has many obscure things to say about the nature of "being" or existence, but for our introductory purposes his most important metaphysical assertion is his denial of the existence of God. Though strongly influenced by Heidegger's *Being and Time*, Sartre's *Being and Nothingness* does not take over the quasi-mystical or religious dimension of "Being" in Heidegger. (However, a posthumously published work by Sartre, *Truth and Existence*, remains somewhat closer to the spirit of Heidegger.)

Sartre claims that the very idea of God is self-contradictory (*Being and Nothingness*, p. 615) and does not spend much further argument on the matter. He seems mainly concerned to consider the consequences of God's nonexistence for the meaning of our lives. Like Nietzsche, he holds the absence of God to be of the utmost significance for human lives; the atheist does not merely differ from the religious believer on a point of metaphysics but must hold a profoundly different view of human existence. If God does not exist, then everything is permitted (as Dostoyevsky once put it). In Sartre's view, there are no transcendent objective values set for us, neither laws of God nor Platonic Forms. There is no ultimate meaning or purpose inherent in our existence; in this sense, human life is "absurd." We are "forlorn" or "abandoned" in this world, and there is no heavenly Father to tell us what to do and to help us do it, as grown-up people, we have to decide for ourselves and look after ourselves. Sartre repeatedly insists that the only foundation for values lies in ourselves, in our human freedom to choose, and that there can be no external or objective justification for the values, actions, and way of life that anyone chooses to adopt (p. 38).

Theory of Human Nature

In one sense, Sartre would deny that there is any such thing as "human nature" for there to be true or false theories about. This is a typically existentialist rejection of general statements about human beings and human lives. Sartre expressed it in the formula "man's existence precedes his essence" (pp. 438–39). By this he means that we have no "essential" nature and have not been created for any particular purpose, by God or evolution or anything else; we simply find ourselves existing by no choice of our own and have to *decide* what to make of ourselves—each of us must create his or her own "essence." Sartre can hardly deny that there are certain human universals—for instance, the necessity to eat to survive, the physiology of our metabolism, and the strength of our sexual impulses. That there are some scientific truths about us is obvious, although as we noticed in discussing Marx there is room for deep dispute about what count as purely biological facts about human nature. Presumably what Sartre means is that there are no general truths about what human beings *want* to be or *ought* to be.

As an existentialist philosopher, however, Sartre has to make *some* general statements about human nature and the human condition. His central assertion is that of human freedom. We are "condemned to be free"; there is no limit to our freedom, except that we cannot cease being free (p. 439). Let us examine how he reaches this conclusion via an analysis of the notion of consciousness. He starts from a radical distinction between consciousness or "human reality" (*l'être-pour-soi*, being-for-itself) and inanimate, nonconscious things (*l'être-en-soi*, being-in-itself; p. xxxix). This basic dualism follows from the necessary truth that consciousness is "intentional" in the sense made famous by the Austrian philosopher Franz Brentano, one of the forerunners of phenomenology. Consciousness always has an object: if one is conscious at all, one is conscious *of* something that one conceives of as distinct from oneself (p. xxxvii). (Even if one is mistaken or doubtful in a particular case, as Macbeth was about the illusory dagger, one is thinking of something that *would* exist independent of oneself if it existed at all.) For Sartre, then, all consciousness is consciousness of the world, or at least of something conceived of as in the world—it involves what he calls "positional" or "thetic" consciousness.

The next point to appreciate is the connection Sartre sees between consciousness and the mysterious concept of "nothingness" that appears in the title of his book. I avoid here any attempt to trace the roots of this concept in previous philosophy and instead see what intelligible points we can interpret from Sartre. We have noted that consciousness is always of something other than itself; Sartre holds that it is always aware of itself as well (pp. xxix, 74–75), so it is distinguished from its objects: the subject is aware in a *non*-reflective ("nonthetic") way that the object is *not* the subject. A judgment about the world can be negative as well as positive; we can recognize and assert what is *not* the case, as when I look for my friend in the café where we arranged to meet and say, "Pierre is not here" (pp. 9–10). If we ask a question, we must understand the possibility that the reply will be "No" (p. 5). Conscious beings who can think and say what is the case can equally well conceive, and may sometimes believe, what is *not* the case (this is a point whose deep implications have been pondered by other philosophers from Plato to Wittgenstein).

Sartre indulges in some mystifying verbal play with his concept of nothingness, in paradoxical phrases such as "the objective existence of a non-being" (p. 5), which perhaps means that there are true negative statements. And he is fond of dark metaphorical sayings such as "Nothingness lies coiled in the heart of being—like a worm" (p. 21). But the crucial role of nothingness in Sartre seems to be to make a conceptual connection between consciousness and freedom. For the ability to conceive of what is not the case involves the freedom to imagine other possibilities (pp. 24–25), and the freedom to try to bring them about (p. 433ff). One can never reach a state in which there remain no other possibilities unimaginable or unfulfilled, for, whatever situation we are in, we can always conceive of its being otherwise in the future. Desire involves recognition of the *lack* of something (p. 87), as does intentional action (p. 433), for I can try to bring about a change in the world only if I believe that what I intend is not already the case. The mental power of negation is, then, the same thing as freedom—both freedom of mind (to imagine possibilities) and freedom of action (to try to actualize them). To be a concious being is to be continually faced with choices about what to believe and what to do. To be conscious is to be free.

Note how this position of Sartre's directly contradicts two of Freud's. It is incompatible with Freud's belief in complete psychic determinism (p. 458ff). But it also conflicts with the postulate of unconscious mental states, for Sartre holds that consciousness is necessarily transparent to itself (p. 49ff). I explore this difference a bit more more later.

Every aspect of our mental lives is, in Sartre's view, in some sense chosen, and ultimately our own responsibility. Emotions are often thought to be outside the control of the will, but Sartre maintains that if I am sad, it is only because I choose to make myself sad (p. 61). His view, outlined more fully in his *Sketch for a Theory of Emotions*, is that emotions are not just moods that "come over us" but ways in which we apprehend the world. What distinguishes emotions from other ways of being aware of things is that they involve an attempt to transform the world by magic—when one cannot reach the bunch of grapes, one dismisses them as "too green," attributing this quality to them although one knows quite well that their ripeness does not depend on their reachability. So we are *responsible* for our emotions; they are ways in which we choose to react to the world (p. 445). We are equally responsible for longer-lasting features of our character. We cannot just assert, "I am shy" as if this were an unchangeable physiological fact about us like "I am black," for our shyness is the way we behave in company, and we can choose to behave differently. Even to say "I am ugly" or "I am stupid" is not to assert a fact already in existence but to anticipate how people will react to me in future, and this can be tested only by actual experience (p. 459).

So even though we are often not aware of it, our freedom and our responsibility extend to everything we think, feel, and do. There are times, however, when this radical freedom is clearly manifested to us. In moments of temptation or indecision—for example, when the man who has resolved not to gamble any more is confronted with the gaming tables once again—one realizes, painfully, that no motive and no past resolution, however strong, determines what one will do *next* (p. 33). Every moment requires a new or renewed choice. Following Kierkegaard and Heidegger, Sartre uses the term "anguish" to describe this consciousness of one's own freedom (pp. 29, 464). Anguish is not fear of an external object but the awareness of the ultimate unpredictability of one's own behavior. The soldier fears injury or death, but he feels anguish when he wonders whether he is going to be able to "hold up" in the coming battle. The person walking on a dangerous cliffpath fears falling but feels anguish because she knows that there is nothing to stop her throwing herself over (pp. 29–32).

Diagnosis

Anguish, the consciousness of our freedom, is painful, and we typically try to avoid it (p. 40). Sartre thinks that we would like to achieve a state in which there are no options left open for us, in which we simply "coincide with ourselves" like inanimate objects (*être-en-soi*), rather than conscious beings. But such escape is illusory, for it is a necessary truth that we are conscious beings (*être-pour-soi*), and therefore free. Such is Sartre's metaphysical diagnosis of the human condition. Hence his description of human life as "an unhappy consciousness with no possibility of surpassing its unhappy state" (p. 90), "a useless passion" (p. 615).

A crucial concept in Sartre's diagnosis is that of "bad faith"(*mauvaise foi*, sometimes translated as "self-deception"). Bad faith is the attempt to escape anguish by thinking that one's attitudes and actions are determined by one's situation, one's character, one's relationship to others, or one's social role—by anything other than one's own choices. Sartre believes that bad faith is a characteristic of most human life; it is not confined to those who philosophize (p. 556).

He gives two famous examples of bad faith, both of them scenes from the Parisian cafés that were his favorite haunts (pp. 55–60). He pictures a young girl sitting with a man who, she has every reason to suspect, would like to seduce her. But when he takes her hand, she tries to avoid the necessity of a decision to accept or reject his advances by seeming not to notice: she carries on their intellectual conversation while leaving her hand in his as if she were not aware of his holding it. In Sartre's interpretation, she is in bad faith because she somehow pretends—not just to her companion but *to herself*—that she can be distinguished from her bodily actions and postures, that her hand is a passive object, a mere thing, whereas she is, of course, a conscious embodied being who knows what is going on and is responsible for her actions, or lack of action.

The second illustration is of the café waiter who is doing his job just a little too keenly; his movements with the trays and cups are full of flourishes and are overdramatic, he is obviously "acting the part" of waiter. If there is bad faith here at all (and maybe there is not), it lies in his identifying himself completely with the role of waiter, thinking that this role determines his every action and attitude, whereas the truth is, of course, that he has chosen to take on the job and is free to give it up at any time, even if he would face unemployment. He is not *essentially* a waiter, for nobody is essentially anything. "The waiter cannot be immediately a café waiter in the sense that this inkwell *is* an inkwell"; "it is necessary that we *make ourselves* what we are" (p. 59). Anything we do, any role we play, even (Sartre wants to say) any emotion we feel or any value we respect (pp. 38, 627) is sustained in being only by our own constantly remade decision.

Sartre emphatically rejects any explanation of bad faith in terms of unconscious mental states (pp. 50-54). A Freudian might try to describe the cases just given as examples of repression into the unconscious—the girl might be said to be repressing the knowledge that her companion has made a sexual advance to her; the waiter might be repressing the knowledge that he is a free agent who does not have to continue acting as a waiter any longer than he decides to. But Sartre points out an apparent self-contradiction in the very idea of repression. We must attribute the act or process of repressing to some element within the mind ("the censor"); yet this censor must be able to make distinctions between what to repress and what to retain in consciousness, so it must be aware of the repressed idea, but supposedly in order *not* to be aware of it. Sartre concludes that the censor itself is in bad faith and that we have not gained any explanation of how bad faith is possible by localizing it in one part of the mind, rather than in the person as a whole (pp. 52–53).

Sartre goes on to claim that what he calls "good faith" or "sincerity" presents just as much of a conceptual problem. For as soon as one describes oneself in some way (e.g., "I am a waiter," "I am shy," "I am gay"), in that very act a distinction is involved between the self doing the describing and the self described. The ideal of complete sincerity seems doomed to failure (p. 62), for we can never be mere objects to be observed and described: the attempt to achieve sincerity thus becomes merely another form of bad faith. The example Sartre offers here is of someone who has a clear record of homosexual activity but who resists description of himself as a homosexual (p. 63). His friend, "a champion of sincerity," demands that he recognize himself as a homosexual. But Sartre points out that nobody just *is* gay in the way that a table is a table or a person is red-haired (even if we think that someone's homosexual *inclinations* are in the same category as being red-haired, Sartre's point applies to *actions*). If someone were to admit reflectively that he is gay, and mean by that that he cannot cease his homosexual activity, he would be in bad faith—and so would any "champion of sincerity" who demanded such an admission (p. 63). We have here another kind of bad faith, which consists in not admitting one's freedom to do otherwise than one does.

Sartre is touching here on the deep difficulties of self-knowledge, what others have called "the systematic elusiveness of the self." But his account threatens to make these matters even more confusing and perplexing than they are, for he displays an inordinate fondness for the paradoxical formula that "human reality must be what it is not, and not be what it is" (e.g., pp. xli, 67). This is, of course, a self-contradiction, so we cannot take it literally. But Sartre rests too easily in such paradoxical statements and thereby seems to shirk the difficult task of explaining in clear, consistent terms what it is about the concept of consciousness that generates the possibility of bad faith. (Did he repeat his slogan "consciousness is what it is not, and is not what it is" with the deliberate intention of infuriating philosophers? Or did he deceive himself into thinking that by its incantation he had achieved insight?) I suggest that we take it as misleading shorthand for "human reality is not *necessarily* what it is, but must be *able* to be what it is not" (which is my paraphrase of the way he puts in on p. 58). The crucial point is that we are always free to *try* to become different from what we presently are.

The problem remains to explain how bad faith is possible. Sartre may have something to offer here when he distinguishes between reflective (positional, thetic) consciousness and prereflective (nonpositional, nonthetic) consciousness. This distinction plays a not very well signposted but seemingly fundamental role in his analysis. As we have noted, he says that all consciousness is "positional" consciousness of some object taken to be distinct from the subject. But, he adds, "the necessary and sufficient condition for a knowing consciousness to be knowledge of its objects, is that it be consciousness of itself as being that knowledge" (p. xxvii). He rejects the suggestion that this implies "To know is to know that one knows," which would imply that all consciousness involves *reflective* consciousness of itself. He suggests instead that "every positional consciousness of an object is at the same time a non-positional consciousness of itself" (p. xxix). In his example, if I am counting the cigarettes in my case, I am conscious of the cigarettes and that there are a dozen of them; what is more, I am *prereflectively* conscious that I am counting them (as is shown by the answer I could unhesitatingly give when asked what I am doing), but I need not be *reflectively* conscious of my activity of counting—though presumably I will become so as soon as someone asks the question.

Whether we can make good sense of this distinction between pre-reflective and reflective consciousness is a difficult philosophical problem, which I cannot pursue further here. But we may note the irony that Sartre rejects the Freudian distinction between conscious and unconscious, only to invoke what may be an equally obscure and controversial distinction within consciousness.

Sartre gives an apparently pessimistic analysis of interpersonal relations in Part Three of *Being and Nothingness*. He throws some new light on the much discussed philosophical problem of other minds, arguing by appeal to common experience that we often have an immediate, noninferential awareness of other people's mental states. When we see two human eyes directed at us, we believe that we are being observed, and we know this with as much certainty as we know anything about purely physical events in the world. If one is engrossed in doing something not socially approved of, such as spying on someone through a keyhole, and one then hears (or merely *thinks* one hears) a footstep behind one, one suddenly feels vividly *ashamed*. One becomes aware that someone else is (or might be) critical of one's actions (if one is witnessed doing something admirable, one may feel *pride*). Many emotional states thus involve, in their very conceptual structure, the existence of other people.

But Sartre goes on to argue for the much more dubious thesis that the relationship between any two conscious beings is necessarily one of conflict in that each must want to "possess" the other, to make the other into a mere object. In these terms, he gives a persuasive version of Hegel's famous dialectical relation between master and slave in which, paradoxically, the slave ends up with more power because the master needs the slave to *accept* him as master. Sartre is able to apply this analysis to sadism and masochism quite plausibly, but he goes on to suggest that genuine respect for the freedom of others, nonpossessive love, is an impossible ideal (pp. 394ff, 429ff). At this stage of his writing, the outlook seems bleak indeed.

But is there not a contradiction between Sartre's insistence on our freedom and his analysis of the human condition as necessarily determined in these respects? He holds that we are always wanting to fill the "nothingness" that is the essence of our being conscious; we want to become inanimate objects, rather than remain in the state of having possibilities unfulfilled and decisions to make (p. 90). He holds, as we have just seen, that the relationship between two conscious beings is necessarily one of conflict. In these two ways, he analyzes human life as a perpetual attempt to achieve the logically impossible. But *must* it be like that? Can't someone choose *not* to aspire to become an object, or to make other people into objects? If even "good faith" is a kind of "bad faith," how is any kind of authenticity possible? It is not clear how Sartre resolves these tensions at the heart of his theory.

Prescription

In view of his rejection of objective values, Sartre's prescription appears a peculiarly empty one. There is no *particular* way of life that he can recommend. All that he can condemn is bad faith, any attempt to pretend that one is not free. And all that he can praise is "authenticity": he would have us each make our individual choices with full awareness that nothing determines them for us. We must accept our responsibility for everything about ourselves—not just our actions, but our attitudes, our emotions, our dispositions, and our characters. The "spirit of seriousness," which is the illusion that values are objectively in the world rather than sustained only by human choice, must be decisively repudiated (pp. 580, 626). Consciousness contains a permanent risk of bad faith; yet Sartre suggests that it is *possible* to avoid this and achieve authenticity (p. 70). Bad faith may be common, but presumably it is possible (even if rarer and more difficult) reflectively to *affirm* one's own freedom.

In his lecture *Existentialism and Humanism*, Sartre illustrated the impossibility of rational prescription through the case of a young Frenchman at the time of the Nazi occupation. The man was faced with the choice of joining the free French forces in England or staying at home to be with his mother, who lived only for him. One course of action would be directed to what he saw as the national good but would make little difference to the total war effort. The other would be of immediate practical effect but directed to the happiness of only one individual. Sartre holds that no ethical doctrine can arbitrate between such incommensurate claims. Nor can strength of feeling settle the matter, for there is no measure of such feeling except in terms of what the subject actually does, which is precisely what is at stake. To choose an adviser or moral authority is only another sort of choice. So when Sartre was consulted by this young man, he could only say: "You are free; therefore choose." However, not even the most objective system of ethical values (Platonic, Christian, or Kantian) can claim to offer a single, determinate right answer to *every* individual human dilemma. To admit that not every choice has a right answer is not to say that *no* choice ever has a right answer, that all moral rules or values are merely "subjective."

Sartre does clearly commit himself to the intrinsic value of authentic choice. His descriptions of particular cases of bad faith are not morally neutral but implicitly condemn any self-deception, any refusal to face the reality of one's freedom and to affirm one's own choices. He thus offers another perspective on the ancient virtue of self-knowledge prescribed by Socrates, Spinoza, Freud, and many others.

Sartre's understanding of the nature and possibility of self-knowledge differs in crucial ways from Freud's. We have seen that psychoanalysis is based on the hypothesis of unconscious mental states that have causal effects on people's mental life. Freud conceived of these causes as acting in a quasi-mechanical way, like flows of energy, and he thought of his task in psychoanalysis as the uncovering of these hidden causes. Sartre rejects the idea of unconscious causes of mental events; for him, everything is already out in the open, available to consciousness (p. 571). In what Sartre calls "existential psychoanalysis" we look not for the *causes* of a person's behavior but for the *meaning* of it, for intelligible reasons (pp. 568–75). (Some contemporary psychiatrists have followed him on this point.) Sartre holds that since a person is a unity, not just a bundle of unrelated desires or habits, there must be for each person a fundamental choice (the "original project") that gives the ultimate meaning or purpose behind every particular aspect of his or her life (pp. 561–65). Sartre's biographies of Baudelaire, Genet, and Flaubert are particular exercises in interpreting the fundamental meaning of a person's life.

But it is not clear that for every person there must be a *single* fundamental choice. Sartre allows that one can sometimes make a "radical conversion" of one's "original project." Need there be just one such project in each period of someone's life? Can't one have two or more simultaneous projects that are incommensurable, not derivable from any common formula—e.g., family, career, and hobbies?

Sartre implores us to avoid bad faith and to live authentically. But how does authenticity differ from the good faith or "sincerity" that he diagnoses as only another form of bad faith? Here is another perplexing conceptual question to which he did not devote sufficient attention. A promising suggestion is that authenticity consists in *reflective* choice, self-consciously making one's own freedom a value, whereas good faith—the absence of deception—remains at the prereflective level. Sartre occasionally uses quasi-religious language, if only in evasive footnotes: he talks of "a self-recovery of being which was previously corrupted" (p. 70), an ethics of "deliverance and salvation" (p. 412), and, indeed, of "radical conversion" (pp. 475–76). Elsewhere, he talks of what he calls "pure" or "purifying" reflection (p. 155ff), and the whole trend of his argument seems to be to attribute a peculiarly moral power to reflective awareness.

But if no reasons whatever can be given for choosing one way rather than another, human choices would seem to remain totally arbitrary. It looks as if on his own premises Sartre would have to commend the man who "authentically" chooses to devote his life to exterminating Jews, seducing women, or playing computer games, provided that he chooses this with full, "purifying," reflective awareness that this is what he is choosing to do. Could Sartre find within his own philosophy any reason to criticize a would-be Nietzschian "Superman" (or superwoman) who resolutely and reflectively develops his or her own freedom at the cost of other, less-than-super human beings? Conversely, if someone devotes himself to looking after his children, helping the poor, or playing music, but does not reflect on his own motivation for doing so, Sartre would apparently have to condemn him as inauthentic.

Or can it be argued that authenticity must involve respecting the freedom of others, that valuing one's own freedom somehow implies equal value for the freedom of all other conscious, rational beings? Sartre made a suggestion in this Kantian direction in his lecture *Existentialism and Humanism.* One way to develop his thought would indeed be to embrace Kant's formula of the "Kingdom of Ends"—

that rational beings stand under the moral law that each of them should treat himself and all others, never merely as a means, but always at the same time as and end in himself (*Groundwork*, Chap. 2). But Sartre did not endorse this route. He ended *Being and Nothingness* with a promise to write another book on the ethical plane, but he never completed it—and some have taken this to show his realization of the impossibility of any distinctively existentialist morality. His *Notebooks for an Ethics* have now been published posthumously, and his *War Diaries*, which also touch on ethics and authenticity. In his later thought, he came to adopt a more Marxist standpoint, analyzing the social conditions that restrict freedom and seeking changes would make it possible for *all* human beings to exercise their freedom.

For all its obscurities, there is something important to learn from Sartre's analysis of how the very notion of consciousness involves freedom. We have seen that he wants to extend the concept of choice far beyond its normal use, to hold us responsible not just for our actions but for our emotions and even for our characters. If I am angry, it is because I have chosen to be angry; if I am the kind of person who tends to be passively resigned to the prevailing conditions, that too is a disposition that I choose to maintain. Sartre's view is not just a perverse misuse of language. For we do commonly reproach each other for our emotions and characters—"How *could* you feel like that?" "*Must* you be so selfish, or so impatient?" And such reproaches are not always useless. For to make people *aware* that they are feeling or behaving in a certain way does make a difference to them. The more they are aware of their anger or pride or self-centeredness, the more they are not *just* angry or proud or self-centered, and the more they are capable of change. Surely this is the essence of Sartre's point. The vast verbiage of his philosophy issues in a directly practical and intimate challenge to us all, to become more truly self-aware and to exercise our freedom to change ourselves.

For Further Reading:

For thought-provoking introductions to existentialism generally, see William Barrett, *Irrational Man: A Study in Existential Philosophy* (London:

Heinemann, 1961), now unfortunately out of print; and David E. Cooper, *Existentialism: A Reconstruction* (Oxford: Blackwell, 1990).

For admirable short guides to particular existentialist thinkers, see Patrick Gardiner, *Kierkegaard* [(Oxford: Oxford University Press, 1988); Michael Tanner, *Nietzsche* (Oxford: Oxford University Press, 1994), in the Past Master series; George Steiner, *Heidegger* (London: Fontana, 1978); Arthur C. Danto, *Sartre* (London: Fontana, 1975), in the Modern Master series.

Those who want to read Sartre's early philosophy for themselves might start with his novel *Nausea* or his lecture *Existentialism and Humanism* (London: Methuen, 1948), then the short books *The Transcendence of the Ego*, (New York: Farrar, Straus & Giroux, 1957) and *Sketch for a Theory of the Emotions* (London: Methuen, 1962), before launching into the depths of *Being and Nothingness*, trans. Hazel Barnes (London: Methuen, 1957; New York: Philosophical Library, 1956).

M. Jeanson, *Sartre and the Problem of Morality* (Bloomington: Indiana University Press, 1980), first published in French in 1947, is an interpretation of Sartre's early philosophy that was enthusiastically endorsed by Sartre himself at the time.

My own short paper "Sartre on Bad Faith" in *Philosophy* 58 (1983), pp. 253–58, attempts to put Sartre's reflective/nonreflective distinction to work; it is criticized by Jeffrey Gordon in the same journal, vol. 60 (1985), pp. 258–62.

Ronald E. Santoni, *Bad Faith, Good Faith, and Authenticity in Sartre's Early Philosophy* (Philadelphia: Temple University Press, 1995), makes a valiant attempt to distinguish the three notions in its title, taking into account Sartre's posthumously published work. This book is somewhat infected with Sartre's habits of verbosity, repetition, and undue abstraction, but the Introduction gives a useful survey of Santoni's interpretation of Sartre.

PART

IV

Two Samples of Scientific Theorizing about Human Nature

10

Behavioral Psychology: Skinner on Conditioning

Some readers may be wondering by now whether it is worth giving so much attention to the religious traditions, philosophers, and speculative theorists of the past. Now that scientific method has established itself as the proper way of understanding and explaining the world, should we not look to the sciences, and in particular to psychology, for the truth about human nature? This thought has inspired many thinkers since the rise of modern science, especially since the Enlightenment. In the twentieth century, psychology has established itself as an independent branch of empirical science, institutionally demarcated from its early philosophical ancestry. So, it will be said, surely we can now expect some proper scientific answers to our questions about human nature?

There have, however, been a variety of schools of thought and methodologies within psychology, and differences of approach still remain: psychology is not nearly as free from philosophical assumptions and problems as many of its practitioners would like to think, nor is it clearly demarcated from other disciplines such as sociology and linguistics on one side, or from biology and physiology, on the other. Most academic psychologists have been chary of talking about anything as general as "human nature." When figures like Skinner and Lorenz lift their heads above their specialized disciplines and venture to offer some sort of general diagnosis and prescription for human problems, their statements are likely to be as speculative as those of the other broad theorists of human nature we have considered. To review what all kinds of psychology have to say about human nature is far too big a task for this introductory book, though in the final chapter I attempt a brief survey of the main trends. In the next two chapters I concentrate on a critical evaluation of what Skinner and Lorenz have said about human nature, in the hope that the lessons thereby learned may be useful whenever we evaluate recent and future psychological theorizing.

First of all, some historical background should help set the scene. Toward the end of the nineteenth century, psychology began to emerge as an empirical science, and the first psychological laboratories were set up under the leadership of people like Wundt in Germany and William James in the United States. They defined psychology as the study not of soul or mind but of states of consciousness. They assumed that since each of us is aware of our own conscious states, we can describe them by introspection and thus produce empirical data for psychology. But it was soon found that such reports seldom agreed on the description and classification of sensations, images, and feelings, so the introspective method ran into an impasse. At the same time, Freud's work was suggesting that important aspects of the mind were not accessible to consciousness. In the study of animals, introspection is obviously not available; yet (since Darwin) one would expect the mental life of animals to be related to that of men.

So when J. B. Watson (1878–1958) proclaimed, in a famous set of lectures in 1912, that the subject matter of psychology should be *behavior*, rather than consciousness, his views found some eager converts who began to reorientate academic psychology in the English-speaking world. Watson is generally recognized as the founder of the "behaviorist" movement in psychology. The behavior of animals and men is publicly observable, so reports and descriptions of behavior under observed and controlled conditions can yield agreed-upon, objective data for analysis. And there was the extra attraction that the concept of behavior seemed to involve no question-

able philosophical assumptions about soul, mind, or consciousness—
just observable stimuli and responses.

This rejection of the introspective method was the most fundamental point of Watson's new program; it was a purely *methodological* dictum about what psychology ought to study, the *data* that are
its subject matter. As such, it does not exclude appeal to mental states
and processes in explaining the data. But Watson and many of his
followers, such as Skinner, tended to impose this restriction on psychological theorizing, too. The stipulation about data for psychology
does not imply the *metaphysical* statement that consciousness does
not exist or that it is nothing but the material processes inside a person's skull. It is also independent of the philosophical thesis (called
logical or *analytical* behaviorism) that the meaning of all our ordinary words for various sorts of mental state can be defined entirely
in terms of behavior or dispositions to behave. Watson tended to go
beyond his methodological point to the metaphysical claim that belief in consciousness is a hangover from our superstitious, prescien-
tific past, akin to a belief in witchcraft. He asserted that there are
internal contradictions in our ordinary mental concepts, but he never
gave reasons for this conceptual claim.

Watson's creed contained two other main points, which are really
empirical theories within psychology. The first was his belief that environment is much more important than heredity in the determination of behavior. This was a natural concomitant of his methodology,
for the external influences on an organism's behavior are relatively
easily observable and manipulable, whereas the internal influences
(in particular, the genes) are much more difficult to discover and manipulate (though new technical possibilities have opened up since
Watson's time). These differences do not rule out the influence of
heredity on behavior, but Watson assumed that the only inherited features of behavior were simple physiological reflexes; he attributed
everything else to learning. Hence his claim (which he admitted went
beyond the known facts):

> Give me a dozen healthy infants, well-formed, and my own specified
> world to bring them up in and I'll guarantee to take any one at ran-
> dom and train him to become any kind of specialist I might select—

doctor, lawyer, artist, merchant-chief, and yes even beggar-man and thief, regardless of his talents, penchants, abilities, vocations, and race of his ancestors. (*Behaviorism*, 1924, rev. ed. 1930, p. 104)

He hoped that psychology could show us how to *affect* (and even control) human behavior (e.g., in advertising, the field in which he later made his living, after leaving his academic position).

Watson's other empirical guess was a particular theory of how learning takes place, namely by the conditioning of reflexes. This was suggested by Pavlov's famous experiments in which dogs were trained to salivate at the sound of a bell by regular ringing of a bell just before feeding them. Watson's research program sought to explain all the complex behavior of animals and men as the result of such conditioning by their environment.

Work in experimental psychology since Watson's time has cast doubt both on his extreme emphasis on environment and on his particular theory of learning by the conditioning of reflexes. However, B. F. Skinner (1904–1990), who was Professor of Psychology at Harvard University from 1948 to 1974, took the behaviorist program to new standards of technical exactness and became one of the most influential experimental psychologists of his generation. He also wrote in quite a readable, stylish manner for a wider public, offering diagnoses of social problems and suggestions for how to solve them. We will thus find plenty to discuss without being drawn into the more technical details of his experimental work. The behavioral psychology of which Skinner was a foremost representative dominated academic psychology, at least in the English-speaking world, in the middle of the twentieth century, but in recent years it has been largely superseded by cognitive psychology.

The Behavior of Organisms: An Experimental Analysis (1938) was Skinner's fundamental technical work on conditioning. He tried to apply his theories to human life and society in *Science and Human Behavior* (1953), and to human language in particular in *Verbal Behavior* (1957). He wrote a novel, *Walden Two* (1948), in which he describes a utopian community organized on his principles of behavioral conditioning. And he later produced another would-be popular book with the sinister-sounding title *Beyond Freedom and Dignity* (1971) in which he claimed again that a technology of behavior could solve the problems of human life and society, if only people would give up their illusions about individual free will, responsibility for action, and dignity. In what follows I make page references to Skinner's *Science and Human Behavior*, which is the most wide-ranging and perhaps the most readable of these works.

Background Theoretical Assumptions

Skinner has enormous faith in science; he would have probably liked to represent himself as the most rigorously "scientific" of all the thinkers considered in this book. He believed that only science can tell us the truth about nature, including human nature, and he made audacious claims for the potential of science to solve human problems. When he writes, "It is possible that science has come to the rescue and that order will eventually be achieved in the field of human affairs" (p. 5), one hears modern echoes of two themes from Plato— the yearning for "order" and the hope that a special kind of knowledge will enable us (or rather, the elite subgroup who can attain it) to reorganize human society (perhaps even to *impose* "order"). Skinner carried on with the main lines of Watson's behaviorism, sticking rigorously to the methodology, eschewing all appeal to unobservable entities in psychological explanation. He retained faith in the program of explaining all the behavior of animals and humans in terms of their past and present environment, mediated by a few basic mechanisms of conditioning.

In trying to support these huge claims, Skinner remarks that science is unique in human activity in showing cumulative progress (p. 11). What is fundamental to science is neither instruments nor measurement but scientific *method*—the disposition to get at the facts, whether expected or surprising, pleasant or repugnant. All statements must be submitted to the test of observation or experiment, and where there is insufficient evidence we must admit our ignorance. The scientist tries to find uniformities or lawful relations between phenomena and to construct general theories that will successfully explain all particular cases (pp. 13–14). Furthermore, Skinner sees no clear distinction between science and technology; he says that the job of science is not just to predict but to *control* the world.

Most scientists and philosophers of science would find little to quarrel with in Skinner's brief outline of scientific method, though many might want to make a clearer distinction between science and technology, prediction and control. But some scientists are Christians, while others are humanists, some are left-wing and others right-wing. Skinner seems to think that there is no basis except in science for *any* sort of belief. He finds no scientific basis for belief in God and treats religion as merely one of the social institutions for manipulating human behavior (pp. 350–58). Value judgments are, he thinks, typically an expression of the pressure to conform that is exerted by any social group (pp. 415–18), a kind of concealed command (p. 429). They can be given an objective scientific basis if they concern means to ends. "You ought to take an umbrella" can be roughly translated as "You want to keep dry, umbrellas keep you dry in the rain, and it's going to rain" (though Skinner proposes to replace the ordinary notion of "want" or "desire" by his supposedly more scientific notion of "reinforcement"). The only objective basis he can see for evaluating cultural practices as a whole is their survival value for the culture (pp. 430–36). But even here he says that we do not really *choose* survival as a basic value; it is just that our past has so conditioned us that we do tend to seek the survival of our culture.

Skinner is an extreme example of the tendency to think that *all* questions—even those about human nature and about what is worth doing or striving for—can be answered purely scientifically, insofar as they are genuine questions at all. "Scientism" is a convenient label for this position, but it is, of course, an extremely controversial *philosophical* view; it is not itself a scientific theory, and certainly not something that can be tested by observable evidence.

Theory of Human Nature

Skinner proposes that the empirical, scientific study of human *behavior* is the only way to arrive at a true theory of human nature. Science, he says, is a search for order, for lawful relations among the events in nature:

> We are concerned, then, with the causes of human behavior. We want to know why men behave as they do. Any condition or event which

can be shown to have an effect upon behavior must be taken into account. By discovering and analysing these causes we can predict behavior; to the extent that we can manipulate them, we can control behavior. (p. 23)

What then, are the causes of human behavior? Skinner firmly rejects all attempts to explain what we do in terms of "inner" mental entities. He admits the possibility of discovering physiological preconditions of behavior (the literally "inner" states inside the body, especially the brain). One day we shall know, he suggests, the precise neurological conditions that immediately precede, e.g., the response "No, thank you" (p. 28). But he claims that even when the progress of physiology tells us about brain states in immense detail, we shall still have to trace *their* causation back to the environment, so we may as well bypass the physiology and look directly for the environmental causes of behavior: "the objection to inner states is not that they do not exist, but that they are not relevant in a functional analysis" (p. 35). Skinner thus takes it that for any given bit of behavior, although there must be some physiological cause—a total state of the body at the time—there must also be some preceding set of environmental conditions (whether in the present, the immediate past, or the longer-term history of conditioning of that individual) that is the cause of that inner bodily state. So we should in principle be able to cut out the middleman here and state general causal laws that connect the relevant environmental conditions with that type of behavior.

Skinner is hostile to all attempts to explain human behavior in terms of mental entities, whether everyday concepts of beliefs, desires, emotions, intentions or decisions, or more theoretical postulates such as unconscious cognitive states and processes, or the Freudian id, ego, and superego (pp. 29–30). He rejects such mental entities not only because they are unobservable but because he thinks they can never be of any explanatory value, anyway. In his view, to say that a man eats because he is hungry is not to assign a cause to his behavior but simply to redescribe it (p. 31). It is no more explanatory than saying that opium puts you to sleep *because* it has a "dormitive power" or that Jill tells good jokes *because* she has "a sense of humor."

Skinner has to admit that genetic factors are relevant, for it is obvious that different animal species behave in very different ways. And among humans, it is pretty obvious to common sense that different individuals are born with different innate capacities, e.g., for mathematics, music, and art. But Skinner dismisses the layman's use of "heredity" as a purely fictional explanation of behavior, and he says that genetic factors are of little value in "experimental analysis" because they cannot be manipulated by the experimenter (p. 26).

Skinner's account of basic human nature is a potentially confusing combination of methodological precept and empirical theory, both derived from Watson's behaviorism. We must try to sort out the different components in the mixture. Obviously, he defines psychology as the study of behavior—that is the basic methodological point. We must ask, however, what exactly "behavior" means in the case of human beings. But let us first note that saying that behavior constitutes the observable *data* for psychology does not settle whether psychologists may postulate unobservable entities to *explain* the data.

Most psychologists, before and after the heyday of behaviorism in the mid-twentieth century, have been quite happy to talk in terms of drives, emotions, memory (short term and long term), and many other "mental" entities. Skinner adopted a very austere methodology, rejecting all mention of unobservables in explanation. In that respect he was trying to be more "scientific" than most scientists and philosophers of science, for the physical sciences typically postulate theoretical entities such as magnetic fields, mechanical forces, and subatomic particles. Some philosophers, influenced by logical positivism, have doubted whether this was really proper procedure and proposed "instrumentalist" or "operationalist" interpretations of theoretical entities in science, but it is now generally acknowledged that this is an implausible restriction on scientific method. Provided that what is said about unobservable entities is testable by observation, there is no objection to them in principle. So if Skinner rejects mental causes of behavior *just* because they are unobservable, we must judge this to be an unnecessarily restrictive methodology for any science, including psychology.

However, he does offer another reason for rejecting what he calls "conceptual" inner causes for behavior (p. 31), namely, that they are of no explanatory value. He seems to think that there is something *especially* unexplanatory about unobservable entities in psychology, as putative mental causes of behavior. But has he shown that such conceptual inner causes must be merely redescriptive of what they are supposed to explain? All he does is give a few examples in which he thinks this to be true and invite the reader to generalize from them. Certainly, an inner state S can be a genuine explanation of behavior B only if we can have some evidence for the existence of S other than the occurrence of B—but surely this condition is sometimes satisfied. For instance (in Skinner's own example), we can have good evidence for saying that someone is hungry even though he is not *actually* eating, if we know that he has not eaten for twenty-four hours (perhaps he even *says* he is hungry!). It is just not true that a single set of facts is described by the two statements: "He eats" and "He is hungry." As Plato noticed, Reason can conflict with Appetite: one can be hungry but not eat even when food is presented, and one can eat when one is not hungry (e.g., out of politeness). Skinner has not given adequate reason for the rejection of all conceptual causes of behavior.

What of his rejection of physiological states as causes? The fact that these are not easily observable or manipulable does nothing to show that they do not play a crucial role in the causation of behavior. Skinner assumes that physiological states inside an organism merely mediate the effect of its environment (past and present) on its behavior. So he thinks that psychology can confine its attention to the laws that connect environmental influences directly with behavior. But is this true of animals, or even of complex inanimate systems like computers, let alone of human beings? What a computer does in reaction to a certain key stroke typically depends on what internal state it is in at the time—there are no universal laws connecting single keystrokes with what comes up on the screen, without taking into account the present inner state. Skinner would presumably say that it is the whole past history of key strokes that have caused the computer to go into whatever inner state it is in now, so there must surely be laws connecting this total history with its present state. But we can reply that: (a) for any such complete explanation we will also have to take into account the programming of the computer—the software, and perhaps also features of the hardware, such as breakdown and replacement of components; (b) in practice, it is much simpler, and gives a much more readily available explanation of the computer's reaction to a keystroke, to appeal to present inner states such as "a certain portion of text has been selected."

Skinner makes two separable assumptions here: first, that human behavior is governed by scientific laws of *some* kind: "If we are to use the methods of science in the field of human affairs, we must assume that behavior is lawful and determined" (pp. 6, 447), second, that these laws state causal connections between *environmental* factors and human behavior: "Our 'independent variables'—the causes of behavior—are the external conditions of which behavior is a function" (p. 35). These two assumptions could be taken in a purely methodological interpretation, as expressing a program of *looking* for laws governing human behavior and specifically for laws connecting environment with behavior. As such, there can be no decisive objection to them. But it is fairly clear that Skinner also takes them as general claims about what is actually the case. As such, we must ask whether there is any good reason to think that they are true, for these are the crucial assumptions on which Skinner's theory of human nature is based.

First, do we have to assume that *all* human behavior is governed by causal laws if we are to study that behavior scientifically? There is no more reason to assume this than there is for Marx to maintain that if we are to study history scientifically, there must be laws that determine the detail of everything which happens. Universal determinism is not a necessary presupposition of scientific knowledge (*pace* Kant!), although the *search* for causal laws is central to science. Admittedly, it would be rather disappointing if psychology could not proceed beyond the mere reporting of statistical regularities. But how far there are strict causal laws governing behavior is something that we must leave psychology to discover empirically. That *all* behavior is governed by such laws is a metaphysical assumption that ill befits a supposedly strict empiricist such as Skinner.

The more specific assumption that all behavior is a function of *environmental* variables is even more dubious. What it means, in detail, is that for any piece of behavior, there is a finite set of environmental conditions (past or present) such that it is a causal law that anyone to whom all those conditions apply will perform that behavior. This is reminiscent of Watson's claim that he could take any infant and make of it anything he liked, given an appropriate environment and denies that inherited factors make any significant difference to the behavior of human beings. So any healthy child could be trained to become a four-minute miler, a nuclear physicist, or anything else? In its full generality, the claim is obviously false. The fact that the differences in ability between identical twins brought up apart are much less than the average range of ability in the whole population is clear evidence against it. Heredity does play *some* part, though this is not to deny the huge importance of environment. To attribute all or most differences to the environment is another empirical assumption that Skinner does not submit to empirical test.

We should now pay some brief attention to the specific mechanisms of conditioning by which Skinner thinks the environment controls behavior. Although his theory is descended from the ideas of Pavlov and Watson, this is the area in which Skinner made his own contributions to the advancement of detailed psychological knowledge. In the "classical" conditioning of Pavlov's experiments, the "reinforcer" (food) is repeatedly presented together with a "stimulus" (the ringing of a bell), and the "response" (salivation) then appears for the bell without the food. The main difference in Skinner's "operant" conditioning is that what is conditioned is not a reflex response like salivation but any kind of behavior that the animal may perform quite spontaneously, without any particular stimulus. For instance, rats can be trained to press levers, and pigeons to hold their heads abnormally high, in each case simply by feeding the animal whenever it happens to press the lever or to raise its head above a certain level. When the environment is arranged so that the reinforcer follows a certain kind of behavior (which Skinner called the "operant," because the animal thus operates on its environment), then that behavior will be performed more frequently (pp. 62–66). (This is, of course, the general principle on which most animal training works.) By careful experimental work, Skinner and his followers discovered many new details about the effectiveness of various processes of conditioning ("schedules of reinforcement," in the jargon). For instance, intermittent reinforcement tends to produce a greater rate of response, so if we want a rat to do as much lever-pressing as possible, we should feed it irregularly, not after every press.

Skinner's experimental work on animals (mainly with rats and pigeons) in artificial laboratory conditions is impressive, and may be unimpugnable except by specialists in that sort of work, but what we can and must criticize is his extrapolation from it to human nature in general. In Section 2 of *Science and Human Behavior* he outlines the understanding of behavior that he gained from his animal experiments. He then goes on, in Section 3, to apply this understanding to individual human beings and, in Sections 4 through 6, to human groups and institutions such as government, religion, psychotherapy, economics, and education. But the whole method of inference is highly questionable. It may well be that Skinner's discoveries about rats and pigeons apply only to those animals (and to closely related species) but not to human beings. Or it might be that Skinner has identified some conditioning mechanisms that apply to animals (including us) but that he ignored all sorts of *other* ways in which behavior can be produced or affected, even in pigeons and rats, let alone in humans. Although he rightly points out that we cannot assume that human behavior is different in kind from animal behavior (pp. 38–39), his whole approach seems to make the equally unjustified assumption that what applies to laboratory animals will apply (with only a difference of complexity) to human beings (pp. 205 ff.).

One especially important area in which Skinner attempted to apply his theories to distinctively human behavior is our use of language. In his book *Verbal Behavior*, he proposed to show that all human speech can be explained in terms of the conditioning of speakers by their environment (including as the crucial elements in this case their early social environments, the noises made by surrounding humans, and the reactions made to noises emitted by them as children). Thus, a baby born in a Spanish-speaking family and culture is subjected to many samples of the Spanish language in use. Skinner suggests that when its responses are reasonably accurate reproductions of what it has heard, they are "reinforced" by approval and reward, and thus the child learns to speak Spanish. Adult speech, too, is analyzed by Skinner as a series of responses to stimuli from the environment, including verbal stimuli from other people.

The crucial defects in Skinner's account of language have been pointed out by Noam Chomsky, whose work has given new direction to research in linguistics and psychology since the 1960s. Chomsky argues that, although Skinner has tried to describe *how* language is learned, his account is of little value because he pays no attention to the question of *what* it is that we learn when we acquire the ability to speak a language as our native tongue. Clearly, we can hardly ask how we learn X unless we first know what X is: we must have a criterion for someone having *succeeded* in learning X. Human language is a very different sort of phenomenon from rats pressing levers or pigeons raising their heads to peck. Skinner can hardly deny this, but he would suggest that the differences are only a matter of degree of complexity. Chomsky suggests that the *creative* and *structural* features of human language—the way in which we can all speak and understand sentences we have never heard before, just by our knowledge of the vocabulary and grammar of our language—make it quite different in kind from any known animal behavior. If so, the attempt to analyze human speech in terms derived from the behavior of lower animals appears to be doomed from the start. And the same may well apply to other distinctively human forms of behavior.

Even the suggestions Skinner does make for how linguistic behavior is learned can be seen to be based on very shaky analogies. For instance, the "reinforcement" that may encourage correct speech by an infant is not feeding but is usually some sort of social approval. He suggests that we can be "reinforced" by having attention paid to us—or even by merely saying something that is satisfying to ourselves, perhaps just because it is an accurate reproduction of what we have heard. But this is merely speculation. The use of a term like "reinforcement," which has a strictly defined meaning for certain experiments with animals—it usually means the satisfaction of an obvious biological desire, such as food or sex—in no way guarantees scientific objectivity for its use in allegedly analogous human situations. Once again, Skinner's supposedly strictly empirical approach turns out to conceal a large element of unempirical speculation.

There is another important respect in which Chomsky argues that Skinner's theories fall down when applied to human language. This is the matter of inherited factors, the contribution made by the speaker rather than by the environment to the learning of language. Obviously, French children learn French, and Chinese children learn Chinese, so the social environment does have a major effect. But again, all normal human children learn one of the human languages, while no other animal learns anything that resembles human languages in the crucial respect of forming an indefinite number of complex sentences according to rules of grammar (not even the chimpanzees who allegedly have been taught a sign system). So it seems that the capacity to learn a language is peculiar to the human species.

Skinner holds that our language learning must be due to a complex set of reinforcements from our human environment. Chomsky argues that the amazing speed with which children learn the grammatical rules of the language they hear from a very limited and imperfect sample of that language can be explained only by the assumption that there is in the human species an *innate* capacity to process language according to such rules. So, behind all the apparent variety of human languages, there must be a certain basic systematic structure common to all, and we must suppose that we do not *learn* this structure from our environment but process whatever linguistic stimulation we receive in terms of this structure. This fascinating hypothesis, rather than Skinner's extreme environmentalism, has been supported by increasing evidence.

Speech is not the only human activity. But it is especially important as a representative of the "higher" human mental abilities (it is the manifestation of the faculty of understanding and reasoning that Plato and Kant emphasized). So if Skinner's theories fail to explain language adequately, we must conclude that, even if they explain some features of human behavior, they cannot give an adequate account of human nature in general. There remains the possibility that other important aspects of human behavior are not learned from the environment but are primarily innate (see Chapter 11).

Diagnosis

Skinner's diagnosis can be seen as the exact opposite of Sartre's. As we saw in Chapter 9, Sartre maintains that we are free but that we keep pretending that we are not. Skinner says we are determined but still like to think that we are free. He claims that our current social practices are based on theoretical confusion. We increasingly realize how environment determines behavior, and hence we exonerate people from blame by pointing to all the circumstances that have influenced them—their upbringing, schooling, their culture generally. Yet we also tend to maintain that individual people are still responsible for their actions—we blame criminals and say that they deserve punishment. Skinner claims that we are thus in an unstable transitional stage and, moreover, that "the present unhappy condition of the world may in large measure be traced to our vacillation"; "we shall almost certainly remain ineffective in solving these problems until we adopt a consistent point of view" (p. 9). "A sweeping revision of the concept of responsibility is needed" (p. 241), for our present practice of punishment is remarkably inefficient in controlling behavior (p. 342). "We will have to abandon the illusion that human beings are free agents, in control of their own behavior, for whether we like it or not we are all 'controlled' " (p. 438).

This sweeping diagnosis of "the unhappy condition of the world" seems very dubious. Admittedly, there are important practical and ethical problems about deciding the extent of responsibility, and these are closely connected with deep theoretical and philosophical questions about the concept of freedom. But Skinner's dismissal of the concept is an inadequate and unargued response to these problems. In *Beyond Freedom and Dignity*, he seems to be saying that just as it was the mistake of animism to treat inanimate things as if they were people and to attribute thoughts and intentions to them, so it is a mistake to treat *people* as people and attribute desires and decisions to them! This is surely absurd.

One first move toward getting out of this confusion is as follows. The thesis of universal determinism is that every event (including all human choices) has a set of sufficient preceding causes. Even if this thesis is true—and remember that Skinner has given us no reason to believe it—we are not precluded from picking out as "free" those human actions that include among their causes the *choice* of the person. The concept of a free action surely does not imply that the action has no causes at all (that would make it random, and hence hardly attributable to its "agent"), but instead suggests that it is caused by the agent's choice. We might still hold people responsible for the actions they choose, even if we think that those choices themselves have causes. Skinner himself seems to believe it important to use methods of social control that depend on individual awareness and hence choice in some sense of the word, rather than concealed, sub-liminal forms of conditioning of which people are not aware. Free will remains a source of deeper philosophical perplexity, however.

Prescription

Like Marx, Skinner holds that human circumstances can and should be humanly formed. If it is the social environment that largely makes us what we are, that produces the most important individual and cultural differences, then we should 'change the social environment deliberately so that the human product will meet more acceptable specifications' (p. 427). Skinner claimed that psychology has reached the point where it can offer techniques for the manipulation and control of human behavior and hence for changing human society, for better or for worse (p. 437). If we will only give up the "illusions" of individual freedom and dignity, we can create a happier life by conditioning everyone's behavior in appropriate ways. For instance, we would cease the inefficient practice of punishment and instead induce people to act morally and legally by making them *want* to conform to the standards of society (p. 345). This can be done by a combination of education and positive inducements ("reinforcement"), not necessarily by propaganda or concealed manipulation. Thus, science could lead to the design of a government that will really promote the well-being of the governed, and perhaps even to a set of "moral values" (which Skinner fastidiously puts in quotation marks!) that may be generally accepted. Provided that control is diversified between different individuals and institutions, there need be no danger of despotism (pp. 440–46).

This vague program sounds naively optimistic, and yet somewhat worrying in its jaunty dismissal of individual freedom. What Skinner has in mind comes out a bit more clearly in his less-than-riveting novel *Walden Two*, in which his ideal community combines the culture-vulture atmosphere of an adult-education summer school with the political system of Plato's *Republic* (for there is a wise designer of the community who has arranged everything along "correct" behaviorist principles from the start).

Skinner's utopia is open to the same objections as Plato's. On what basis are the designers of a culture to decide what is best for everyone? And how can misuse of their power be prevented? Despite his mention of safeguards against despotism, Skinner seems politically naive. His very terminology of "designing a culture" and "the human product" suggests that he makes the highly questionable assumption that it should be the aim of politics to produce an ideal kind of society and individual. But an important alternative view is that the aim should be understood in more limited, indeed, negative terms—namely, to eliminate specific causes of human unhappiness such as poverty, disease, and perceived injustice—and that to try to produce people according to some blueprint is to trespass on what should be the area of individual choice. (This is the distinction that Popper made, in his criticisms of Plato and Marx, between "utopian" and "piecemeal" social engineering.)

So we do not have to accept Skinner's judgment that individual freedom is a myth and therefore not important. There are immediate practical issues involved here, for behavior therapy based on Skinnerian principles of conditioning has been applied to neurotics and criminals. But in cases of behavior that is judged "abnormal" or "deviant" by some criterion, when (if ever) does anyone have the right to condition someone else's behavior? As we have seen in Chapter 6 on Kant, there are deep problems—factual, conceptual, and ethical—with how the purely scientific approach to people, as organisms whose behavior has identifiable and manipulable causes, can be combined with our ordinary treatment of each other as rational beings who are responsible for our actions. Skinner assumes that the two are simply incompatible and that the latter must give way to the former. But this is just the dogmatic position taken by one particular psychologist in the heyday of behaviorism. (Chomsky has taken a very different attitude to social and political issues, based on a passionate concern for the freedom of individuals and groups; the differences between these two theorists thus extends beyond academic theory to practical politics.)

It would be a pity if the failings of Skinner's overambitious and—let's face it—somewhat amateurish generalizations about human nature discouraged us from seeking better understanding of ourselves from empirical psychology. In Chapter 11 I examine a different type of approach, and in the concluding chapter I essay a more general review of prospects.

For Further Reading

Two wide-ranging, thought-provoking histories of psychology are G. A. Millar and R. Buckout, *Psychology: The Science of Mental Life*, 2d ed. (New York: Harper & Row, 1973; London: Penguin, 1966), which concentrates on the twentieth century; and L. S. Hearnshaw, *The Shaping of Modern Psychology: An Historical Introduction* (London: Routledge, 1987), which covers the whole story since ancient times. In *Behaviour* (London: Methuen, 1961), D. E. Broadbent reviewed the progress of the behaviorist movement in psychology.

The main text referred to in this chapter is B. F. Skinner, *Science and Human Behavior* (New York: Macmillan, 1953).

Skinner's utopian novel *Walden Two* (New York: Macmillan, 1953) and his *Beyond Freedom and Dignity* (New York: Bantam Books, 1972; London: Penguin, 1973) outline his ideal society and the means by which he thought we could achieve it.

Beyond the Punitive Society: Operant Conditioning and Political Aspects, ed. by Harvey Wheeler (London: Wildwood House, 1973) is a collection of critical essays on Skinner's social program.

For an introduction to Chomsky's theories, see his *Language and Mind*, enlarged ed. (New York: Harcourt Brace Jovanovich, 1972; J. Lyons, *Chomsky* (New York: Viking, 1970; London: Fontana, 1970, Modern Masters series). Steven Pinker gives a lively survey of recent developments in *The Language Instinct: The New Science of Language and Mind* (New York: Morrow, 1994; London: Penguin, 1995).

11

Evolutionary Psychology: Lorenz on Aggression

I have criticized the behaviorists for neglecting the possibility that certain important features of behavior are innate in the species rather than learned from experience. I now turn to Konrad Lorenz (1903–1989), who offers a diagnosis of human social problems based on precisely this claim. Lorenz was one of the founding fathers of the branch of biology called "ethology." Etymologically, the term means the study of character, but it has come to stand for one particular tradition in the scientific study of animal behavior.

We have seen that the behaviorists were committed to wide-ranging empirical assumptions that behavior is caused almost entirely by environmental influences mediated through conditioning mechanisms, and their experiments studied how artificial laboratory environments can *modify* behavior. The early ethologists realized that many animal behavior patterns could not be explained in the behaviorist way. What was distinctive of much behavior was that it was innate or *fixed*; it could not be eliminated or significantly modified, however much the environment was experimentally manipulated. The ethologists concentrated on these "instinctual" behavior patterns and thought it important carefully to observe the behavior of animals in their natural environment before intervening to perform experiments. To explain such innate behavior, ethologists appeal not to the past experience of the *individual* animal but to the process of evolution, which has given rise to the *species*. To account for the presence of an instinctive behavior pattern in a species, we must say what survival value it has for the genes that contribute to that behavior. Ethology is based, more directly than behaviorist psychology, on evolution. This, therefore, seems the appropriate place to sketch the essentials of the Darwinian theory of evolution, which no adequate theory of human nature can neglect.

Background Theory: Evolution

After a long period of observation and thought, Darwin arrived at his world-shaking theory of evolution, first published in his *Origin of Species* in 1859. The full title of that book is *The Origin of Species by Means of Natural Selection: or the Preservation of Favored Races in the Struggle of Life*, which effectively summarizes its key idea—the gradual divergence of different species from common ancestors by natural selection. The *Origin* was written for the general educated public, and it documents the main argument with an immense wealth of detailed empirical evidence, which Darwin had accumulated from his research over the previous twenty years. Being a cautious character, well aware of the revolutionary implications of his theory, Darwin did not at first state that human beings are also descended from animal ancestors—but this obvious entailment aroused intense controversy, whose reverberations continue even now. In later books, *The Descent of Man* (1871) and *The Expression of the Emotions in Man and Animals* (1872), Darwin explicitly applied his theories to humans. *The Expression of the Emotions*, as its title suggests, was a pioneering work in ethology.

Darwin's theory is in essence an elegant logical deduction from four empirical generalizations. The first two concern matters of genetics:

1. that there is variation in the traits of individuals of a given species, and

2. that traits of parents tend in general to be passed on to their offspring.

These two truths emerge from a wide variety of observations, and
they had long been utilized in the breeding of new varieties of domestic animals and plants. Their theoretical explanation was first offered in Mendel's theory of genes, and the biochemical basis of
genetics in the DNA molecule was elucidated in the early 1950s. The
remaining premises of Darwin's argument are these:

3. that species are in principle capable of a geometric rate of increase of population, whereas

4. the resources of the environment typically cannot support such
an increase.

It follows from (3) and (4) that a very small proportion of seeds,
eggs, and young reach maturity, so there is competition for survival
and reproduction, primarily between members of the same species.
From the inevitablity of such competition, and from (1) variation
within a species, we can deduce that there will be certain individuals (those whose characteristics are "fittest" in the given environment) that will have the best chance of living long enough to
reproduce and leave offspring; therefore, given (2) the fact of inheritance, their traits will tend to be passed on, and less advantageous
traits will tend to die out. Thus, over many generations the typical
characteristics of a population of animals can change. So, given the
immensity of geological time (first confirmed by the geologists of
the early nineteenth century), and the distribution of plants and animals throughout the wide variety of environments around the world,
different species can thus evolve from common ancestors. All that is
needed is the constant pressure of natural selection acting on the vari-
ations caused by random mutations. There is no need to postulate the
biologically implausible inheritance of "acquired" characteristics that
Lamarck had suggested (though Darwin himself muddied the clarity
of his theory by appealing to this idea in some stages of his work).

Apart from this very general argument for the mechanism of evolution, there is much direct empirical evidence for our common ancestry with other animals. Comparative anatomy shows the human

body to have the same general plan as other vertebrates—e.g., four limbs with five digits on each. The human embryo goes through stages of development in which it resembles those of the various lower forms of life. In the adult human body there are "remnants" of such lower forms—e.g., a vestigial tail. The chemistry of our bodies—e.g., blood, proteins, genes—is similar to that of other creatures. Finally, we are discovering more and more fossil remains of creatures that were ape-like but resembled humans more than any existing apes. So our animal ancestry is overwhelmingly confirmed by the evidence. Interesting scientific questions remain about the detailed mechanism of evolution in general, and about human origins in particular, but that human beings have evolved from more primitive ancestors is now as well established a fact as anything else in science.

Admittedly, some religious believers (especially fundamentalist Christians in the United States) have reopened nineteenth-century debates about human evolution. The very fact that it is thus contested is interesting, for it shows just how difficult it is to maintain scientific objectivity when discussing human nature. As noted in Chapter 1, those with firmly rooted religious or political beliefs will not be ready to change them just because some scientific theory goes against them; they will typically challenge the scientific evidence and its interpretation. Of course, one cannot adequately answer the creationists' assertions just by diagnosing ideological motives behind them—that would be to put oneself in danger of maintaining Darwinian theory as a "closed system" in just the way we condemned in Chapter 1. What needs to be done is to consider each of their objections to evolutionary theory in detail and to show that in the light of all available evidence it does not stand up. But this is hardly the place to do that (the job has been effectively done by Philip Kitcher).

I would not want to suggest that evolutionary theory is without problems: no scientific theory can enjoy complete certainty, and the history of science shows that all theories develop and change. But, as I understand it, there is no serious present competitor to a basically Darwinian story about human evolution. Any adequate understanding of human nature must therefore take our evolutionary origin into account. What I have in mind here is not just that we must admit this (as many Christian theologians have done for more than a century) but that we must reckon with the possibility that our evolution may *explain* much about human nature.

But exactly what the implications of the theory of evolution are for our understanding of contemporary human nature, society, and culture is a matter of deep religious, philosophical, and political dispute that cannot be settled by the scientific theory itself. Marx welcomed Darwin's theory, taking it as a confirmation of his view of the progressive development of human history but perhaps not appreciating that biological evolution is something different in kind from economic and cultural change. (Marx even wanted to dedicate the English edition of *Das Kapital* to Darwin, but the latter, with typical caution, politely declined the honor.) On the other side of politics, right-wing thinkers such as Sumner have claimed that unrestrained economic competition is as "natural" as survival of the fittest in the evolution of speces, and therefore right (such doctrine was called "social Darwinism").

Among scientists and social theorists, and Christians who accept evolution, there remains plenty of controversy about how far our evolutionary origin can explain our present condition and our problems. In the 1960s and 70s several best-selling books were based on the idea that our evolution from ape-like ancestors is the key to our true nature: examples are Robert Ardrey's *The Territorial Imperative*, and Desmond Morris's *The Naked Ape*. (In his own amateur way, Arthur Koestler in *The Ghost in the Machine* offered his diagnosis that something has gone wrong in our brains in the process of human evolution.) Since Edward O. Wilson's work in the 1970s, there has been a veritable explosion of evolution-based theorizing about human nature, but I cannot review all this theorizing here. I propose to concentrate on the particular case of Konrad Lorenz, one of the pioneers of this approach, in the hope that a critical examination of his controversial ideas will help us look at more recent work with a sympathetic but skeptical eye.

Lorenz's Theory of Animal Nature

Like Freud, Konrad Lorenz was a product of the great scientific and cultural traditions of Vienna. He pioneered a new area of scientific study, which he also saw as having deep implications for mankind. The allegation that he applied for Nazi Party membership in the early years of that movement should make us look critically at his assertions about human affairs (as, of course, we should about any such assertions)—but it does not entitle us to reject them without a hearing. In World War II Lorenz had a dramatically mixed career—appointed as the last of Kant's successors in a professorial chair in Königsberg, he was absorbed into the German army as a doctor and, in defeat, taken prisoner by the Russians. When he was allowed to return to Austria, he resumed his scientific profession and rose to international fame. In his technical papers on animal behavior, he reported and interpreted his extensive and careful observations of many species, and some of the concepts he introduced passed into the common currency of biological science, at least in his own generation. He was awarded a Nobel Prize for his ethological work.

Lorenz also wote for the general reader, and in *King Solomon's Ring* (1950), *Man Meets Dog* (1954), and *On Aggression* (1963), he displays style, a sense of humor, an engaging personality, an awareness of deep issues in philosophy, human psychology, and sociology, and a certain missionary zeal to apply his expertise to human problems. The first two books introduce ethological themes by a variety of anecdotal descriptions, in many cases of pets Lorenz himself kept. He was a great reader of German philosophy and literature and could quote Kant and Goethe as readily as the latest technical papers in biology. In *Behind the Mirror: a Search for a Natural History of Human Knowledge* (1973) he applied his biological approach to philosophical questions, relating his ideas to some of Kant's and sketching a kind of "evolutionary epistemology" that has since been developed by philosophers and cognitive scientists. He promised a second volume in which he would offer a fundamental diagnosis of social and cultural problems, but he did not live to complete it. *On Aggression* describes patterns of aggressive behavior in many animal species and offers a diagnosis of human problems that stem from our supposedly innate aggressive tendencies. I concentrate on this book here, first expounding its main arguments, then criticizing them.

Lorenz was a biological scientist, so the most important of his background assumptions is the theory of evolution. To explain the existence of any particular organ or behavior pattern, he looks for its survival value for the species. As an ethologist, he introduced the two important concepts of a fixed action pattern and an innate releasing mechanism. There are certain patterns of movement that are typical of each species and that seem clearly to be innate. Often they are performed in response to certain specific kind of stimuli, but only when the animal is in a certain kind of state, e.g., hungry, frightened, or sexually excited. The behavior thus seems to be caused by the combination of external stimulus and internal state.

Lorenz holds that there are many such patterns of animal behavior that are "hereditary co-ordinations" or "instinct movements"; they are innate rather than learned, and for each there is a "drive" that causes the behavior to appear spontaneously. But he also suggests, somewhat vaguely and tentatively, that such fixed action patterns are often at the disposal of one or more of the "four big drives"— feeding, reproduction, flight, and fighting or aggression. He says that any one piece of behavior is usually caused by at least two drives or inner causes and that conflict between independent impulses can give firmness to the whole organism, like a balance of power within a political system (*On Aggression*, Ch. 6).

Lorenz believes that what he picks out as aggressive behavior is instinctive, powered by one of the major drives. He is concerned not with all behavior that might at first sight be called "aggressive," however, but with fighting and threats between members of the *same* species. The attacks of predators on prey, and the self-defense of a cornered animal, including the mobbing of predators by potential prey, do not count as aggression for him. Concentrating on intraspecies aggression, he asks what its species-preserving function can be and comes up with several answers. It can spread out the individuals of a species over the available territory, so that there is enough food for each. On a coral reef, each kind of fish has its own peculiar source of food, and each individual will defend its "territory" against members of the same species, although it tolerates fish of other species. Second, aggression between rival males of a species ensures that the strongest individuals leave offspring and are available for defense of family and herd. Last, aggression can serve to establish and maintain a "pecking order" or hierarchy in an animal community, which can be beneficial in that the oldest and most experienced animals can lead the group and pass on what they have learned (Ch. 2).

But how can intraspecies aggression have such survival value without leading to injury and death, which obviously contradict survival? The remarkable fact is that despite the ubiquity of aggression among vertebrate animals, it is rare for an animal to be killed or seriously injured in the wild by members of its own species. Much aggressive behavior takes the form of threats or pursuits, rather than actual physical combat. Lorenz argues that evolution has produced a "ritualization" of fighting so that it can produce biological advantages without actually causing injury. Especially in heavily armored animals, which must cooperate for breeding and perhaps for hunting, there is a need for a mechanism by which aggression can be inhibited. So typically there is an appeasement gesture or ritual submission by which one animal can inhibit the aggression of another. Beaten dogs, for instance, offer their vulnerable neck to the jaws of their opponent, and this seems to activate some specific inhibition mechanism, for it is as if the victor cannot then bring himself to administer a fatal bite, he just seems to accept that victory has been conceded (Ch. 7).

According to Lorenz, there is an innate drive for intraspecies aggression, with its own unique store of energy and its own innate releasing mechanisms. What he offers here can be described as a hydraulic model for explaining innate behavior. When pressure builds up in an internal system (rather like water in a toilet-cistern or, indeed, like pressure increasing in the bladder), the threshold for the relevant behavior is reduced, and the behavior may be "released" by a small stimulus. In extreme cases, it may "overflow" with no external stimulus. The fixed action patterns sometimes occur spontaneously, as if driven by causes within the animal itself. Thus, a male dove deprived of its mate will begin to perform its courtship dance to a stuffed pigeon, a piece of cloth, or even the empty corner of its cage, and a hand-reared starling that has never caught flies or seen any other bird do so will go through fly-catching movements even when no flies are present (Ch. 4).

Theory of Human Nature

Lorenz sees human beings as one particular animal species that has evolved from others. Just as our bodies and their physiology show a recognizable continuity with those of other animals, so he expects

our behavior patterns to be fundamentally similar. To think of ourselves as different in kind, whether in virtue of our consciousness or
our supposed free will, is an illusion. Our behavior is subject to the
same causal laws as is all animal behavior, and it will be the worse
for us, he suggests, if we fail to recognize this. Of course, we are different in *degree* from the rest of the animal world; we are the "highest" achievement so far reached by evolution. To explain our behavior
causally does not necessarily take away from our "dignity" or
"value," nor does it show us not to be free, for any increase in our
knowledge of our own nature increases our power to control ourselves (*On Aggression*, Ch. 12–13). Though Lorenz does not take discussion of these philosophical questions very far in this book, he
shows himself much more sensitive to them than Skinner.

A crucial point of Lorenz's view of human nature is the theory
that, like many other animals, we have an innate drive to aggressive
behavior toward our own species. He thinks that this is the only possible explanation of the conflicts and wars throughout all human history, of the continuing unreasonable behavior of supposedly
reasonable beings. He suggests that Freud's theory of the death instinct is an interpretation of the same unattractive fact of human nature. Lorenz seeks an evolutionary explanation for our innate
aggressiveness and for its peculiarly *communal* nature (the most de-
structive human fighting is not between individuals but between
groups, whether organized as in war or unorganized as in communal
massacres). He speculates that at a certain stage of their evolution,
our ancestors had more or less mastered the dangers of their nonhu-
man environment; the main threat facing them came from other
human groups. (Recent theorizing has raised the idea of competition
with related but different hominoids such as Neanderthals.) The competition between tribes would have been the main factor in natural
selection, so there would be survival value in the "warrior virtues."
At this postulated prehistoric stage, those groups that banded together
best to fight other groups would tend to survive longest. Thus Lorenz
offers to explain what he calls "militant enthusiasm," in which a
human crowd becomes excitedly aggressive against another group
perceived as alien and loses all rational control and moral inhibitions.
This tendency, he suggests, has evolved from the communal defense
response of our prehuman ancestors.

Diagnosis

"All the great dangers threatening humanity with extinction are direct consequences of conceptual thought and verbal speech." Our greatest gifts are very mixed blessings. Men are omnivorous creatures, physically quite weak, with no dangerous claws, beak, horns, or teeth, so it is quite difficult for one man to kill another in unarmed combat. Accordingly, there was no evolutionary need for very strong inhibition mechanisms to stop fighting between ape-men. The more heavily armed animals need such inhibitions to prevent injury to each other, but others do not, at least in their normal environments. But the dove—the very symbol of peace—can uninhibitedly peck to death a second dove if they are unnaturally enclosed in the same cage and cannot escape from each other. With human beings, cultural and technological development puts artificial weapons in our hands—from the sticks and stones of prehuman ancestors, through the arrows and swords of history, to the bullets and bombs, the chemical and nuclear weapons of today. The biological equilibrium between killing potential and inhibition is upset. Thus Lorenz suggests how it is that human beings are the only animals to indulge in mass slaughter of their own species.

Appeals to rationality and moral responsibility have been notoriously ineffective in controlling human conflict. Lorenz asserts that aggression is innate in us; like the instincts in the Freudian id, it must find an outlet in one way or another. Reason alone is powerless; it can only devise means to ends that we decide on in other ways, and it can exert control over our behavior only when it is backed by some instinctual motivation. So, like Freud, Lorenz sees a conflict between the instincts implanted in us by evolution and the new moral restraints necessary to civilized society. He speculates that in prehuman groups there must have been a primitive morality that condemned aggression within the group but encouraged "militant enthusiasm" against any group perceived as alien. Our technology of weapons has far outstripped instinctive restraints on their use, and so we find ourselves in the highly dangerous situation of today, with both the power to destroy millions of people, even the whole world, and the *willingness* to do so in certain situations.

Prescription

If aggression is really so innate in us, there might seem to be little hope for the human race. Appeals to reason and morality are of little use, and if we try to eliminate all stimuli that provoke aggression, the inner drive will still seek outlets. Theoretically, we might try to breed it out by deliberate eugenic planning of human reproduction. But even if this were morally and politically possible, Lorenz thinks it would be highly inadvisable, since we do not know how essential the aggressive drive may be to the makeup of human personality as a whole. If we tried to eliminate aggression, we might destroy at the same time many of the highest forms of human achievement.

Nevertheless, Lorenz avows optimism in the final chapter of *On Aggression*. He believes that "reason can and will exert a selection-pressure in the right direction." The more we begin to understand the nature of our aggressive drive, the more we can take rational steps to redirect it. Self-knowledge is the first step to salvation (another echo of Freud, Sartre, and Socrates). One possibility is sublimation, the redirection of aggression to substitute objects in harmless ways. We can smash cheap crockery to express rage, and we can channel group competitiveness into team games. We must break down mistrust between groups by promoting personal acquaintance between individuals of different nations, classes, cultures, and parties. And we must redirect our enthusiasm to causes that can be universally acceptable—art, science, and medicine. Last, Lorenz expresses great confidence in the human sense of humor as a tool for promoting friendship, attacking fraud, and releasing tension without getting out of rational control. Humor and knowledge are his great hopes of civilization. He thus claims to see grounds for hope that in future centuries our aggressive drive can be reduced to a tolerable level without disturbing its essential function.

Critical Discussion

Lorenz writes eloquently, and he can make his ideas sound very persuasive: he seems to combine the human insight of Freud with the scientific rigor of Skinner. But there are important questions about his theory and diagnosis. Other biologists have raised doubts about some of Lorenz's theorizing—Dawkins finds him guilty of an un-Darwinian understanding of evolution as "group selection," implausibly operating on groups rather than on individuals. And some of his claims about certain species, e.g., the alleged "bloody mass-battles" of the rat, have been disputed.

What we can discuss here without getting involved in detailed scientific controversies is the methodology of postulating instincts or inner drives to explain behavior. We found this to be one of the weakest parts of Freud's theories, yet we could not agree with Skinner's total rejection of such postulation. Has Lorenz found the right middle path between these extremes? The crucial question is whether his application of the concepts of drive and instinct is testable by observation and experiment. When he postulates a drive to explain a specific fixed-action pattern in a particular species, like the fly-catching routine of the starling, there do seem to be clear ways to test the proposition. We can establish that a given action pattern is innate by showing that all normal individuals of the species of the relevant age and sex perform it, without previous learning from other individuals or by trial and error. If we also find that the stimulus that usually releases the action does not always do so with the same effectiveness (e.g., mating behavior varies with the season) and if we also find that the action can sometimes be produced by less than the usual stimulus (as with the lonely bird courting the corner of its cage), then it is reasonable to say that there is some internal driving factor that varies in its strength.

What is more dubious about Lorenz's methodology is his suggestion that such "little partial drives" are often at the service of one or more of the "four big drives" (feeding, reproduction, flight, and aggression). He holds that a "self-contained function" is never the result of one single drive and even suggests that aggression is one of the driving powers that "lie behind behavior patterns that outwardly have nothing to do with aggression, and even appear to be its very opposite" (*On Aggression*, Ch. 3). On the face of it, this seems to permit us to attribute any kind of behavior at all to aggression and thus makes such attribution untestable and unscientific. (It sounds suspiciously like Freud's theory of "reaction formation," by which an inner tendency can be expressed in the opposite behavior.) Unless there are ways of testing this talk of basic drives, intermingling of drives, and diversion of drives to different behavior, such theorizing is not scientific. And until the tests confirm such theories, there is no reason to suppose them true.

Is aggression innate, "spontaneous," driven by a distinct reservoir of energy that builds up inside? The hydraulic pressure model can be applied to some behavior, such as defecation, the sexual urge (at least in the males of many species), and hunger-driven behavior such as hunting. But it is not clear that there is an internal store of energy for other forms of behavior that would seem to be mere *reactions* to external stimuli. For example, it is implausible to say that creatures have an internal need to *flee*, a need that is released by a threatening stimulus. And whether any creatures have an internal *need* to fight, rather than just a disposition to fight in certain circumstances, is controversial.

As well as these methodological questions about his general theory, there must be considerable doubt about the way in which Lorenz extrapolates from animals to humans. (This was also a major criticism of Skinner.) In *On Aggression*, Lorenz takes most of his examples from fish and birds, rather fewer from mammals, and hardly any from our closest relatives, the great apes. Yet he is prepared to argue by analogy that if fish and birds are innately aggressive, then human behavior is subject to the same basic laws. Aggression may be innate in territorial fish, or in stags in the rutting season—but whether this is true of human beings is, to say the least, highly debatable. The analogy must surely be judged a weak one. It would be stronger if Lorenz had made detailed studies of our closest relatives, chimpanzees and gorillas, as more recent ethologists like Jane van Lawick-Goodall and Diane Fossey have done.

But even evidence about the great apes is far from proving the essential nature of humanity, although many popular evolutionary writers would have us believe so, for the *differences* between humans and other animals may be as important as the similarities. In general, to show that X has evolved out of Y does not show that X is Y, or is nothing but Y, or is essentially Y. Even if it could be proved that sectarian, ethnic, or racial conflict (e.g., in Los Angeles, Northern Ireland, or Bosnia) has evolved from the territorial defense mecha-

nism of tribes of ape-men, this does not show the former to be nothing but the latter. In any case, theories about prehuman behavior, such
as Lorenz's suggestions about competition between hostile tribes are
highly speculative, and it is hard to see how we can now find solid
evidence for or against them.

These doubts must therefore infect the crucial feature of Lorenz's
theory of human nature—the idea of innate aggression. For if the
analogy from animals does not prove this point, we must make direct observation of human behavior to test it. At this level, Lorenz is
as amateur as the rest of us who are not social anthropologists or sociologists. We must look not to his speculations but to the facts. Social
anthropologists have described some societies in which aggression
is notably absent. This suggests that aggression is more socially
learned than innate. In modern industrial societies, overt violence
varies according to social background. Some may suggest that mid-
dle-class economic competition is just as "aggressive" as working-
class gang warfare, but in such usage the term is being extended to
cover more than physical violence and the threat of it. A clearer conceptual definition of aggression is a prerequisite of further inquiry,
and that inquiry looks like being at least as much sociological as biological. We must judge Lorenz's theory of innate human aggressiveness as an unproven speculative generalization from his
observation of animals.

Aggression certainly poses urgent problems for humanity.
Throughout history, tribes, races, and nations have done the most terrible things to each other, and every day the news bulletins give more
instances from all over the planet. The most insoluble political and
military problems around the world involve intercommunal hostility,
and the very survival of the human species on earth is still threat-
ened by the availability of nuclear, chemical, and biological weapons.
There may be hope in the fact that hostility between nations or al-
liances can sometimes change relatively quickly; for example, the
Cold War went on for less than fifty years, which is not long in historical terms. But at the ethnic level, it is depressing to reflect on the
hostility passed on down over centuries from one generation to the
next in so many parts of the world.

Aggression is not easy to understand and explain, or even to define. The Freudian/Lorenzian hypothesis of a specific aggressive

drive or instinct that is constantly seeking release now looks over-simplified, at best. A more plausible view, which allows a crucial role for social environment, is that we are predisposed by our genes to become highly aggressive toward each other in distinctively communal ways, but only in certain social conditions.

Evolutionary theorists like Lorenz who inquire into human ethology or sociobiology have been criticized by those who maintain that, apart from the most obvious biological universals like eating, sleeping, and copulation, human behavior depends on culture much more than on biology. Some of this protest may reflect sociologists' and social anthropologists' resentment of other academics who are seen as "invading their territory." But critics have also expressed suspicion about the ideological motives behind theories that certain forms of human behavior, such aggression and competition, are innate in our biological nature. They perceive danger that such claims can be used to justify as "natural" or "inevitable" certain social practices, such as the encouragement of aggressiveness, male dominance, wars and preparation for war, or competitive economic systems. But, of course, there might be social and political motives behind some of the *resistance* to sociobiological claims. In this case, as elsewhere, we cannot rest content with attacking each other's motives: we have to do the hard work of investigating the evidence for the claims themselves.

For Further Reading

For Darwin's classic first statement of the theory of evolution, see his *Origin of Species*, reprinted in the Pelican classics series in 1968, and in a Mentor paperback from the New American Library, New York.

For a careful critical discussion of the scientific pretensions of "creationism," see Philip Kitcher, *Abusing Science: the Case against Creationism* (Cambridge, Mass., MIT Press, 1982; Milton Keynes: Open University Press, 1983).

For a useful survey of ethology and its relation to other disciplines, see Robert A. Hinde, *Ethology* (London: Fontana, 1982).

The main text referred to here is Konrad Lorenz, *On Aggression*, trans.

Marjorie Latzke (London: Methuen, 1966; New York: Bantam Books, 1974). Lorenz's late work *Behind the Mirror: A Search for a Natural History of Human Knowledge* (London: Methuen, 1973) promised a more general diagnosis of the malaise of civilization but seems to have remained uncompleted.

For criticism of Lorenz and other ethological diagnoses of the human condition, see Erich Fromm, *The Anatomy of Human Destructiveness* (Greenwich, Conn., Fawcett Publications, 1973); *Man and Aggression*, 2d ed., ed. M. F. Ashley Montagu (New York: Oxford University Press, 1973); and Steven Rose, R. C. Lewontin, and Leon J. Kamin, *Not in Our Genes: Biology, Ideology and Human and Nature* (Harmondsworth: Penguin, 1984).

P A R T

V

Conclusion

12

Toward a Unified Understanding: Nine Types of Psychology

To hope to finish this book with some final or complete truth about human nature would be foolish. Final truths do not seem to be given to us finite human beings, except perhaps in mathematics—and least of all about a topic as complex and controversial as human nature. So I have no eleventh theory to offer but rather an invitation to try to put together what seems most acceptable from those we have considered here—and from many others. Although some readers may think of the various theories as rivals for our allegiance, they are not incompatible with each other on all points. Each of them can surely make some positive contribution to our understanding of ourselves and our place in the universe. Unless one has a special commitment to a particular framework of thought, the sort of total and exclusive allegiance to a "closed system" that we discussed in Chapter 1, one can see each conception as emphasizing (though perhaps *over*-emphasizing) different aspects of the total, complicated truth about human nature. In this way, one can begin to see the different theories as adding up, rather than canceling out.

For this irenical project, I venture to suggest that Kant's system of thought (allowing for some modernizations) is the most comprehensive, the most able to include what is acceptable in other conceptions into one coherent overall view. His distinction between different kinds of truth or levels of theorizing—a priori and a posteriori—allows us to recognize a place for both purely philosophical reflection and scientific results based on observation. Kant wrote before Darwin, of course, but there is nothing to prevent us integrating evolutionary theory into the empirical side of his thought. Thus, we can have both an a priori account of what distinguishes human beings as rational thinkers and moral agents and a posteriori accounts of how these faculties of perception, thought, feeling, and agency have evolved and come to be embodied in our biological species. By the empirical study of history and anthropology, we can come to understand how the expression of human faculties has developed through various human cultures. And perhaps we can entertain some hopes for ethical, political, and social progress in future.

One of the big questions that Kant raised is how far human actions and thoughts are amenable to scientific explanation. A host of difficult philosophical problems arises here. Someone who believes, like Plato and Descartes, that we are essentially nonmaterial souls is going to see our most distinctively human nature as beyond all scientific investigation. This metaphysical issue of dualism or monism has to be faced—are we made of matter alone, or is consciousness necessarily nonmaterial in nature? Are mental states (e.g., sensations, emotions, beliefs, desires) and brain states (the electrical and chemical goings-on investigated by neurophysiologists) two different sorts of thing, or just two aspects of one set of events? Of the theories considered in this book, only Plato's is unambiguously dualist, and that only in some parts of his work: I argued that dualism of body and soul is not essential to his theory of three conflicting elements within human nature.

Even if we reject a dualism of two substances, there still seems to be something distinctive about human action and thought that makes scientific explanation in terms of causes and laws of nature inadequate. We find a duality of human mental and physical *aspects* (properties, or vocabularies) unavoidable in practice, but this too gives rise to philosophical puzzlement. One traditional way of raising this set of issues is to ask how there is room for free will in a world of determining causes, but recently this has been seen as part of another question: how there is room for *rationality* in a physical world, how people whose brain functioning consists in neuron firings can have reasons for their beliefs and actions. As we have seen, these issues are fundamental in the thought of Kant, they are involved in the critical evaluation of Freud and Skinner, and they are presented in a dramatic though idiosyncratic way by Sartre. They are at the center of contemporary philosophy of mind and action and are fundamental for psychology and all study of human nature.

It is still a matter of deep difficulty and controversy how exactly psychology and the other would-be sciences of human nature are to be understood—what they study, what their data and methods are, and what sorts of results and theories they can hope to arrive at. In the two preceding chapters I examined two supposedly scientific theories of human nature, those proposed by Skinner and Lorenz, but these represent only two particular kinds of psychology. There has been a wide variety of schools of thought and methodologies within psychology, and significant differences still remain. Taking a long historical overview, here are some of the main answers to the question What is psychology?

1. Study of the *soul*, as the etymology of the word "psychology" suggests. (One way of interpreting this is as the love of wisdom—*philo-sophia*—about how to live, how to prepare for death and perhaps an afterlife, practical methods of self-discipline, teaching, psychotherapy, spiritual development or guidance, meditation or prayer, as in the various religious traditions and to some extent in Socrates and Plato)

2. Study of the *concepts of mental powers and operations* ("moral psychology," "philosophical psychology," or philosophy of mind. Religious traditions involve some such conceptions, but they are most systematically developed in Plato, Aristotle, Kant, and modern philosophy)

3. Study of *states of consciousness* (as envisaged by the classic empiricists such as Locke, Hume, and J. S. Mill; the introspectionist psychologists such as Wundt and William James; and Freud, in interpreting dreams and phantasies; some Gestalt psychology and phenomenology)

4. Study of *human actions* in their social context, as defined by
   their intentions (e.g., social psychology and much of sociology
   and social anthropology; Freud's study of errors, jokes, and neurotic behavior; Sartre's existential psychoanalysis)

5. Study of *behavior*, understood as physical movements of the
   body, with no interpretation in terms of intentions or purposes
   (e.g., Pavlov and the American behaviorists such as Skinner,
   who studied the behavior of animals in controlled conditions in
   the laboratory)

6. Study of *behavior*, understood as physical movements of the
   body, not involving intentions but allowing interpretation in
   terms of *biological function* and *evolutionary origin* (the ethologists, including Tinbergen and Lorenz, who studied the natural behaviour of animals in the wild)

7. Study of the nature and development of *cognitive structures and
   processes*, which are thought to underlie and explain behavior
   and states of consciousness (the high-level theorizing of Piaget,
   Chomsky, and contemporary "cognitive science")

8. Study of the nature and development of *motivational and emotional states and processes*, which are thought to underlie and
   explain behavior and states of consciousness (the high-level theorizing of Freud and of later developmental psychoanalysts such
   as Bowlby, as well as of some ethologists such as Lorenz)

9. Study of *physiological states and processes* in the brain and the
   central nervous system, which are thought to underlie and explain behavior and consciousness

William James's definition of psychology was "the scientific study
of mental life," which is broad and vague enough to encompass all
of these. But the academic discipline of psychology as it has developed in university departments in the twentieth century has tended
to confine itself to very carefully defined questions on specific topics. Much of it concentrated for some time on (5) and, more recently,
on (7) and (9). The emotive and the social—let alone the philosophical or spiritual—have often been seen as not amenable to precise
scientific treatment. Thus, most experimental psychologists have
been chary of talking about anything as general as "human nature."

The topics in (1) and (2) have typically been dismissed as "off limits," professionally speaking. Recently, there has been some widening of approach, for example in Jerome Bruner's conception of "cultural psychology," which proposes to make (4) its heartland, with (7) and (8) very much involved in the explanation.

Lorenz's evolutionary concentration on (6) has, for all its faults, proved more fertile than Skinner's restriction to (5). In 1975 E. O. Wilson published his *Sociobiology: The New Synthesis*, in the last chapter of which he claims that the new methods of what he calls "sociobiology" can be applied to human beings and will revolutionize the social sciences. In his next book, ambitiously entitled *On Human Nature*, Wilson applied his evolutionary approach to some specific categories of human behavior, including aggression, sex, altruism, and religion. Other biologists have hotly criticized both the scientific claims of sociobiology and what they see as the reactionary social and political pronouncements that have been made on a supposedly scientific basis.

We here touch again on the matter of ideology (raised in Chapter 1, and in our discussion of Marx). Every human way of life presupposes some beliefs about human nature, and, when such a fundamental belief informs their ways of thought and action, people typically resist changing it. Proponents of social change may appeal to their own claims about human nature, perhaps inspired by Marx's emphasis on the plasticity of human nature by human culture. So whenever supposedly scientific evidence is adduced for claims about our evolution, or about differences between human races, sexes, or social classes, we must be alert to the possibility that such assertions may serve the interest of certain social groups rather than others. Factual evidence can show only how people have so far behaved in certain forms of society, which we may want to change. For example, the feminist movement has raised important questions about how far differences between men and women are a matter of innate, biological, "natural" tendencies and how far they are the result of cultural conditioning that serves the interests of men.

In the 1980s and 90s there has been quite an explosion of evolution-based theorizing about human nature, and the term "evolutionary psychology" has come into fashion because of the political controversies about "sociobiology." Much of this recent writing, though aiming to be strictly scientific, has a certain popular appeal, because it promises some explanation and diagnosis of the human predicament and perhaps some prescriptions for policy, but it, too, will be morally, politically, and philosophically controversial for just this reason. If we have learned anything from this book, it is that critical philosophical assessment will always be needed when new theories about human nature are proposed.

That there are *some* innate tendencies in human nature is indisputable—for example, human sexual behavior is obviously rooted in our biological nature. But even that inescapable example immediately raises problems and questions, for the forms sexuality takes vary considerably between societies, and in devotedly celibate individuals like monks and nuns, its expression may be deliberately suppressed. We have some innate biological drives, certainly—but we seem to be unique in the way in which our behavior depends on the particular human culture we are brought up in and, to some extent, on individual choices. (Rudimentary cultural differences have been discerned in some of the apes, but to nothing like the human extent.)

Culture is crucial to human nature, then. Although Skinner was surely wrong to see the means of cultural influence as reducible to the mechanisms of operant conditioning he imposed on his experimental animals, he was right to recognize the enormous influence of culture and the social environment on every human individual from birth on. (In the capitalist economies that now dominate the world, much of the influence is obviously exerted through the power of money.)

The study of human evolution itself leads us into the study of human cultures; for example, there may well have been a two-way interaction between tool use and the development of human hands and brains, and between increasing brain size and humans' growing sophistication in language and social organization. But our cultural systems of meaning involve values and beliefs—theories of human nature in the wide sense of the term as used in this book, including some conception of the overall place and purpose of human beings in the universe, and thus some belief that is religious in its scope if not necessarily in transcendent metaphysical content. (Confucianism and Kant's "religion within the limits of reason" are two different examples, in contrast to the transcendent beliefs of Hinduism, Judaism, Christianity, and the Platonic theory of Forms.)

Clearly, religion has immense emotional power over most of humankind compared with the purely rational approach of science and philosophy, which are minority interests. Even for those who would say (with Freud and Marx) that the metaphysical content of religious beliefs is illusory, there arises an obvious question, namely, why is it that all known human societies suffer from some form of this illusion? Can it be explained in terms of pyschoanalytic theory (the wish for a father figure), or in sociological terms as Marx and Durkheim claimed, or in evolutionary terms, as Wilson and others suggest? These various reductive explanations are intellectually interesting, but are any of them really convincing? Is not religion an attempt to cope with problems that confront *any* human being, however comfortably situated, in however reformed a society—how to face up to the inevitability of one's own death and that of loved ones, how to cope with one's awareness of failure and wrongdoing, and how to answer the questions of what to aim for, what to hope for?

Yet the philosophical question of whether the transcendent content of religious assertions is illusory must be faced. We raised such critical questions about Christianity in Chapter 4, and we found Kant expressing them in his final musings on religion. Assessing religious claims is one route into central philosophical inquiries about meaning, epistemology, and metaphysics. Psychological or sociological explanations of religion depend on assumptions about the meaning and truth or falsity of the beliefs to be explained. So the philosophical questions about religion are unavoidable.

At the end of a book that presents such a lot of generalizing and *theorizing*, it is worth reminding ourselves how much understanding of human nature we acquire in a practical nontheoretical, way from our experience of particular cases. Foremost, of course, comes our own individual experiences of life—the people we have had dealings with, and the communities and cultures we have lived in. But the study of history and social anthropology can extend our acquaintance beyond our own limited experience, to other individuals and societies, distant in time or space, with their own particular characters.

Let us also remember how literature presents us with imaginary, but in another sense very "real," particular cases of men and women displaying their human nature in feeling, thought, and action. In the greatest works, our understanding of human nature is extended and deepened, though not necessarily in ways we can put into explicit words. To pick an obvious but unmissable example, consider the plays of Shakespeare, with the aid of perceptive interpreters. The fictions that enjoy wider popularity in the contemporary media of TV and movies tend to present shallow, stereotyped characters and social/ cultural situations and thus restrict rather than exend understanding of human nature. (Plato realized how influential the arts and "media" can be, for better or for worse.) Understanding can, however, be deepened by attention to particular cases, whether encountered in one's own experience, reported from history or anthropology, or presented imaginatively in the arts.

Human nature as a topic breaks down the boundaries between the sciences and the humanities. Social and political problems around the world cry out for better understanding of human nature—how often the technical problems are soluble, but what seem insuperable are the political, social, and psychological obstacles. Even in affluence and peace, individual existential problems, dilemmas, and tensions remain. There is no contradiction between Kant's hope for social progress and his recognition of the need for each person to come to terms with his or her individual destiny, *sub specie eternitatis*. To paraphrase Alexander Pope, the proper study of human beings is human nature and the human condition.

For Further Reading

For surveys of the history of psychology, see the books recommended at the end of the chapter on Skinner. In *Acts of Meaning* (Cambridge, Mass.: Harvard University Press, 1990), Jerome Bruner reviews the progress of psychology and recommends "cultural psychology." For a recent, innovative introduction to a variety of approaches in personality theory and social psychology, see *Understanding the Self*, ed. R. Stevens (London: Sage, 1996). A reference book full of fascinating articles on a huge variety of topics is *The Oxford Companion to the Mind*, ed. by R. L. Gregory (Oxford: Oxford University Press, 1987).

For E. O. Wilson's sociobiological approach to human nature, see the last chapter of his *Sociobiology: The New Synthesis* (Cambridge, Mass.: Harvard

University Press, 1975) and *On Human Nature* (Cambridge, Mass.: Harvard University Press, 1978).

For philosophical overviews of sociobiology, see M. Ruse, *Sociobiology: Sense or Nonsense?* (Dordrecht: Reidel, 1979); Mary Midgeley, *Beast and Man : The Roots of Human Nature* (London: Methuen, 1980); F. von Schilcher and N. Tennant, *Philosophy, Evolution and Human Nature* (London: Routledge, 1984); and Philip Kitcher, *Vaulting Ambition: Sociobiology and the Quest for Human Nature* (Cambridge, Mass.: MIT Press, 1985).

Robert Wright, *The Moral Animal: Evolutionary Psychology and Everyday Life* (New York: Pantheon Books, 1994; London: Abacus, 1996) cleverly interweaves Darwin's ideas, Darwin's life, recent developments in evolutionary theory, and their application to human nature. For lively introductions to contemporary evolutionary theory and genetics, see Richard Dawkins, *The Selfish Gene* (Oxford: Oxford University Press, 1989), and Steve Jones, *The Language of the Genes* (London: Flamingo, 1994).

Two points of entry to the explosion of writing on feminist issues in human nature are: Jean Grimshaw, *Feminist Philosophers: Women's Perspectives on Philosophical Traditions* (Minneapolis: University of Minnesota Press, 1986; Brighton: Wheatsheaf Books, 1986); and Alison Jaggar, *Feminist Politics and Human Nature* (Totawa, N.J.: Rowman and Allenheld, 1983; Brighton: Harvester Press, 1983).

An interesting selection of readings from the seventeenth-century scientific revolution to recent discussions of "postmodernist" themes is *Knowledge and Postmodernism in Historical Perspective*, ed. Joyce Appleby et al. (New York: Routledge, 1996).

Roger Scruton, *An Intelligent Person's Guide to Philosophy* (London: Duckworth, 1996) is an unconventional introduction to the subject, fired by his conviction that "scientific truth has human illusion as its regular by-product, and that philosophy is our surest weapon in the attempt to rescue truth from this predicament"—a message I hope this book has reinforced.

Index

Adler, 166
Aggression, 152, 156–57, 166, 207–22
Alienation, 6, 7, 54, 131–34, 141–44
Analytic, 17–18, 113
Animals, 17–18, 116–17, 121, 140, 153, 166, 190, 199–201, 209–10, 212–16, 219, 228
Anguish, anxiety, 54, 177
Appearances, 49, 54, 57–59, 92–93, 114, 119–20, 171
Aquinas, 84, 110
Ardrey, R., 211
Aristotle, 8, 75–76, 91, 96, 108, 110, 116, 118, 227
Arts, 93, 105, 107, 108, 232
Atheism, 4, 73, 134, 170–74
Atman, 50–52, 56
Augustine, 79, 85, 108, 110, 115, 144, 170
Authentic, authenticity, 170–71, 182–85

Bad faith, 178–81
Bakunin, 132
Behaviourism, 190–202, 227–29
Benevolence. *See* Virtues
Berlin, I., *xi*
Bible, 3, 68–86, 123
Biology, 8, 71, 141, 153, 174–75, 208–12, 221
Bowlby, 228

Brahman, 47–51, 53–54, 57–62, 64–65
Brentano, 150, 175
Breuer, 150–51, 157, 160
Brücke, 150
Bruner, 229, 232

Calvin, 111
Capitalism, 6, 11–12, 130, 133–39, 142–47, 211, 230
Catholicism, 5, 69, 84
Charcot, 150
Children, childhood, 106, 122, 141, 156–59, 167
Chomsky, 200–202, 205, 206, 228
Christianity, 5, 6–7, 10–13, 68–86, 113, 130, 146, 147, 170, 183, 210–11, 230
Chuang-Tzu, 43
Civilization. *See* Culture
Class, 7, 43, 66, 106–7, 139, 141–47, 220
Classics, 34–38
Closed system, 13–15, 162, 210, 225
Communism, 5, 6–7, 11–12, 130, 133–39, 144–47
Conditioning, 191–207, 228–29
Condorcet, 111
Confucianism, Confucius, 8, 9, 25–44, 69, 124, 230
Consciousness, 52, 59, 61, 139–40, 145, 153–54, 171, 175–76, 179–81, 184–85, 190, 215

Creationism, 71, 74–75, 210
Culture, 3, 29, 81, 152, 159, 161,
    204–5, 216, 220–21, 229–32
Cultural relativism, *x*, *xi*, 14–15,
    90, 95, 171

Darwin, 8, 71, 137, 153, 208–11,
    226, 233
Dawkins, 218, 233
de la Mettrie, 134
Decree of Heaven, 26–30, 32,
    36–37
Definition. *See* Analytic
Democracy, 5, 76, 89–90, 102–3,
    107–8
Descartes, 114, 118, 230
Destiny, 26–27, 29, 33
Determinism, 4, 6, 11, 54–55, 114,
    118–20, 144–45, 154, 176,
    198, 202–4
Doing for nothing, 32–33
Dostoyevsky, 174
Dreams, 152, 155, 160–64
Drives, 99, 121, 156, 166, 213–21
Dualism, 75, 78, 84, 96–97, 114,
    118, 153, 175, 230
Durkeim, 132, 231

Economics, 3, 4, 6, 11, 135–39,
    142–47, 211
Education, 33, 41, 94, 104–5, 122,
    146–47, 159, 204
Emotion, 98–99, 116, 121, 151,
    155, 176–77, 228
Empirical, 18–21, 191–92, 198–99
Engels, 132–34, 141
Enlightenment, *x*, 8, 111–13, 128,
    130
Epiphenomenalism, 139
Epistemology. *See* Theory of
    knowledge
Ethology, 207–8, 212–15, 228
Evil, *x*, 10–11, 40–41, 72, 76, 79,
    123–25
Evolution, 4, 8, 9, 71, 74, 137, 153,
    208–11, 226

Existentialism, 5, 104, 134, 169–86
Explanation of behavior, 154,
    164–67, 183–84, 190–202,
    211, 226–30, 232

Falsifiability, falsification, 19–21,
    72–73, 163–65, 218
Family, family values, 31–34, 66,
    106, 141, 155–59
Female, feminism, *x*, 4, 29, 43, 75,
    79, 99–100, 106, 141, 150,
    157, 229, 233
Feuerbach, 132–33, 142, 170
Forms, theory of, 49, 92–96, 105
Fossey, D., 219
Four seeds of virtue, four incipient
    tendencies, 39–41
Freedom, free will, 4, 6, 11, 54–55,
    59, 62–63, 75, 85, 113–14,
    118–20, 144–45, 154, 169–86,
    192–93, 202–4, 215
Freud, Freudian, 8, 12–13, 97, 132,
    147, 149–68, 176, 183, 211,
    215–19, 227–31
Fromm, 159

Galileo, 111
Genes, genetics, 191, 195–96, 209
God, gods, 3, 4, 6, 10–12, 19–20,
    26–27, 47–48, 51, 57–65,
    70–73, 91–92, 95, 113, 115,
    125–27, 132, 170–74, 194
Grace, 62–63, 82, 84–5, 123–28

Hegel, 128, 131–35, 142, 170–73,
    181
Heidegger, 171–74, 177, 186
Hinduism, 9, 45–67, 69
History, 6, 11–12, 19–20, 128,
    131–39, 211, 231
Hobbes, 8, 111
Homosexualtiy, 16–17, 100
Hsun-tzu, 38, 40–43
Human perfection, 27–29, 31–32,
    35–38, 42, 121–28
Hume, 71, 111, 125, 134, 227

Husserl, 171–73
Hypnotism, 150, 164
Hysteria, 150–51, 155, 160

Id, ego, and superego, 152, 155–58, 195
Ideology, 9, 13, 14–15, 134–40, 162, 210, 221, 229
Imagination, 116–17, 172, 176
Innate, 96, 198–99, 201–22
Instincts, 152, 156, 161, 166, 207, 213–21
Introspection. *See* Self-knowledge
Islam, 8, 68, 69, 81, 110, 136

Jaggar, A., 148
James, W., 190, 227, 228
Jeanson, M., 186
Jesus, 6, 7, 11, 78–85, 144
Judaism, 6, 68–78, 152, 230
Jung, 166

Kant, 8, 9, 71, 110–29, 143–44, 183, 184–85, 198, 202, 205, 212, 225–27, 230
Karma, 54, 59
Kierkegaard, 115, 170, 177, 186
Kitcher, P., 210, 221
Knowledge. *See* Theory of knowledge
Koestler, A., 211

Lamarck, 209
Language, 192, 200–202
Lenin, 145
Liberalism, 5, 9
Life after death. *See* Soul
Literature, 169–72, 192, 204, 231–32
Locke, 111, 227
Logical positivism, 20
Lorenz, *xi*, 8, 10, 167, 190, 207–22, 228, 229
Luther, 111

Marx, Marxist, 3–4, 6–7, 10–13, 128, 130–48, 154, 170–75, 185, 198, 204–5, 211, 229, 231
Materialist theory of history, 6, 133–39, 211
Materialist theory of mind, 6, 11, 75, 96–97, 114–15, 118, 139–40, 153–54, 190, 195, 230
Maya, 57–59, 62
Meaning, 17–21, 72–73
Media. *See* Arts
Meditation, 53, 55, 60, 64
Mencius, 38–42
Mendel, 209
Metaphysical, metaphysics, 19–21, 26, 43, 46–50, 57, 71–73, 83–84, 91–93, 113–15, 190, 199, 230, 231
Mill, 227
Moksha, 53
Moral philosophy, morality 15, 26–27, 35–38, 65–66, 75–76, 94–95, 100–104, 118, 120, 122–23, 174, 182–85, 204
Morris, D., 211

Natural, nature, 16–17
Neurosis, 158–59
Newton, 111, 138
Nietzsche, 14–15, 80, 170–71, 174, 184, 186

Oedipus complex, 157

Pantheism, 70, 131
Paradigmatic action, 37–38, 42
Pascal, 115, 170
Paul, 78–82, 97, 123, 170
Pavlov, 192, 199, 228
Pelagius, 85, 144
Persons, 17, 72, 74–75, 84, 181, 203
Phenomenology, 171, 172, 228
Piaget, 228

Plato, *xi*, 8, 9, 18, 75, 79, 89–109, 110, 118, 122–23, 156, 158, 176, 183, 193, 202, 205, 226, 227, 230–31

Politics, 3, 11, 33, 65, 89–91, 105–7, 131–34, 145–47, 172–73, 204–5, 211, 220

Popper, *xi*, 19, 109, 205

Postmodernism, *x*, 14–15, 233

Protestantism. *See* Reformation

Proudhon, 132

Psychoanalysis, 8, 9, 149–68, 173, 183–84

Psychology, *xi*, 8, 118, 150–54, 162, 189–206, 225–33

Ramanuja, 56, 60–66

Rationality, reason, *x*, 13–15, 74–76, 90, 98–101, 111–13, 117–18, 121–22, 164–65, 202, 217, 227

Rectification of names, 34

Redemption, regeneration, 7, 12, 77–78, 81–82, 130, 147

Reformation, 69, 111, 113

Relativism. *See* Cultural relativism

Religion, religious experience, 6, 8, 60–65, 69, 70–73, 125–28, 132, 137, 152, 170–71, 184, 227, 230–31

Renaissance, 109–11, 158–59, 165–66

Renunciation, 46, 60, 63–64

Repression, resistance, 151, 155–60, 179

Resurrection. *See* Soul

Revolution, 7, 11–12, 133, 138–39, 144–46

Rousseau, 112, 124–25

Sages, 27–31, 35–38, 40–42

Salvation. *See* Redemption

Sartre, 4, 10, 147, 166, 169–86, 202, 217, 227, 229

Science, 8, 18–21, 111–15, 118, 135, 138, 153, 163–67, 193–94, 196, 210, 233

Self-knowledge, 90, 118–19, 123, 154, 158, 161, 180–83, 190

Selfishness, 9, 30–31, 39–40, 54, 119–23

Sexuality, 79, 98, 103, 141, 151, 156–59, 166–67, 219, 230

Shakespeare, 232

Shankara, 56–66

Sin, 6, 30–31, 54, 76–81, 123–25

Skinner, *xi*, 8, 10, 189–206, 218, 219, 227–30

Smith, Adam, 132

Social nature of human beings, 3, 30–34, 100, 124–25, 140, 159

Sociobiology, 221, 229–30, 233

Sociology, 135–39, 140, 219–20

Socrates, 89–91, 96–97, 108, 183, 217, 227

Soul, 11, 50–53, 57–59, 62, 73, 75, 79–84, 96–97, 115, 118, 127–28, 226, 227

Spinoza, 111, 183

St-Simon, 138

Sumner, 211

Tao, Taoism, 27–28, 43–44

Theory of knowledge, 15, 53, 55, 73, 92–95, 113–18, 212, 231

Therapy, 150–52, 160–61

Tinbergen, 228

Transcendence, transcendent, 49, 65, 70–73, 83, 231

Transference, 151, 161

Tripartite theories of mind or soul, 97–99, 100–104, 152, 155–56

Unconscious, 151–58, 160–61, 164, 176, 179, 183, 195

Value judgments, 5, 16–17, 94–95, 141, 174, 182–85, 194, 204

Van Lawick-Goodall, 219

Verifiability, verification, 19–21, 163–67
Virtues, 27–42, 75–76, 94–95, 100–104, 118–23, 182–85, 217, 227
Voltaire, 111, 134

Watson, J.B., 190–92, 198–99
Way of the Sages, 27–28, 31

Will, 32, 95, 99, 104
Wilson, E. O., 211, 229, 231
Wittgenstein, 176
Women. *See* Female
Worship, 26, 46, 58–65, 76, 81–82, 92
Wundt, 190, 228

Yajnavalkya, 46–48, 54, 64